D1364832

HORNING IN

HORNING IN

The Grown-Up's Guide
to Making Music for Fun

Jerry and Lucie Germer

FROST HILL PRESS
MARLBOROUGH, NEW HAMPSHIRE

Copyright © 2000 by Jerry and Lucie Germer
Published by Frost Hill Press

Edited by Adrienne Spector
Cover designed by Max Germer O'Carolan
Illustrations by Jerry Germer

Library of Congress Cataloging-in-Publication Data

Germer, Jerry
      Horning In: The Grown-Up's Guide to Making Music
for Fun/Jerry and Lucie Germer.
Includes bibliographical references and index.
ISBN 0-9675517-0-6
Printed and bound in the United States of America.

                                            99-96929
First Edition

Acknowledgements

We didn't just dream up this stuff. We drew upon the help of many folks—amateur musicians to pros, as well as some sources not even involved in music. For this help, we greatly thank the following:

Professional musicians and or teachers who reviewed text and/or provided information or suggestions: Carlson Barrett, Russ and Rita Germer, Miriam Goder, Matthew M. Harre, Bonnie Insull, Tom Jones, Lorraine Larson, Bob Mark, Peter Mose, Doug Nelson, Bill Pardus, John Payne, Ted Rust, Walt Sayre, Gene Uman, Jeremy Youst.

Professionals in other fields who provided information: Richard Dryden, M.D., Knud Keller, Richard Norris, M.D., Gary H. Price, Bernadette Quinn.

For assistance with layout and graphics: Max Germer O'Carolan, Cinda Germer.

For help reviewing and editing text: Adrienne Spector (our editor), Peter Allen, Travis Hiltz.

Amateur musicians who shared their personal journey: Cindi Brooks, Gordon Bennett, Ron Boerger, JoAnn Bulley, Gene Chan, Dick Chase, Miriam Diamond, Chris Goding, Chris Herman, Karen Jackson, Pat Onufrak, Brian Reilly, Peggy Saunders, Heidi Scanlon, Kathy Shaw, John Suta, Scott Swanson, Sandy Van de Kauter, Nathan Winer, Sally Wright.

Contents

Overture:

WHY YOU SHOULD BECOME A MUSICIAN

"I wish I could play the sax," said Vinnie DePalo to his son, Jim, as they sat listening to the riffs of a jazz combo at a nightclub almost twenty years ago. It was the kind of wistful off-hand comment many of us make from time to time, and for most of us it doesn't go any farther than that. But most of us don't have sons who are music teachers.

"Well, why don't you?" asked Jim. Vinnie gave him every possible excuse, but Jim had heard them all and kept encouraging him. He was successful. Today, Vinnie has a great time leading The Comebackers, a swing band composed of adult amateurs.

He's not alone. Adults everywhere are discovering or rediscovering the joys of making music. They, like Vinnie and the others you will meet in this book, share one thing: the joy of discovering how much making music adds to their lives and to the lives of those around them. Much of their enjoyment comes from expressing their art with others, whether it is in a duo or seventy-piece band. In fact, the Association of Concert Bands, founded in 1977, now lists 2,000 active community/concert bands in the U.S. alone. When you add in the numerous amateur community orchestras, chamber ensembles, fiddling groups, brass quintets, jazz, rock and folk bands listed over the Internet, it's obvious that there are a lot of people out there doing something with their free time besides watching television.

A 1997 Gallup poll found that two-thirds of all households include people who play or have played an instrument. Ninety-five percent of the respondents agreed that playing an instrument is a good hobby and provides a sense of accomplishment.

But most important, it's fun. The pleasure that you get out of hearing beautiful music is nothing compared to the sheer joy of making it. As an adult, you can choose what to do for recreation, so why not choose something that makes you feel good?

Say, for example, you learned to play an instrument in school. You grew up, you lived in small apartments with paper-thin walls; or you moved around a lot and couldn't afford the shipping charges for the double bass; or you were working sixty-hour weeks. Somewhere along the line you stopped thinking of yourself as a musician. You still have the sax or trumpet, but it is stashed away somewhere down in the basement with the stationary bike.

Or maybe you didn't take music lessons as a child. You couldn't afford it, or the soccer team practiced at the same time as the band, or (worst of all) someone told you that you didn't have "an ear". Even though you love music, you never thought you could be a musician.

Whatever your reasons, haven't you ever wished you could make music?

We think you can and should.

We, ourselves, are involved in music to the hilt and can't imagine living without making music. Reaching this point wasn't automatic. Sometimes we struggled, though each of us in a different way.

In high school, Jerry considered a career in music and partially paid his college expenses by playing piano in dance bands. Although he eventually ended up an architect and writer, he never really left music, at least emotionally. When we moved to New Hampshire he got back into it in a big way. He joined the local college/community band, playing clarinet, bass clarinet, and bassoon (not all at once). He plays jazz piano in various small combos, bassoon in a trio with two flutes, and most recently french horn in a brass quintet.

Frankly, he's the kind of musician Lucie found threatening at first. She has always loved music, though she never felt she had much talent. She played flute until her second year in high school. When she moved to a school without a band she quit playing. After their marriage, when Jerry played in the evenings Lucie wished that she hadn't quit. It would be lovely to play duets, she thought, but doubted she she could ever be good enough.

Yet when the children were old enough to play and the town band was encouraging family participation, she brought out the flute and the whole family joined. It was fun. A few years later, she began to learn trombone, finding a kind of freedom she'd never felt with the flute. She now belongs to a town band and the brass quintet where Jerry plays. Her musical confidence has grown to the point where she plays duets with Jerry.

Since we've become more involved in music, we've noticed that there are two kinds of people in the world: those who play an instrument and those who say,

"Oh, you're so lucky to play. I've always wished I could play the viola (or clarinet, or drums), but I wouldn't know where to begin." Or, "I used to play, but it's been so long that I can't even remember which end to blow into."

Encouraging these people is largely what inspired us to write this book. Our aims are very simple: we want to get you playing, either going back to an instrument you once played, or taking up something completely new. Beyond that, we want to encourage you to find groups of like-minded musicians to play with. One of the people we talked with in doing our research for this book, Dick Wylie, sums up the value of participating with others thus: "One of the things that our group provides is an escape from the isolation that is part of practicing. This is particularly true of pianists who don't have the outlet provided by community orchestras and bands." Dick went on to join the Montgomery County Chamber Music Society, which "has led me to levels of musical gratification that I hadn't believed possible."

There have been other books on amateur music-making, such as Stephanie Judy's *Making Music for the Joy of It* (Jeremy P. Tarcher, Inc. 1990), but none devoted entirely to instrumental music and none that take into account the growing list of resources now possible through the information revolution.

We make our case largely through spotlighting the experiences of other amateur musicians, who generously shared their stories, and through cartoons.

And naturally, since we are so heavily involved ourselves, it was impossible to write the book without drawing upon our own experiences. Though Jerry plays the occasional gig for pay, most of his musical activity is for pleasure, so he includes himself among the musicians that call themselves "amateurs." We hope we don't need to remind you that "amateur" is a positive term meaning someone who does something for the love of it.

Throughout, we'll refer to our joint experiences and suggestions as coming from "us", but when something comes from only one of us, we'll use the third person: Jerry or Lucie. For example, Jerry put in all the trombone jokes, but Lucie, who doesn't think they're funny, did not reciprocate by inserting some really hilarious bassoon jokes, because she wanted to keep this a high-class book.

On the other hand, we both laugh at accordion jokes.

Throughout we've tried to minimize the technical musical terms and made every effort to explain any we suspected might be unfamiliar in the glossary at the end.

The book is organized into five parts, named as musical movements. You can read the movements that fit your level of musical experience or general interest and skip the others, or simply read straight through.

For example, the first part, **Overture**, aims to stir your desire to get into music. We begin by showing you what it is like to make music for pleasure, with a series of vignettes of amateur musicians in typical situations you might encounter when playing in various kinds of groups. The following two chapters tell how playing an instrument can help you deal with the stresses of modern life. Then we'll talk in more detail about good things that happen musically and non-musically when you get in the habit of playing.

The next part, **First Movement**, is intended to launch you on your own musical journey by shooting down any excuses you may have thought of while reading the first section. We dispel feeble notions you may cling to such as you're too old, too untalented, too lame, or just don't have the time.

Once you're filled with enthusiasm and ready to get going, we'll explore the range of instruments available to you in the **Second Movement**. After dealing with the questions anyone might face in choosing an instrument, we explore the range of instruments available to you as an adult amateur. Which instruments fit your physical abilities? Which fit your lifestyle? Which fit the kinds of music and kinds of group you prefer? If you've never played before this part of the book will open up possibilities you might never have considered. If you once played the trumpet because Uncle John's trumpet was available (and it's now up in the attic), this part will give you an idea of your choices and open you to possibilities you might not have thought of. After all, now that you're a grown up, you can choose what you really want. So it's reasonable to consider what you *do* want?

If, on the other hand, you played sax as a child and still love it, it's worthwhile to review just those parts which are most relevant. (Saxophones can be found among the other "pipes with lots of keys and holes" in Chapter 12).

We have limited our discussion to instruments and excluded voice, not because we don't like singing, but because instrumental music is our own focus and vocal music is already so well covered in other books. While we've tried to be inclusive, we may have missed a few instruments, either because they are still relatively exotic or because of the lack of opportunities to play them in a group (the didgeridoo springs to mind).

Having selected your instrument, you will be ready for the next part, *Learning Music as an Adult*. When you were a child you learned (or didn't learn) what, when, and how the teacher chose. You have a lot more options now. Chapter 15 helps you find and work with a teacher. In Chapter 16 you can find out if teaching your-self is a possibility, and in Chapter 17 we discuss the val-ues and drawbacks of group lessons. Generally speaking, the news is all good — you don't have to spend the next few years playing "The Happy Farmer" and "Lightly Row." Whether or not you've ever played, there are ways to learn which will suit your needs, constraints, and inter-ests.

The final section of the book answers the question, *What Next?,"* with helpful advice on how to chart your musical future. Many amateurs start out full of fire, but the flames weaken, and can die out altogether unless other means are found to keep them alive. The major factor in keeping their enthusiasm, say amateurs we interviewed, is playing and sharing music with others. Chapter 18 tells how to find a group to play with that will meet your level of ability and fit your personality. The final chapter gives other helpful hints on how to keep your zeal for a long and satisfying musical journey.

Bon Voyage!

Jerry and Lucie Germer

Chapter 1

What's It Like?

Scene One: The Town Band

The middle school trumpets look doubt-fully at the fourth-grade flutes while the oboe giggles. The new third clarinet, father of one of the fourth-graders, wor-ries about playing through lips that haven't touched a reed in twenty years. Three young trombones show the only grownup in their section how to make race car noises through their horns. The Marlborough Town Band is warming up for a new season.

The program doesn't vary much from year to year: a show tune medley, some simplified Tchaikovsky, marches from the Karl King Band Book, and "The Stars and Stripes Forever."

The fourth-graders are awed. "Do we have to play all those notes?"

"Just the ones you can reach." The new third clar-inet sighs. What has he let himself in for?

"Don't worry," says the second clarinet player next to him, a retired music teacher. "It'll all come back to you."

The conductor raises her baton, smiles encourag-ingly, and they begin.

Three weeks later, the third clarinet is still won-dering what he's doing there. The main thing that's come back to him is how silly he always felt with a reed hanging

---

out of his mouth as he wet it before rehearsals. His instrument produces squeaks and hoots, seemingly without his input. He'd quit in a minute except that his daughter is having so much fun. He heard her saying importantly on the phone, "No, I can't come over tonight. Me and my dad have our rehearsal, and I can't miss it."

Suddenly it's the dress rehearsal, and the conductor reminds everyone to wear something dark on the bottom and light on the top (no T-shirt and jeans), to keep the music in order, and not to wave at grandpa's video camera. They deal with a few specific problems: the adult flutes all promise that before the show they'll search the youngest flute's mouth for bubble gum. The trombones are moved back a few feet so they can't jab the trumpets with their slides.

The retired music teacher says, "You must have been pretty good in high school. You've really improved. Have you thought about sticking around for the winter season?"

Performance night, and the third clarinet is a bundle of nerves. His daughter is in heaven. "Dad, everyone's here, not just Mom and Kelsey. Grandma and Grandpa, and all my friends."

The conductor gives one last bit of advice. "Here we go, folks. Just relax, have fun, and don't forget to breathe."

He takes a deep breath, and they're off. A good start. Here comes the tricky bit with the triplets. Not bad. Oops, well, maybe no one heard that C—sharp. Now for the Tchaikovsky. We can do that. During a long rest, he looks out over the crowd at the toddlers dancing on the grass. A church group sells refreshments. It looks so Norman Rockwell that the clarinet almost misses his entrance.

Finally it's "The Stars and Stripes Forever" and everyone is clapping.

As they pack up their instruments, his daughter says happily, "This is so much better than music lessons because it's real."

The retired music teacher says, "So, do you think you'll stick around? We're going to start working on some interesting stuff next week."

He thinks about those triplets that finally came out right, the clapping during "The Stars and Stripes", and especially the closeness he feels to his daughter as they go to rehearsal. And he thinks about her comment.

"I guess I just might," he says.

Scene Two: The High School Variety Show

The cafeteria is thinly disguised as a nightclub. Along the wall where the teachers stand during their duty periods at noon is a spot-lighted stage. The long tables are covered with paper tablecloths and crepe paper streamers. An overflow crowd of fellow students, parents, and community members sits at the tables eating ice cream sundaes and drinking sodas. At the end of each act they applaud, sometimes politely, often enthusiastically.

Few of us in the West take part in music making any more, except perhaps in church or at school. Most of us live in big cities, have jobs to do, and are content to let others make music for us. Fortunately for me, I belong to those others, practicing musicians.

Yehudi Menuhin

The energy level in the room is palpable as act follows act. Three girls with bright umbrellas sing "It's Raining Men." A group of very young boys with very loud guitars takes a literal whack at "Proud Mary." A soprano sings "The Rose" while another girl signs it. There are ballads, some jazz, and a lot of inspired choreography obviously inspired by MTV.

By the second half, you might expect the audience to begin to flag, and in fact they're spending a certain amount of time chatting.

"Is that Kim? She's all grown up now. Does she know what she's going to do when she graduates?"

"She's going to college. Right now she can't decide between Musical Theater and Education. She'd be a great teacher, but she's such a ham she might get bored trying to be serious all the time."

"Well, she sounds wonderful. Tell her I said so."

Suddenly the students in the audience cheer as the MC announces, "And here are... The Rolling Drones!"

Electric guitars, a bass, and a saxophone blare out a rock pattern familiar to anyone who remembers the sixties. Several of the more substantial female teachers dressed in black miniskirts, with feather boas over their shoulders, begin to shimmy. The high school's own version of Mick Jagger strides over to the front of the stage, looks down at his students and their families and sings, "I can't get no...." The crowd goes wild.

As a matter of fact, the group is at least as good as most of the other acts in the variety show. The Dronettes flip their boas around; the bass and guitars keep their sound levels just at the edge of discomfort; and the sax hides behind his dark glasses and hunches his shoulders in a parody of Beat musicianship. "Mick Jagger" and the backup singers are having the time of their lives. Each time any of the teachers makes eye contact with a student, the student screams.

As the last "satisfaction" fades, the audience jumps up to give a spontaneous standing ovation.

Back in the classroom that serves as a dressing room, one of the Dronettes grumbles, "Why don't we get a reaction like that when we're teaching?"

"Maybe sines and cosines would go better with a bass line."

Another Dronette comes in laughing. "You'll never believe this, but I was just talking to Kim, you know, that girl in my third period class? She says that after seeing us she's decided. She wants to be a teacher."

Scene Three: A Nursing Home

The audience gathers in the recreation room, some in wheelchairs, others in folding chairs. A six-piece band sets up: two trumpets, two clarinets, a trombone and a tuba.

The leader introduces them. "We were going to call ourselves Dixieschnitzel, but I got outvoted, so instead we're Anything Goes, and we'd like to welcome you to our concert where it just might happen that anything *does* go. We're going to play a variety of music—a bit of oompah, a little Dixieland, some jazz, and even a few original compositions. If you feel like it, you're welcome to get up and dance."

A voice comes from the back, "It'll take a lot to get me up on my feet."

The leader grins, then gives the count, and the group swings into a medley of "Mame" and "Satin Doll." In the audience toes and fingers tap, and one woman sings along. At the end the applause is soft but sincere.

More tunes follow each other in quick succession:

"In München Steht ein Hofbräu Haus", "St. Louis Blues," "Edelweiss," "The Beer Barrel Polka," "The Little Brown Jug." Encouraged by the nursing home's social director, a few people do get up and dance, at first shyly and then with enthusiasm. At the end of each song, the applause is as much for them as for the band.

It's during the medley of "I'm Looking Over a Four-leafed Clover" and "You Are My Sunshine" that the disaster happens. A man in a wheelchair, dancing with the aid of the social director, makes a quick turn, loses control, and plows straight into the music stands. He's brought to a safe halt knee-to-knee with the tuba as sheet music drifts over the dance floor. The band collapses in laughter.

Someone comments, "They got you up on your feet after all, Ella, but George knocked you right back off them."

You never know how an audience will respond to your music.

Ella says, "I think I'll just sit down and listen for a while."

George says to the tuba player, "Well, I wanted a chance to examine this up close anyhow. Always wished I could have played an instrument."

"Tuba's the best. Wait till you hear it on our theme song."

After the music is picked up and sorted back into rough order, the concert continues, though now the audience is content to listen. Afterwards, the band overhears a few comments.

"Now that was a nice change."

"Yes, these guys were better than that last group who came in."

"Louder, too."

These are just a few of the scenes we've experienced on our own paths back into music. None of the musicians we describe is a professional. Most of them are busy people and have only gotten back into music when other parts of their lives have gotten simpler. As one anonymous

Some people find playing an instrument a pleasant, relaxing oasis at the end of a demanding workday.

poster to a horn web page put it, "I have taken several hiatuses (is this a word?) of anywhere from 6 months to 2—3 years (due to having a toddler). Have you ever tried practicing with a little guy biting your ankles?"

Just as they differ in backgrounds and occupations, adult musicians differ in what they get out of making music. Some have discovered inner resources they never knew they had. Making music is a new world for them. Each new piece they take on pushes them into undiscovered territory filled with challenges.

On the other hand, some people find playing an instrument a pleasant, relaxing oasis at the end of a demanding workday. Unless you're a school music teacher or studio musician, picking up an instrument is a change from whatever you did for the past eight hours. You're moving different muscles, using other skills, and even breathing differently.

Some people find that playing in a group provides a unique way to meet and interact with people of other ages and occupations (even when the audience doesn't crash

It's not uncommon to find several generations of the same family playing side-by-side in a community band.

What's It Like?

into you). Carlson Barrett, director of the Westmoreland Town Band, says that people stay in a community music group for several reasons. First of all, it's fun. People have a good time in rehearsals and a good time at the gigs. Then there's the challenge. Band members can push themselves to their own limits musically. Finally, many groups have a mix of older and younger players, and everyone helps each other out. Groups like this tend to think of themselves as families—and sometimes include real family members. It isn't uncommon to find parents and children or even three generations playing together, as has happened in the Westmoreland Town Band.

Sometimes members of such groups find themselves making other kinds of beautiful music together—the After Hours Community Band in St. Louis even boasts of three married couples who met through the band.

What else can you get out of making music? Well, scientists are beginning to investigate how music might affect the brain and help aging people keep their brain cells going. While the jury is still out on the specific relationship between music and general intelligence, it seems obvious that any activity which challenges you intellectually, gets you out of the house, involves you socially, and provides a break from the routine of daily life will help you keep the brain power you already have.

With so much going for it, it's hard to see why everyone isn't out there making a joyful noise. Maybe we're getting carried away, but we do suspect that there are millions of adults who love music and wonder what it would be like to play it. If you are in this group, this book is designed to give you that little push.

Chapter 2

Using Music to Counter Stress

A paradox: as the most well-fed, comfortable, healthy people in the history of civilization, we find ourselves facing all the stresses our ancestors knew *plus* some brand-new ones. How do we deal with them? Not terribly well, despite the mood-altering substances available—everything from coffee to new age nostrums such as kava kava, prescription tranquilizers, and illegal substances. The variety is literally mind-boggling. Some of us try physical means such as yoga or tai chi, or put on running shoes to outrun our problems.

There is another solution.

"I don't know if it's my church or my therapy session; I just know I need it," says Sally Wright, describing her feeling that making music keeps her sane. Sally has good reason. In one short year she battled cancer, faced the end of a long-term relationship, and lost her home. Something must have given her the courage to keep going. Sally credits her flute playing and her membership in a town band.

"Whenever I went in to see my doctor, he said, 'Go home and practice and you'll feel better' and he was right," she says.

Half a world away in Switzerland, Ralf Stangl writes, "Horn-playing is like loading my human battery for next day." The anonymous writer of an e-mail to a horn web page agrees. "As a Navy Captain retiring this summer to practice as a CPA, playing the horn keeps one sane in an otherwise topsy world."

Whether you're confronting the worst life can throw at you or simply trying to deal with the stresses of job and family, music can be what keeps you from shattering. Let's look at some stresses that many of us face and see how making music can help us deal with them. As you read this, think of your own life and what you're going through right now. Making music might be just what you need.

Time

Probably the first stress that most of us think of is the time crunch. If you feel as though you're running faster and faster to stay in the same place, you aren't alone. If the rat race was the metaphor of the world of work for the 1950's, the stair-climbing machine seems more apt for today. It symbolizes the combination of stress and utter boredom that causes us to flip through magazines or listen to a walkman while we climb to get nowhere.

We say that we don't have enough time, but according to John Robinson and Geoffrey Godbey, in *Time for Life*, what we're really doing is "multitasking," watching TV while we read the paper, talk with our family, eat dinner–or, as in the example above, distracting ourselves while we exercise.

What we need is at least one time during the day when we are completely connected. Music gives us that opportunity. Although it is possible to warm up on your instrument without paying much attention, there's no way to work on a new piece while worrying about something else. Remember Transcendental Meditation and all the Zen meditation techniques which require you to focus on the present moment? Well, practicing an instrument can be a kind of moving meditation. As Sally puts it, "When I'm playing, no one else is around. The only thing in my head is what I'm doing. It's like a mini-vacation somewhere else." But even mini-vacations take time you may be in short supply of. In chapter 7 we tackle the the question of how to add music making to your life without adding to the stress imposed by the chronic lack of time.

Technology

Our increasing electronic complexity yields us great benefits, along with its own stresses. One is that every improvement requires its own learning curve, and many of us feel as though we're running after knowledge that expands so fast that we'll never be able to grasp it. Learn Windows 95 so thoroughly that you're comfortable with it, and guess what! While you were on vacation they reorganized and brought in Windows 98. Or 2000. Or something else.

So the solution is to spend your free time learning yet another skill? Strangely enough, it is. When you read music, you're following a notation system which was codified in the early seventeenth century. It hasn't changed much since and isn't likely to in the future, either. Once you have it, your knowledge

When I'm playing, it's like a mini-vacation.

won't become obsolete. You won't have to worry about having to learn Music Notation System 98. Of course, if you prefer folk music, you can follow an even older tradition by memorizing or playing by ear without having to learn to read music at all.

Many instrumentshave changed very little over the centuries. Some, such as French horn or flute, are actually easier to play than their predecessors. The skills you learn or re-learn on the sax that's been gathering dust in the attic for ten years will work just as well on the snazzy new Selmer you buy because you're having so much fun. Music is such a big field of knowledge that you'll never run out of things to learn, but it's all cumulative, so you'll never have to play catch-up with the whole field (we scan the whole field of instruments in the section titled "Second Movement.")

On the other hand, those of us who love what's happening in technology will be glad to know that music hasn't been left behind. From synthesizers to electronic practice mutes for brasses to web pages for almost any instrument you can think of, there is a technology that fits your interests. You can get as involved as you like in the electronic aspects of music-making—or you can ignore them completely. Whatever you choose, you can participate fully with like-minded friends. You can even switch back and forth. For example, Floyd Oster, who owns a computer-hardware distribution business and plays trumpet every chance he gets, moves easily between playing baroque pieces with organ accompaniment for church services and weddings and using a synthesized full band back-up for his jazz gigs.

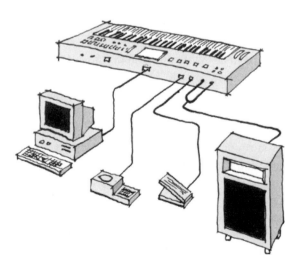

Today, you can get involved in music at any level of technology you like.

Isolation

Another image of the modern business world is the Dilbert cubicle. At a time when there are more of us in the world than at any time in human history, we're becoming more isolated from each other. We sit in front of computers all day at work, then go home and sit in front of TVs (or other computers). We interact via e-mail and telephone calls, and get our entertainment through wires, rather than live performances.

Making music in a group is a wonderful antidote for all this.

Most amateur music groups are warm and supportive environments. They have to be, because, no one is forced to be there. They offer you a chance to get away from whatever is bothering you and be with a group of people who want the best for you and like you for who you are (even if they all wish you didn't always come in a beat early in the third measure). The atmosphere in a group which plays together regularly is usually upbeat (well, what else?) and friendly. You get to know the people who sit close to you fairly well, but in a limited way. You may never find out their jobs, politics, or family situation, except when and where they learned to play. Yet these are people who have joined you in a joint creative effort where the whole is far more than (and different from) the sum of its parts.

Carlson Barrett, who founded the Westmoreland Town Band in the 1970s and has guided it ever since, points out that "in a good band, everybody helps each other out. It's for everyone, and everyone feels like they're a part of it. That leads to a lot of mutual pride and respect for each other, and for the whole group. It's like a family."

And the loss of family solidarity is, sadly, another hallmark of modern life.

Loss of Family Closeness

Sometimes a musical group is literally a family. As we saw in the previous chapter, playing together in a group helps counteract the fragmentation of today's busy families. As we talk to people all over the country about their musical experiences, we're struck by the ways in which musicians involve their spouses, children, parents, and even grandchildren or grandparents in what they do. During our own tenure in the the Westmoreland Town Band, we have seen times where three generations of the same family are all playing in the band. Sometimes parents or spouses of band members are drawn in simply from transporting their their family members to rehearsals or concerts. Joining the band has another benefit, by the way—it's more fun to play the same concert three times than to hear it three times! As the rituals of rehearsal and performance become part of the family experience, other rituals develop to bring the family members even closer together. The ceremonial ice cream cone after a concert ranks high as a popular post-performance ritual.

Aging

Finally, we're all aging. We worry about losing it, with "it" being our brain cells and, ultimately, control. Could it be possible that learning to play an instrument can improve your mind?

The only reason to make music is because you love it. That doesn't mean adoring every squawk that comes out of the instrument, or every moment of practicing and still not getting it right. It means that you're doing this because it makes you happy.

That said, it turns out that there are intellectual benefits to making music, which is rather like finding out that chocolate is good for you after all. This area of study is new, and some of the claims are clearly overblown, but it's nice to know there's something solid enough for scientists to be working on it.

Most of the studies, unfortunately, focus on children, so we have to extrapolate to adults. So far, research suggests that music helps children learn language and reading, enhances their creativity, and improves their attitudes toward school and education, and these benefits seem to last throughout their academic lives. The College Entrance Examination Board compared students who played instruments with those who didn't and discovered that the performers scored an average of 51 points higher on the verbal section and 39 points higher in math than the non-musicians. Another study of college students found that music and music education majors had reading scores even higher than English majors.

Does any of this mean that playing music makes you smarter or that smart people like to play music? You win either way.

A few years ago Don Campbell made a big splash with his book, *The Mozart Effect,* in which he claimed that listening to music–especially that composed by Mozart–can improve peoples' mental functioning, immune system, productivity, and digestion, by affecting brain waves. There were even suggestions that it improves one's sex life–a claim that we're not quite ready to make. Never mind that much of this is from anecdotal or small-scale evidence, and almost none of it from studies of musicians. A problem with studying listeners as opposed to the music-makers is that it's sometimes hard to judge if the closed eyes and deep breathing signify appreciation or sleep. You can usually tell if musicians are awake, at least while they're playing.

While *The Mozart Effect* was raising questions about the relationship between music and intelligence, another researcher came out with the idea that the concept of "intelligence," itself, was overly simple. Howard Gardner, a Harvard professor of education, suggested that there are actually many intelligences, including musical intelligence.

What we need now are studies on how music making affects the brains of adults. And they're coming out. Dr. Oliver Sachs and Dr. Frank Wilson, both neurologists, writers, and speakers, point out ways in which music making helps mental function as we age. You've probably heard depressing "facts" about how many irreplaceable brain cells we lose a day, about shrinkage of brain tissue, and about how there isn't much we can do to stop intellectual entropy.

Afterwards, one player asked..."Did they like us because we're good or because we're old?" It was a joy to be able to reply that the applause had been genuine—...because this band of senior adults had played so musically.

Don D. Coffman
and Katherine M. Levy
Music Educator Journal

Nonsense! Even if these facts are true, they are irrelevant. The amount of brain shrinkage is minimal and the normal amount doesn't seem to have that much to do with loss of intellectual functioning. Similarly, most of the brain cells we lose we can manage without. And we can do a lot to keep things going—such as making music. This isn't just propaganda. A study at Beth Israel Deaconess Medical Center in Boston discovered that the cerebellum of expert male musicians was significantly larger than that of non-musicians. This suggests that musical training leads to an increase in the size of the brain, though the researchers haven't gone so far as to say that musicians are therefore smarter than everyone else.

We haven't actually found any musicians who are willing to tell us that they were pretty dumb until they took up the cello, but now they read books on calculus for fun. Too bad. That would be great propaganda.

The Power of Music

The Music Making and Wellness Project is studying how music making affects the brains and immune systems of older adults. The study wants to find out if participating in music will improve three areas of the lives of older persons:

❑ Overall quality of life
❑ Resistance to disease
❑ Response to stress

The first round of results showed that elderly participants who took keyboard lessons showed significant decreases in anxiety, depression, and loneliness. Further research continues, and while we don't know yet how this project and others will come out, we can speculate on why music might be so good at helping us deal with stress.

First, consider the the nature of music itself. As a patterned, rhythmic activity, it can be either relaxing or stimulating —but it is always involving. Mothers sing to soothe colicky babies. Slightly older children under stress rock and suck their thumbs.

Unfortunately, most cultures discourage adults

from grabbing a comfort blanket, twisting their hair, and rocking. But on the other hand, most cultures do approve of making music (it's interesting that fundamentalist Muslims, who detest music because it stirs the lower emotions, constantly finger their worry beads in a relaxing rhythm). In holding a musical instrument and moving our arms and hands in a pattern, we begin to let go of whatever bothered us. If we're really fortunate, we play a brass or woodwind, which, by giving us something to put in our mouth, can be the next best thing to sucking a thumb.

It isn't just the oral stimulation which relaxes brass and woodwind players, though. Any wind player knows that the quality of the music depends on breathing. Stressed breathing is shallow and irregular. In fact, if you are upset or frightened, you may forget to breathe entirely for a moment–bad enough in the middle of a presentation, but fatal if you're aiming for a high G. In order to make the sounds come out of the horn, you have to breathe, and as you breathe more deeply and regularly, you relax.

This effect is less obvious for string, percussion, and keyboard players, but it is still there. Madeline Bruser, in *The Art of Practicing*, returns again and again to the importance of breathing/relaxation for any musician. Musicians who breathe deeply and smoothly, relax, and as they relax they make better sounds, which makes them relax even more.

But what if you're so upset that you simply can't relax? Lucie isn't sure if this works for everyone, but she finds that playing something badly and very loudly can help. She can get much louder sounds on the trombone than with anything less than a scream, and a smeared, violent solo rendition of a song usually improves her mood. Of course, this approach isn't without hitches. Her furious playing is guaranteed to put those around her into the mood she's managed to get rid of; and the system works best with a noisy instrument. A flutist who isn't continuosly serene might do well to keep a horn around in case of need.

Of course, if you've been yelled at by the boss, jammed the copier, gotten a parking ticket, and generally had a miserable day, sitting down to play something too challenging may just set you up for more stress. Walt Sayre, a music teacher, emphasizes the point made by all of the music teachers we talked to. "Music is not to add stress to your life; it's to add enjoyment. If you're stressed, back off to something easier for a bit. But keep playing."

And this leads to another reason that music-making is such a good stress-reliever. The size of the repertoire open to most instruments is so great that there is always something you can play that will lift your spirits. Play something loud, as Lucie likes to, play something sad. Play something easy. If you're feeling so bad that you can't even make a choice, just play some scales. Whatever you play will help you musically as well as psychologically, and the better you play, the better you'll feel. Outside of, say, sex, there aren't too many pursuits that can offer this much.

At the beginning of this chapter we asked you to think about your own life and the kinds of stress you deal with every day. If right now you're overwhelmed by the result, you probably need more help than this book can provide. Get it—then come back to the book! If, however, you're basically okay, except for sometimes feeling a lack of focus and time, pressure from your job and technology, bored and isolated, you already know what we're going to recommend. But you don't learn to play an instrument just because it's good for you, like taking your vitamins. There are many other perks, as we'll see in the next chapter.

Chapter 3

More Wonderful Things About Making Music

If your life is already good, you'll see in this chapter how it can become even better. By engaging in music making, you, you can expand your horizons, discover and push your limits, re-invent yourself, give something back to your community, show off, have fun, and make something beautiful. Not bad for one activity, is it? Now let's see if and how each of these extravagant-sounding claims holds up.

Expanding Your Horizons

Music making can take you in directions you never expected to go. Miriam Diamond studied cello through high school and college, but, as with so many others, she packed her instrument away as demands of career and life steered her in other directions. An attraction to Cajun dancing is what brought her back to music. One night, while attending the Monday night Cajun dancing at Johnny D's, a club in Sommerville, MA, Miriam noticed that the band, Krewe de Rous, was missing its rub-board player. A rub-board is a kind of wearable washboard played by stroking and tapping with special picks or the backs of spoons. At break time, Miriam asked what had happened to Christine, the regular rub-board player. The drummer said Christine had another gig. Then he surprised Miriam by asking her if she wanted to sit in. Miriam said, "Why not?" The next thing she knew, she was off the dance floor and on the bandstand as part of the band's rhythm section. The band liked her well enough to offer her rub-board lessons if she would fill in when needed. Miriam thus found a new duality. When she wasn't dancing, she was often sitting in with the Krew de Rous and even with Cajun bands in Providence, RI. Miriam's high school cello teacher would probably have been horrified, but then encouraged by an ironic twist to this story: Miriam's joy in playing rub board has somehow re-invigorated her interest in the cello. She recently had it refurbished and is gearing up to tackle it anew.

Sometimes you literally end up in unexpected places. Ron Boerger played horn through high school and college, then then stopped for the next ten years. When he one day picked up a used flugelhorn and started noodling around for fun, he enjoyed it so much that he ordered a new horn. "When the horn arrived I talked to a co-worker who I knew was in a community band and found out their first rehearsal was that night, so I went and picked up the horn, practiced for about 20 minutes at home, and had the nerve to show up at rehearsal that night and play."

Ron stayed. One of the unexpected benefits of his participation was meeting his wife through the band and the chance for the two of them to tour the UK with the Lakeshore Concert band of Montreal, Canada. He now plays in the Austin (Texas) Symphonic Band and maintains the Community Music Mailing List on the Internet, a wonderful resource for amateur musicians.

If you studied an instrument in school, you may not have had the kinds of opportunities that awakened an interest in music in Miriam and Ron, but it's amazing what is open to you, if you look around a bit. Like Miriam you may find yourself playing a new kind of music on an unexpected instrument. Or, like Ron, you may come back to a loved instrument and discover social and travel opportunities you could never have anticipated.

Suppose you've never played before? Then, obviously, everything is going to be new, and by definition, your horizons will be wider than they were before.

Pushing Your Limits

An inspirational poster with a picture of a hang glider taking off from the side of a mountain is captioned "Limits Exist Only in Your Mind." Amateur musicians spend a lot of time discovering their limits, then finding out either that they don't really exist after all or that within the limits there is still plenty of room to grow.

An anonymous e-mail writer says ruefully, "Now I'm trying to re-establish myself at some reasonable level of technical mediocrity, and saving my pennies to buy myself a good horn."

Dick Chase first picked up a baritone in 1927. "I wanted to play trumpet, like every kid my age. The Band director said, 'All we have is a baritone, how would you like to play that?' I disliked the looks of the horn, but took a few lessons from a trumpet player and got to the point where I could play in the band."

He changed his opinion of the instrument as he became more competent, and eventually got a music scholarship to Middlebury College in Vermont. After playing through college and briefly while in the Navy, he left the baritone behind for forty years, though he continued participating in music by singing in church choirs and other groups with his wife.

When a local town band started up in the early 80's, he borrowed a baritone and joined. "It was a great experience picking up a horn again. I have never been an accomplished musician, but the whole idea of the sociability and being able to produce some music in an organization is a wonderful experience."

When Lucie came back to music, all she could see was her limits. What helped her grow beyond them was a combination of setting small goals and her family's blithe assumption that of course she could play. Joining the Westmoreland Town Band was a big step. There she found sympathetic associates and a gentle conductor. Immediately appreciating her lack of confidence, Carlson Barrett put no pressure on her except to show up. His criticisms were put generally to the section, or even more courteously, to half the band: "Low brasses, could you play a bit more softly here?" Another trombone player pointed out in an aside, "It sounds really nice when he puts

Your self-confidence will grow with experience.

it like that until you look around and realize you're the only low brass at the rehearsal."

Lucie's self-confidence has grown to the point where she's been known to grab a solo away from a better player, butcher it, and shrug. There's always another chance to get it right.

Recreation as Re-creation

Miriam, the demure cellist, and Miriam, the riot of the rub-board, are two very different people. Part of Lucie's enjoyment of the trombone is that she is playing against a stereotype. After all, no one expects a sweet, white-haired lady to honk. As an adult amateur musician, you don't have to fit any stereotype. You can be more *yourself* than you ever were before or, perhaps, can allow yourself to be, in other areas of your life.

This isn't to suggest that knocking down the preconceptions will be easy. People's ideas start young and tend to be firm. Even elementary school children know that drums, trombone, or trumpet are "what boys play" and that clarinet, flute, or violin are "girls' instruments." Not only do children have rigidly-defined ideas of what instruments are appropriate for boys or girls, but they will try to force their friends to play the "right" instruments. Pity the poor boy who wants to play flute, or the girl who loves the tuba.

Even among adults in symphony orchestras, there are stereotypes and self-stereotypes. String players say that brasses are noisy, stupid heavy drinkers. The brasses counter that the strings are oversensitive, delicate, and too high-minded to be any fun. Percussion players are seen as fun-loving, loud, and insensitive, while everyone agrees that the woodwinds are quiet, intelligent, and meticulous.

Some scientists have even given musicians personality tests, checking to see if they're true. Are string players neurotic? Woodwinds controlled and shy? Brasses insensitive? Percussion players extroverted?

Not necessarily. The personality tests suggest, for example, that string players aren't always more neurotic than brass and woodwind players, which should be a relief if you love the viola but would rather spend your money on lessons than on sessions with a shrink.

None of the personality tests given to woodwinds turn up any outstanding defining characteristics. This makes sense, because the instruments aren't all alike, and neither are the people who play them. They're a varied bunch of players on a varied bunch of instruments. The only exceptions are that oboe players appear to be more tranquil than other woodwinds, and bassoon players somewhat more anxious. The tests also say that bassoon players tend to be the practical jokers of the orchestra, presumably as a way of diffusing the anxiety of dealing with all those keys plus two temperamental reeds.

The research did seem to back up the stereotype that the brasses are the first into the bar during the intermission. Brass players are generally extroverts, although horns are more anxious and less social, perhaps because they play such a hard instrument (do horn players keep their hand stuck in the bell of the horn for tuning or for security?).

How do these stereotypes affect you? Perhaps when you were a child you chose an instrument because "girls play…" or "boys play…", or perhaps you avoided all instruments because musicians were somehow a bit weird. Isn't it great to be a grownup and, especially, an amateur? You can be a shy and retiring bass drummer, play down-and-dirty French horn, or sensitive tuba. You can give another side of your personality a chance, or follow your deepest instincts.

In the end, personality stereotypes, as they relate to musical instruments, are fun to read, but little else. Playing the oboe won't make you tranquil if you don't have tranquility or at least the potential for tranquility in yourself. Playing tuba won't suddenly turn you into a hard-drinking practical joker, unless you already have that tendency.

On the other hand, to the extent that the stereotypes ring true, they can tell you something about the musicians around you. Do the string players tell as many jokes as the brasses? Are the flute players dreamy and imaginative? When you are part of an ensemble, your interaction with the players you sit by can affect your enjoyment in the whole process. One of the things to look forward to as you choose an instrument is the people you'll eventually be hanging out with during rehearsals and concerts. Whether you, yourself, fit the stereotypes and the results of the research, there are all those other people to consider. Let's say that you're rather aloof and shy, and are trying to choose between cello and euphonium, two beautifully mellow instruments. All other things being equal, this research would suggest that you'll be happier with the string section of the orchestra than having to put up with the noisy brasses.

As you choose your instrument and the kind of music you want to play, you're opening up a whole new side of yourself. You're creating yourself as a new person.

Are flute players really dreamy and imaginative?

Giving Back

How often do you get a chance to give something back to your community? If you're like most of us, it's probably not as much as you'd like to. Who has time to volunteer on a regular basis?

Almost every music group finds itself playing for worthy causes at one time or another. Every community has a long list of worthy candidates, in nursing homes and schools, for fund-raisers or non-profit events, or for church services or celebrations. Playing in these settings can be wonderfully heart-warming. Think of Anything Goes playing at the nursing home we told about in chapter 1. Think of a town band playing for The Special Olympics as the Special

Olympians march across the field.

Chris Goding, a trombone player and computer programmer, has found a way to mix music, volunteering, and family closeness. A job change a few years ago gave him one day of the work week at home. Because he worked in Boston, several hours away from his home in a small Vermont town, he wanted more of an opportunity to spend time with his sixth-grade son, who had recently taken up the trombone. Chris volunteered to help the music teacher in the local middle school with the instrumental program. The music teacher was delighted to have knowledgeable extra help, and Chris has been a part of the music program ever since. Now he spends his Fridays at the school, working with particular groups or sections of the band. He enjoys working with the kids, and points out that the school has been able to add another concert to their calendar.

Is playing oboe a tranquilizing experience?

Showing Off and Having Fun

When Jerry's family gets together, they always end up in a jam session. His brother Russ usually starts them off by saying, "Let's make some memories." And they do.

Playing music with the people you love is wonderful, but the musicians we talked to describe other magical moments. Chris Goding suggested, "Every once in a while the situation will come up where I'll sit down with a bunch of strangers, and boom, we're making music. It's a neat feeling that we can just do that."

Brian Reilly, a family practice doctor, would agree. "I just like getting together with a friendly group of people. It's the atmosphere."

Making Beautiful Sounds

When it comes right down to it, all of the stress-busting or self-fulfilling aspects of music are secondary to the music itself. Some people can remember the moment they learned to read, when letters became words and words suddenly had meaning. It's the same sensation when you play an instrument, when instead of playing a sequence of notes you find yourself playing a song. If you once played an instrument and you felt this sensation, we're sure you can remember how exciting it was. It's good to know that you can recapture that excitement. If you have never played, you have an incredible moment to look forward to.

We hope we've persuaded you to get that horn out of the attic and dust it off, or to try a new and different instrument. If so, we invite you to skip ahead to the **Second Movement: Getting the Right Instrument**. If you need more persuading because of specific physical or psychological concerns, keep reading right ahead.

First Movement

ME, A MUSICIAN?

Middle age has its own momentum. A lot of the major life decisions are now history. All we have to do is carry on, finding a certain amount of comfort in following a predictable routine. Sometimes, however, we may get the disquieting feeling that the smooth paths we're following are actually ruts. A small imp occasionally pokes its head up out of the subconscious to ask "Is this all there is?" We quickly slap the imp back down. Why risk changing a comfortable status quo in favor of a risky alternative?

It's easier to stay the course, backed up by the assumptions we have about ourselves and our capacity for change. Let's face it: some of the assumptions may be true, but others may be based on our early experiences, extrapolations from other parts of our life, or even laziness.

It's worthwhile to drag these assumptions out from time to time and examine them in the light of day. Which ones apply? Which are only useful in keeping us going in the direction we were heading anyhow? Which keep us from doing something which would enrich our lives? We (the authors) do this kind of examination on long walks along a nearby country road, usually coinciding with an unusual period of stress or some sort of crisis. The conversations may start out with the immediate problem, but then we find ourselves asking, "What are we doing?", "Where are we going?", or "Is this the best way to get there?" We don't always come back home with the answers, but the exercise clears the air and helps point us toward the future.

The assumptions you have about yourself as a musician are also worth examining. You may surprise yourself to find that you have held onto some simply for comfort and to avoid having to try something new. In the following five chapters we'll take on some of the most prevalent reasons other adults give for not learning a new instrument. They may help you see where your true limits lie and where the assumptions are just convenient excuses.

Chapter 4

I'm Too Old

You probably know of famous musicians who maintain mastery of their instrument well beyond middle age. Several years ago we saw Lionel Hampton knocking out rapid licks on the vibes (vibraphone) at a summer concert at Stratton Mountain, Vermont. He was in his early eighties then, and is still going strong as this is being written. Jazz pianist Marian McPartland, at 79, seems as sharp as ever on her NPR weekly radio show "Piano Jazz." Dave Brubeck, who ushered in "cool" jazz in the 1950s, is still making the rounds on the concert circuit. Similar examples could be cited from the world of classical music (Rubenstein, Horowitz, Menuhin, Toscanini) or folk music (Pete Seeger, Bob Dylan, Joan Baez). With a few notable exceptions such as the Rolling Stones and Greatful Dead, the world of rock seems to stand alone as the only genre that is so bound to youth that it consigns its practitioners to the junk heap even before they reach middle age.

Granted, well-known professional musicians who started late are exceptions rather than the rule. For every one who began at 40 there are probably 100 who started in their teens. But these examples are people who reached the top in a highly competitive environment. They had to be among the best, or we wouldn't be hearing about them. Amateur musicians live in a different world and need only to be good enough to please themselves or meet the minimum level for any group they want to play with. If your goal is to get good enough to play for pleasure rather than fame, you have a lot of company.

Our piccolo player turns 90 this Sunday. We happen to have a band concert that day and guess what we'll finish up with? If you want to hear an audience go nuts, have a 90-year-old piccolo player take the solo in "Stars and Stripes Forever."

Larry Hamberlin,
Director, Rochester, Vt.
Town Band

John Suta, a retired pipe fitter from Eugene, Oregon, started from scratch on the French horn at the age of 73. John had always loved music and had studied opera singing in his youth. No horn player himself, he nevertheless recalled his brother and a friend going house-to-house playing Christmas carols on a violin and French horn. The fond memories came to the fore one day when he spotted a

Age, in itself, is no handicap.

used French horn in a Salvation Army store. After buying the horn for $75, John enrolled in an adult music class at the University of Oregon and took eight lessons over the summer. He was invited to join the Emerald Horn Club, a group of 16 horn enthusiasts, who would be starting their season in the fall. But eight lessons on a difficult instrument wasn't enough preparation, he felt, to qualify him for the group. A friend suggested he contact the band director of the Roosevelt Middle School, who was also a horn teacher. John asked the teacher if he could learn alongside the students. The teacher said, "Take a seat."

John made steady progress, moving from *Mary Had a Little Lamb* to Beethoven, and advancing from the sixth grade to the eighth-grade band. Meanwhile, the young band members, who found him an oddity at first, came to see him as an inspiration. The progress John made along the way gave him the ability and confidence to join the Emerald Horn Club.

Admittedly, John Suta starting out on a difficult instrument in his 70s is a bit unusual. But we discovered many examples of people beginning in middle age. Consider Gene Chan, who took up trumpet at 50.

A computer information systems engineer in Burnaby, BC, Gene always loved but never engaged in music. He and his wife cultivated this passion in their two sons, who played in the high school band and Summer Pops Youth Orchestra. By the time the youngest son was off to college, Gene had attended several years of concerts. The experience sparked a desire to get into music himself. He took his first tentative step by joining a community choir. "I walked in, they handed me the term's selection of SATB [four-part] music, and they started the practice. I didn't even know what I was supposed to be looking at on the sheets! That was my introduction to reading music."

Gene toughed it out with the choir, gaining confidence to take the next step, which came two years later with the coincidence of two events. His younger son moved on to a better trumpet, leaving the student-model one unused. At the same time, the Little Mountain Brass Band (LMBB) was being formed. Gene saw opportunity here. He already had the motive, and found the means in his son's abandoned trumpet. He started taking trumpet lessons from Jim Littleford, the director of LMBB. Six lessons later, he was playing in the band's trumpet section. Now, three years later, Gene has added two more ensembles to his schedule: a big swing band and a brass quartet.

When we asked Gene how far he had come musically, he replied, "It's a little discouraging to think that an average high school player would be much further along than I am after three years, but you have to put it into perspective.....[they] go to band every day." His goal is to play as well as a high school senior. In the meantime, Gene says, "Playing has given me something I never had before, the ability to create something that others can enjoy."

Fiddlers play by ear. Violinists play from the written note.

Karen Jackson had wanted to play the fiddle since the fifth grade, when she had a friend who was learning the instrument. She pressed her parents to get her a fiddle and start her on lessons. They didn't go for it, but the dream didn't die. In 1998, at 51, she brought it to life. Karen had always been interested in Gaelic songs and poetry. She was intrigued by an item she ran across on the Internet, a week-long session in Gaelic language and singing at the Gaelic College in St. Ann, on the Island of Cape Breton, Nova Scotia. Most of the participants were learning instruments, and Karen met one who let her try out her fiddle. "What a noise, but I was hooked," she said. Back home in Montpelier, Vermont, she noticed an ad on the bulletin board of her food cooperative offering a free one-hour lesson to the first ten people to sign up. It started the wheels churning. Karen figured if she didn't do it then, she would

never do it. On the day before the offer expired, she rented an instrument and signed up. She has since bought a
student-grade fiddle of her own and is taking bi-weekly
fiddle lessons.

At this point in our interview with Karen we asked
her exactly what the difference was, between a fiddle and a
violin. "Fiddles are the same as violins," she said, "except
they use more rosin and go more places. Fiddlers play by
ear. Violinists play from written music." Rosin is the
gummy stuff violinists put on their bows to make them grip
the strings better. Karen explained that you need a lot of
rosin for Scottish music, to give it the staccato lilt it is
known for. Karen has been an avid Contra dancer until
recently, when problems with her back have made dancing
more of a task. Now, she wants to get good enough on the
fiddle to be able to play for other Contra dancers.

Is this in the cards? Now into her 10th month,
Karen describes what she produces as mostly noise, but
says, "Like ski-mobiles, it's only noise to others, not the
one making the sounds." She elaborates on her progress by
describing the feelings she comes away with after attending the occasional Saturday afternoon fiddle jam session at
a restaurant called "Fiddleheads." Fiddlers, pipers,
harpists and assorted other amateur musicians show up on

You need a lot of rosin to play Scottish music.

the first Saturday of each month. They park their coats and cases in one corner of the dining room and pull up chairs. Someone starts off on an Irish tune and those who know it join in. Others quickly pick up the thread. All the while, the patrons either listen to or ignore the music. Karen says the abilities range from musicians who sit in the back and join in as they are able, to very accomplished fiddlers. "When I watch those guys I feel limp and useless, but when I think about how bad I was when I started, I feel like I have really come a long way."

Learning to read music is another milestone. Karen has sung all her life, often in groups that used music written with each part. Though she learned in grade school music class that the lines of the staff were E, G, B, D, F and the spaces F, A, C, E, she wasn't able to correlate this with musical sounds. When it came to reading the notes in choruses, "I pretended to follow the music. What I knew was that if the notes are going up the staff, they're going higher; down the staff is lower; and if it's a big jump, it's a big change in pitch." Now, she is not only learning to read notes written by someone else, but to accurately record the Celtic melodies she plays by ear.

Karen hopes soon to move from "noise" to music, but in the meantime is enchanted by the sounds she can get from her fiddle. "I just love the sound of it, the feel of the buzz on my jaw that comes out of wire on wood." Her long-term goals are to learn enough tunes to be able to play for Contra dancers and to branch out into other types of violin music, such as Stravinski's *A Soldier's Tale,* which she says has a funky fiddle part. Looking back, she says, "When I am tempted to wish I had started fiddling long ago and become as good at it as I am at things I've done for a long time, I realize I am glad I saved some pleasures for my allegedly mature years."

Young players have to contend with instruments designed for full-grown people.

The Real Limits of Age

By citing examples of people successfully taking up a new instrument in mid life and others who continue playing into old age, we don't mean to imply that aging poses no natural limits to making music. It does. As we grow older we stand to encounter any number of physical changes that can

It's only noise to others.

limit what we do. Arthritis in the hands makes it difficult to finger any instrument that requires the use of fingers. Supporting the weight of an instrument can quickly fatigue a person weakened by age. Seeing notes on a page gets increasingly hard as our eyes deteriorate. And there are any number of physical conditions associated with aging that can leave our heart or lungs too weak to cope with the demands of a wind instrument.

But these conditions vary widely from person to person. There are often very effective ways to compensate. Indeed one of the best ones is to use your mind and body in creative activity. Mounting evidence suggests that making music ranks high on the list of candidates. Naturally, we agree. Frank Wilson makes the case better in *Tone Deaf & All Thumbs:* "The answer to when it is too late to begin is that it is never too late, if your interest is recreational."

The Advantages of Age

Many of the consequences of aging are positive—perks you can turn to advantage as you launch yourself into music. Think for a moment of the real advantages you have over young people starting out:

- ❏ You have a goal—you are not simply going through the motions to please someone else.
- ❏ Your superior motivation makes you willing to invest time, money, and your energy in pursuit

of your goal.

❑ Your longer attention span enables you to stay on task longer than a younger person.

❑ Superior analytical powers and ability to concentrate puts you in better stead to assimilate and retain new information.

❑ Your physical growth is complete—young players have to contend with instruments designed for fully-grown people.

❑ Your finger, eye, and hand coordination is better developed than in young people.

❑ Your emotional maturity enables you to put things in perspective and deal with frustration.

❑ You know a lot about how music is supposed to sound just from having listened to it for all those years.

Age gives you these advantages at the starting gate. Once you get going there is very good reason to believe that playing will help you *as you age*. Joanne Bulley, a physician and violinist tells of a comment she overheard after a concert of the Keene (N.H.) Chamber Orchestra, "Look around—the people that are older than 50 don't look that much different that the ones who are 40 or 45." Joanne believes there is something about making music that keeps you younger.

This belief may not be very different from conclusions emerging from solid research. A multi-year study currently underway at the University of Miami is seeking to find how music making affects the brains and immune systems of healthy older adults. The researchers hypothesize that the participants will show:

❑ Higher quality-of-life scores on accepted tests

❑ Better relaxation and response to stress

❑ Increased resistance to disease and enhanced immune system function

If the study bears out even one of these conclusions, it's enough reason to get off your duff and grab a horn.

Another study, from Michigan State University, shows that elderly piano students had an increase in growth hormones, which fight osteoporosis, increase muscle mass, and help with sexual functioning. The levels of these hormones generally drop dramatically with age.

Stan Hinden, writing in the *Washington Post,* listed ten suggestions for growing old successfully. It occurred to us that making music was a natural way to satisfy most of them. Hinden's ten points are summarized below with our tie-in to music making at right.

	Tips for Successful Aging	Relevance to Making Music
1	Find an activity you really love.	Love of music easily translates into love of making music.
2	Maintain your independence.	Choosing an instrument, a style of music, and a setting for playing puts you in control of a part of your life.
3	Exercise regularly--it's good for the mind as well as the body.	Many instruments exercise the arms, hands or lungs. All exercise the mind.
4	Eat healthfully.	No particular relevance to music, but good advice for anyone.
5	Keep your brain in gear.	Making music is an excellent way to focus the mind on a specific activity.
6	Stay involved with people.	Playing an instrument opens the door to becoming an integral part of a musical group.
7	Use your experience and inner strength to survive crises.	Developing skill on an instrument yields confidence and inner strength.
8	Pace yourself--don't feel compelled to rush through life.	As an amateur musician, you can choose your instrument and type of music. You have a lot of say as to how fast you play it.
9	Keep your sense of humor.	Learning an instrument requires a sense of perspective and tolerance for one's mistakes. A sense of humor is part of the process.
10	Reach out to other generations.	Playing in a musical ensemble is an excellent way to connect to people both younger and older.

Chapter 5

I Don't Have Any Talent

Every Monday morning the classroom next to Lucie's erupts with honks, squeaks, and buzzes which eventually resolve themselves into something faintly resembling that great musical classic, *Lightly Row*. In the Franklin Elementary School beginner's band, the only thing more impressive than the noise is the enthusiasm of the children.

"Boy, did you hear that? I bet I can play louder than anybody."

"That's nothing, listen to *this*."

Lucie has no choice but to listen. The experience makes her wonder how she can in good conscience recommend to adults that they put themselves in the position of playing inane melodies badly in front of other people. But she does, claiming she is probably the best person to make that recommendation. When she began trombone after 30 years of no musical involvement, she did so with extreme trepidation. She married into a very musical family who couldn't seem to get together for any occasion without ending up in a jam session. Jerry would look at a strange, unknown, instrument with curiosity and be playing it a half hour later. The rest of the family have played everything from viola to blues harmonica. Within this setting it was more natural for Lucie to cower in the corner than approach the trombone with any confidence. Looking back, she must have had enough confidence in her own innate talent to at least begin on a new and strange instrument. But her confidence wavered. On a bad day she measured her own talent in inverse proportion to her stage fright.

The common belief is that, "some of us have it, some of us don't." Implicit in that statement is the assumption that "most of us don't.".....My belief is that, if you can talk, you can play.

Kenny Werner,
Effortless Mastery: Liberating the Master Musician Within

Ten years later, she sees things differently. Her confidence has grown with each advance in technical proficiency. In the six years she has played trombone in the Westmoreland Town Band, she has gone from the point where a solo would scare her out of her wits to the point where she plays them comfortably and with increasing conviction. She firmly believes that if she can do it, anyone can.

What is Talent, Anyway?

Peter Mose specializes in teaching adult beginners how to play the piano in Toronto, Ontario. Many of them have worked up the courage to pursue a long-held dream, but aren't convinced they have the talent to achieve it. Mose tells them, "Forget about this word 'talent.' We are all musical. What it takes to play the piano is not talent, but thirty minutes a day of diligent practice, and weekly lessons with a teacher you like."

If you don't concur that the value of talent is overestimated, listen to some of the musicians who have made it big. Talent seems definitely optional and, in some cases, may even get in the way. Just think of (fill in the blank with a successful musical personality you can't stand). More seriously, though, the term "musical talent" is a composite of two characteristics:

1. Aptitude
2. Achievement

Aptitude is the stuff you are born with. Like all other aptitudes, you either have it or you don't. It's the genetic predisposition that gives you the potential to make music. The achievement itself comes from applying the aptitude through practice and training. Or, as Ethan Winer, a computer programmer who started the cello at 43 puts it, "I'm convinced that what is often mistaken for musical talent or aptitude is really persistence and enough belief in one's self to keep at it." But even if practice and persistence make up the bulk of what it takes to play an instrument, you have to start out with something. What is the "something" and how much of it do you need?

It was more natural for me to cower in the corner than to approach the trombone with any confidence.

There's no easy answer to that one. The branch of psychology that includes aptitudes is expanding as psychologists continue to identify new aptitudes, or intelligences. **Pitch and rhythm** are two raw materials of sounds we recognize as musical. Wouldn't it be logical, then, to assume that a person's musical aptitude should be defined by their innate sense of these traits? Yes, but. Music is a complex, highly subjective form of human expression that escapes attempts to stuff it into a rigid scientific straitjacket. Music teachers and psychologists generally agree on the raw ingredients that go into the final product, but differ on how important each one is in predicting one's musicality, or aptitude for making music. Other traits, such as **intensity, duration, and timbre** are also important in music. How much of each aptitude should you start out with?

Aptitude is the stuff you are born with. Achievement comes from applying it.

Pitch

No one disagrees that sensitivity to pitch is a bedrock requirement of music making. All musical tones have some place on the scale that makes them higher or lower than other tones. This relative highness or lowness called pitch is caused by the rate of vibration, or frequency, and measured in vibrations per second, or "Hertz" (Hz). The higher the pitch of the tone, the higher the frequency.

A poor opinion of your own pitch sensitivity may be what has kept you out of music. You may have even labeled yourself as "**tone deaf.**" If so, you're probably wrong. At least, if what you mean is that you really can't tell one pitch from another, you may be underestimating your capability. After all, you depend on pitch differences in speech to understand what people mean. If you need convincing of this, say the following sentence out loud:

You're pregnant.

Now say the following:

You're pregnant?

The first example was a statement of fact; the second a question. Say the two in succession and note how the pitch of your voice rises and falls. If you are a native speaker of English, the pitch of your voice rose and fell something like the following:

          preg-
You're   **-nant**

          -nant?
You're preg-

The point is that the same two words in the same order can convey two entirely different meanings by little more than a change of pitch of the voice. If you can manipulate your voice to do this well enough to communicate different meanings to another person, you are not tone deaf. Nor are most people, according to Atarah Ben-Tovim and Douglas Boyd, who in their book *You Can Make Music*, hold that tone deafness is rarer than color-blindness. They claim that if you can get pleasure from music, you are not tone deaf, whatever you have been told. Frank Wilson, a neurosurgeon and amateur pianist, backs this up in *Tone Deaf & All*

Thumbs: An Invitation to Music-Making, a most interesting book for anyone interested in the physiological basis of hearing. Wilson says that what most people mean when they say they are tone deaf is that they can't regulate the pitch of their own voice closely enough to match it to a standard. He suggests that even people who fall into this category can still get into music. The key is to pick an instrument that makes fixed pitch intervals rather than one that depends on the player to temper the pitch. If this fits you, you might do well to steer clear of oboes, bassoons, French horns, or any stringed instruments lacking frets on the neck, and consider a keyboard instrument or one with fretted strings, such as a guitar or banjo.

Bonnie Insull, an accomplished flutist and participating teacher in the *Music for People* workshops, doesn't think there is such a thing as tone deafness. As evidence, she cites the many reversals of workshop participants who thought themselves tone deaf. "People such as this have probably just stopped listening, somewhere at a crucial time, such as the time where we learn languages," she says, and describes a simple test she employs: "If you say you are tone deaf, I would ask you to sing a note, then I would match your note. If you could hear that we are together, I would go up and down from this note. You would signal when you hear me coming into sync."

At the other end of the spectrum from tone deafness are a few gifted people who have what is called "perfect pitch," the ability to recognize the pitch of a tone without the aid of a reference. You can hear a note and say with accuracy, "that's a C." If you are so endowed, you are probably already engaged in making music. If not, you should be. Perfect pitch is a great help. Meanwhile, the rest of us shouldn't get worked up too much. The ability to recognize one pitch in its relationship to another is much more important. You'll need it in order to play an instrument that doesn't have fixed pitch intervals (bowed strings, French horns) and in order to play any wind or string instrument in tune with other players.

Pitch sensitivity can be improved with the proper ear training, say some experts. You can access one training program, *EarTest,* free online (see Brent Hugh's Music Instruction Software, in the Resources section of the appendix). The computer plays a tone of the scale and you

After a long immunity from the dreadful insanity that moves a man to become a musician in defiance of the will of God that he should confine himself to sawing wood, I finally fell a victim to the instrument they call the accordion.

Mark Twain, *A Touching Story of George Washington's Boyhood* indicate with your mouse which note you think it is. When you master the easiest levels you can move on to more difficult ones.

Rhythm

Rhythm is the glue that binds the sounds of music in time, according to their duration and intervening silences. It is a primal urge in all of us that cries out to be expressed. It finds expression in many ways. The steady thud of a pow-wow drum sets the scene for chanting in Native American ritual. Another world apart, a group of African drummers beat out highly intricate rhythmic patterns to dancing and singing. Western music uses different rhythmical patterns to differentiate a waltz from a polka, a march from a minuet, a fox-trot from a two-step. Rhythm is so important to music that it must be perceived and manipulated when playing most any type of music. Miriam Goder, a retired music professor and piano teacher, ranks it even above pitch discrimination as a must for anyone aspiring to make music and not one that everyone has in equal measure.

Author Frank Wilson tells the story of two amateur musicians who often played chamber music together. The amateurs were the famed humanitarian and missionary Albert Schweitzer and the great mathematician-theoretical physicist Albert Einstein. Einstein was having a rough time negotiating a particular passage. Even after several attempts, the rhythm failed to come out right. Exasperated, Schweitzer blurted out: "Count! Count! Dammit, Albert, can't you count?"

Most of us demonstrate sensitivity to rhythm in ways we may not even be aware of. Even if you have never played an instrument, you most likely have tapped your feet to the sound of stirring music. If you do this you probably have the raw stuff of rhythm. Developed and refined in the process of learning an instrument, the raw stuff can become the polished seasoning of your own music.

Most of us demonstrate rhythm in ways we may not even be aware of.

Other Aptitudes

The little story about Albert Einstein makes an important point about music aptitudes: As with all aptitudes, you can have a high degree in one, but not another, even in the same field. No one knows the exact mix of aptitudes that makes one person a more capable musician than another. Those that have been identified most always include sensitivity to pitch and rhythm. Sensitivity to duration, intensity, and timbre also figure in as somehow important parts of the mix, as does the ability to remember sequences of tones.

Duration. What's the main difference between *Yankee Doodle* and *Old Man River*? Tempting as it is to give a joke response, the answer we are looking for is *duration*. The melody of *Yankee Doodle* pops out in rapid-fire sequence, each tone can't seem to wait to exit, to make way for the next one. The tones of *Old Man River* issue forth in a more leisurely manner that evokes a gently flowing river. Each tone is sustained, in no hurry to move along. Singing or playing these pieces in a way that will make them recognizable and appreciated by a listener requires a certain judgment of the length of tones, as well as the length of the spaces between them.

Intensity (Loudness). Except for the most ear-splitting, in-your-face, flavors of rock, all music uses changes in volume as part of the palette of expression. Orchestras and bands evoke calm or excited feelings by varying the intensity from one phrase to the next and by varying the loudness of different instruments to change the balance. Most people with normal hearing can discern these changes. If you can, you can probably learn to enhance the music you play as an amateur musician by varying the intensity.

Timbre. Though it will cause some teeth gnashing among music pros, we'll refer to this quality throughout this book as "tone quality" in most cases, because it is a French word used to mark the difference between the tone of a sax from that of a piano. The differences in tone that make one instrument sound different from another come from a unique pattern of sound wave vibrations—combinations of the fundamental pitch and overtones—that create a signature.

Tonal Memory. Music is more than tone, howev-

Q: What's the difference between bagpipes and a chain saw?

A: A chain saw has better timbre.

er, it is a sequence of tones. The ability to recognize sequences is a key to both appreciating and making music, but in different proportions. Most of us can remember the sequence of tones in *Mary Had a Little Lamb* accurately enough to hum them. But we probably can't reproduce the notes of *The Flight of the Bumblebee* or a symphony, though we may appreciate them and have heard them many times. This is because they contain more complicated sequences of tones, sometimes lacking the repetition that aids memory. Tonal memory is an important aptitude to playing some, but not all, music. Playing a piece with written music in front of you every time doesn't require it; memorizing the piece does. Any kind of improvisation depends on a high degree of tonal memory.

Most people can discern changes in intensity.

Horning In

Rating Your Talent

We have tried to dispel some of the popular misconceptions concerning musical talent and suggest how much of each component aptitude you may need for success in making music. If you are still in doubt about what you have at the starting gate, you can get a more definite idea by taking a musical aptitude test.

Formal testing in musical aptitude has been around since the 1920s and has spawned several standardized tests of pitch, rhythm, intensity, duration, timbre, and tonal memory. The most widely known test is the *Seashore Measures of Musical Talents,* conceived by Carl Seashore in 1919. These tests are mainly aimed at young children and to a lesser extent at college students considering a music major. Though they can be applied to any adult, they are not intended for this purpose, so if you want to take one, you will have to do it through a college or aptitude testing agency.

Musical aptitude tests typically use pairs of sound items heard through earphones. After hearing each pair, you must indicate your answer to the question, such as "same," "different," "higher," or "lower." The results don't typically add up to a total that tells you how much musical aptitude you have, but are put together in some kind of a profile. These tests are time-consuming, tedious, and frustrating, and will appeal mainly to persons who have a crying need to quantify things. Jerry took such a test in the course of research for a prior book on fitting people to careers. It was part of a larger battery of aptitude tests administered by the Johnson-O'Connor Company.

The part that measured pitch sensitivity started innocently enough with two tones played consecutively by an electronic device. He had but a few seconds to mark a response to indicate whether the second tone was higher or lower than the first. The first few examples were a piece of cake. He sailed through them feeling cocky. Then they got harder, as the notes of each pair got increasingly closer in pitch. At one point they converged—or at least he thought they did and would have sworn to that effect. But they kept coming. Why in the hell are they jerking me around like this? he wondered.

The next portion dealt with rhythm sensitivity.

The drill here was administered in much the same way, in pairs of sound bytes. Again, the first few examples were easy to tell apart. Dum-di-dum was obviously not the same as dum-di-di. But before long, he scratched his head trying to decide whether he heard "dum-di-di-di-dum" and "dum-di-di-dum-dum" as same or different. He had reached the drop-out point for his own ability to discern.

A similar series tested tonal memory by airing combinations of tones, asking whether they were same or different. After the last session of acoustic torture he walked out somewhat shaken, convinced that the tests would show he had the musical aptitude necessary to qualify him to operate a jackhammer. On the following day the counselor went over the results of the complete battery (the term is well chosen). He had scored in the 90th percentile in all categories.

If you can't see yourself undergoing this kind of ordeal, you can get an approximate idea of your musical talent from our completely un-scientific quick-and-dirty shotgun test.

The Germer Shotgun Test of Musical Aptitude

- Do you get pleasure from listening to music?
- Can you recognize the differences between the sounds of different instruments, such as a trumpet and flute?
- Can you whistle or hum a melody so that others recognize it?
- Can you tell when someone else is humming a tune off key?
- Can you clap your hands in time to a song with a regular beat, such as *Yankee Doodle* or *When the Saints Go Marching In*?

If you answered each question with a "yes" you probably have enough innate talent to learn a musical instrument. Go for it.

Chapter 6

I Have Physical Disabilities

An auto accident in 1976 left National Public Radio commentator John Hockenberry without the use of his legs. Confined to a wheelchair, but with full use of his arms and hands, he took up the digital electronic piano. He got good enough to audition for entrance into the School of Music at the University of Oregon—except for one thing: he had no way to operate the foot pedal that sustains notes. He compensated somewhat by holding the notes longer with his fingers, but the effort wasn't convincing enough to gain him entry into the program. Undaunted, John fashioned a device out of a rubber bulb that he held between his teeth. When he bit down on the bulb, it compressed air that drove a piston that pushed the pedal down and held it until he unclenched his teeth. Though encouraged, he realized it would take major engineering to make the device practical. He eventually abandoned the piano.

Physical disabilities can undeniably get in the way of playing an instrument. Creative people such as John Hockenberry often devise ingenious ways to compensate for chronic conditions, some of which work, some of which don't. But before you let your physical handicap stand in the way of making music, we encourage you to assess your situation. How does it affect your chances of playing a particular instrument? Are there ways to get around the obstacles? If not, are there other instruments you could play? In this chapter we'll discuss some of the possible impairments you may have and the options they leave you.

Loss of Limbs

Missing limbs can limit your choices but don't necessarily exclude you from playing an instrument. Even John Hockenberry had choices other than the piano. With two arms and hands, he could have chosen an instrument that didn't require his feet to work a pedal. The choices include many small stringed instruments, woodwinds, or brass.

With only one arm, your options are somewhat more limited. You may have heard about the famous piano concerto for the left hand that Maurice Ravel wrote for a friend who had been a renowned concert pianist until his arm was shot off in the First World War. The piece is remarkable not only in that it can be played entirely with one hand, but as a wonderful piece in its own right.

Other pieces have been written for pianists who have only one hand, but there are probably better choices of instruments than piano for a one-armed person. Most woodwinds are out, since they require both hands to cover all the holes or keys. One exception we found is a series of woodwind recorders fitted with extra keys, specially designed for players who have the use of only one hand. The *Gold Series,* made by Dolmetsch, are available for right and/or left hand, in descant and treble recorders.

Better all-round candidates are brass instruments that are fingered by three fingers of one hand. Large brass instruments such as euphoniums and tubas sit in your lap while you operate the valves with one hand. You could both hold and play smaller brass, such as trumpets and cornets, with one hand, either the right or left. The percussion instruments you could play with one hand include bass drums, bells (lyres) and many auxiliary percussive instruments commonly found in community bands.

Diminished Eyesight

George Shearing, Ray Charles, and Stevie Wonder have shown dramatically that you can make wonderful music without the use of the eyes. Music, after all, is an aural rather than visual experience, and people were making it for several thousand years before they got around to devising a way to communicate it by writing. Even today, some genres of music are communicated without writing, such as jazz, folk, and rock. So if your interests are in these areas, you can very likely find your way in by using your ears instead of your eyes.

Jazz, folk, and rock, however, are played largely in small groups where only one person plays a particular part. With larger groups, communication gets more difficult and the likelihood of musical conflict increases. For example, a jazz combo consisting of three melody-line instruments—trumpet, sax, and trombone, plus three rhythm instruments—piano, bass, and drums—can get along quite well playing by ear, following the unwritten traditions that have evolved around this type of music. A 15-piece big band, though, may contain 12 lead instruments—4 saxes, 4 trumpets, and 4 trombones. Given free rein and without the benefit of a written arrangement, their sound would more likely be cacophony, not music.

Thus, the need for written music.

Fortunately, lack of eyesight does not have to preclude one from reading music. Music can be transcribed in Braille and there are ample resources for anyone interested in exploring this medium. Braille music and materials are obtainable, free of charge, from the National Library Service (800-424-8567) and the National Braille Association (716-427-8260). The latter also maintains a transcription service. Computer software, such as the *Goodfeel Braille Music Translator* makes it possible to convert standard music into Braille. Opus Technologies publishes an interactive computer program , *How to Read Braille Music, Second Edition,* which comes with a multimedia CD-ROM disk.

There are also aural self-instructional media for visually impaired persons. *Bill Brown's Introduction to the Piano for the Visually Impaired* and *Introduction to the Guitar for the Visually Impaired* (e-mail: BillBrown@guitarbyear.com) are teach-yourself courses consisting of four cassette tapes, fully Brailled on the tapes and spine. The piano method talks the student through basics such as posture, finding the notes, the names and locations of the flats and sharps, scales and cadences—all by using no Braille or visual references.

Complete blindness, however, isn't the concern of most adults—it's eyes that don't focus as well as they once did. Glasses or contact lenses can usually provide correction, but may need to be augmented to serve your musical endeavors. If you wear bifocals or trifocals and aim to play in a group, you may need a second pair of glasses with a focal length set to the distance between you eyes and the music stand. If your present glasses or contact lenses are not adjusted for that focal length, you can get an auxiliary pair to be used just for playing. That works well for piano playing but what do you do in a band or orchestra? There you need to be able to shift your focus from the music stand to the conductor. No problem if your glasses are monofocle, but this task gets harder if you wear bifocal or trifocal lenses. The angle at which you must hold your head to play your instrument may force you to view the music out of the wrong part of the lens. This constantly plagues Jerry when he plays bassoon or bass clarinet in the band. His trifocals are set so that the top lens corrects for distant objects, while the bottom lens corrects for close-up. Because the middle lens is neutral—set for objects approximately 3 feet from his eyes—he doesn't need its help to see music on the stand. So he simply takes off his glasses. The downside is that he can't see the conductor clearly, though this is an advantage with some conductors.

Hearing Loss

Even with the violin, if one plays delicately, one gets the sense of vibrations in one's bones, and you know where it should be placed.

Yehudi Menuhin

Like eyesight, hearing also decreases with age, as well as with long-term exposure to the loud noises many of us encounter in the workplace. The distinctive and powerful tone that distinguishes Steinway pianos may be due to the fact that the Steinways' own hearing had been impaired by long exposure to the noise in the piano factory, target shooting, and the effects of alcohol, according to Noah Adams, in his book, *Piano Lessons*. Adams suggests that the Steinways were simply trying to make pianos that they could hear.

If you work in an office your ears are probably spared the injurious effects of loud workplace noise. How loud is loud? Sound levels exceeding 85 decibels (db), according to the Consensus Development Conference on Noise and Hearing Loss of the National Institutes of Health. The panel says people exposed to sounds louder than 85 db for 8 hours a day will eventually suffer permanent hearing loss. About a third of the 28 million people in the U.S. with hearing loss have it because of long-term exposure to noise in the workplace. Especially vulnerable are firefighters, police officers, military personnel, construction and factory workers, farmers, truck drivers and—musicians.

That musicians risk hearing loss by plying their craft should come as no surprise. We all know of the tragic irony that beset Beethoven. Just as he was reaching the pinnacle of his musical prowess he had to struggle ever harder to hear the product of his genius. Professional musicians often incur diminished hearing over the long haul, depending on the type of sonic assault they are prey to. Flutists, for example, may get hearing loss in the right ear, which is the one closest to the instrument.

When Harry didn't like the music the band was playing, he simply turned off his hearing aid.

But, sadly, those who make the music are only a small part of the people whose hearing may be endangered by it. If you have ever been to a live rock concert, you have probably been exposed to sounds that frequently exceed the 85 db level, crossing the threshold of pain. Curt Taipale, a sound engineer and ex-rock musician drives this point home poignantly in an article he wrote for *Soundcheck Magazine.* His ears were already starting to hurt, at a Michal W. Smith concert, when he noticed a family two rows up—two parents, a teenage daughter and young son about 3 years old. While mom, dad, and the daughter bopped to the music, the little boy tucked himself into a ball in his seat, his hands covering his ears. Dad occasionally picked him up, pried his hands from his ears, and tried to jolly him into the euphoria, which only caused the kid to scream in terror. But during the quieter songs the boy was also quiet. The dad's attempts to inflict this aural pain on his young son infuriated Taipale. "I wanted to punch the guy's lights out and rescue the kid. This little 3 year old had more sense than the combined intelligence of the other 2,000 people attending the concert."

Our own son now 28, has played in rock groups for about six years. For much of his time in rehearsal or on stage he wears earplugs. But the kids in the audience don't, and it remains to be seen how their hearing will fare by the time they reach their 40s. An even greater threat to their hearing comes from the portable sound sets consisting of earphones-plus-playing device, according to Bernadette Quinn, an audiologist at the Hitchcock Clinic, Keene, N.H. A sound of 90 db delivered through earphones has more potential for injury to the eardrum than a 100 db sound in a concert hall, she says.

We start out being able to hear sounds ranging from 20 to 20,000 cycles per second, or Hertz (Hz). To put this into perspective, a piano's range is 27.5 Hz to 4,186 Hz. With age, hearing tends to decrease, particularly in the higher frequencies. Age-related hearing loss (presbycusis) tends to run in families and affects about one in every four people aged 65—75 and half of those over 75. Ironically, as electronic technology has increased the ability to reproduce sounds in all frequencies, it has also given us the devices that ruin our hearing. So we end up with expensive and very accurate home entertainment systems whose highest and lowest sounds we can't even hear. The condition is progressive and without cure. You may not notice any hearing loss until your spouse gets mad after having to tell you what was said in a movie one too many times. Other clues to hearing loss include:

❏ You find it hard to understand phone conversations
❏ You lose track of conversations that involve more than one other person
❏ Others complain that you turn up the TV too loud
❏ Background noise makes it hard for you to discern other sounds
❏ You have a harder time understanding the speech of women and children than men

You should have your hearing tested by a competent audiologist if you suspect you have hearing loss. Select one who doesn't sell hearing aids and who can give you an honest appraisal of your hearing and how it should affect your playing an instrument.

Deafness is a matter of degree. Hearing aids can often amplify the incident sounds enough to restore a range of hearing that will enable you to both enjoy and play music. Four members of our town band get along quite well with the help of hearing aids. One of these, Cindi Brooks, has worn a hearing aid for 23 years. She grew up in a musical environment, has played a tenor sax for much of her adult life, and intends to continue as long as she is able. Cindi's hearing aid is not directional, so it doesn't allow her to hear with the same acuity the ear. She says she compensates by watching the conductor for cues as to whether she is playing too loud or soft. The only other adjustment she makes is an occasional twist of her volume button, when the trumpets are too loud.

There is good news for musicians and other people who must discern a wide range of frequencies in their hearing, according to audiologist Bernadette Quinn. Where standard analog hearing aids dropped off for frequencies above 4,000 Hz, the new digital hearing aids extend amplification to 6,000 Hz with even better potential in the future. Present costs of these units are expensive, however: $2,500-$4,000, versus $600-$700 for an analog device.

About one-third of Americans between age 65 and 74 and one-half of those age 85 and older have hearing problems. They may mistake words in a conversation, miss musical notes at a concert, or leave a ringing door bell unanswered.

Hearing and Older People
www.agenet.com

Stiff Joints

All instruments require movement of various muscles and bones, but in different degrees. Assuming your mouth is up to the task, you can play a valved brass instrument using only three fingers of your right hand. Woodwinds call for the use of both hands and all ten fingers. An organ involves both hands and both feet. The free movement of these joints can lessen with age and be aggravated by activities we engage in as part of our work.

Carpal Tunnel Syndrome. Office workers exposed to nothing louder than low-level Muzak and the gentle tapping of computer keyboards may escape noise-induced hearing loss only to find they are vulnerable to another injurious consequence of modern life—carpal tunnel syndrome (CTS). The result of repetitive motions of the hands and wrists over a period of time, CTS occurs when a nerve that runs from the arm to the fingers gets compressed inside the narrow passage in the wrist called the carpal tunnel. Symptoms include pain, numbness, tingling, and muscle atrophy in the thumb and fingers in severe cases. Cures begin at the cause. If working at a keyboard is the culprit, better posture, a more ergonomically sensitive keyboard, and varying the work pattern with wrist exercises can help. Wrist splints that stabilize the wrist but leave the fingers free are a mainstay treatment device for mild cases. In extreme cases, surgery is warranted.

You can get or worsen CTS by playing certain instruments. Violins, violas, and pianos are heavy contenders, because of the repetitive fine motor control they exact on the fingers. Joanne Bulley, an obstetrician and gynecologist, is an accomplished amateur violinist who has played for more than 20 years. During her pregnancy 11 years ago, both hands went numb for two months, victims of CTS. The effect was profound. "Everything I had done in my life involve my hands and wrist, whether it's violin, piano, being a surgeon, being a gynecologist," she said. She recently had surgery in both wrists, in which the ligaments were cut and the hand put in a cast to allow the ligaments to heal across the cut, but farther away from the nerve. She reported that the feeling returned within 24 hours of the surgery. She intends, in the future, to use biofeedback to sense the correct way to hold her violin and not practice for extended periods.

Joanne's story is not meant to scare you off of taking up an instrument that requires repetitive use of your hands and wrists if you are at risk because of your work. She suggests you consult with a physical therapist or sports medicine specialist, rather than a physician. If you are going to be paying $40-$60 to take lessons anyway, it's

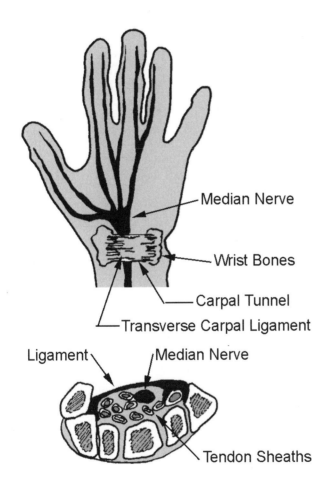

The carpal tunnel is a two-inch-long enclosed region at the undersurface of the wrist and base of the palm. This region contains nine flexor tendons that flex the fingers and thumb-- each of which is surrounded by a sheath to allow easy gliding when moving.

I Have Physical Disabilities

worth paying $60 for a therapy session to learn how to avoid damage. In his book, *The Musician's Survival Manual: A Guide to Preventing and Treating Injuries in Instrumentalists*, Richard Norris, an amateur flutist and M.D. who specializes in performing arts medicine, recommends other precautions: pay careful attention to the technique with which you play, especially your wrist position, limit the time your fingers are in the extremes of flexion or extension.

Arthritis. Affecting many people in their 40s and beyond, arthritis is actually not a single disease at all, but an umbrella term that covers a number of medical conditions that cause painful movement and inflammation of the joints, which can impede playing any instrument needing hand control. The effects can be mildly to extremely debilitating and the response to treatment varies in equal measure. The Arthritis Foundation advises patients to take an active role in managing their care. Exercise helps in many cases, resulting in stronger muscles which stabilize joints, a stronger heart, more stamina and better sleep. But it must be done at the time of day when you have the least pain and stiffness. Start slowly, gradually increasing the time and number of repetitions.

Lucie chose the trombone partly because she suffered bouts of rheumatoid arthritis in her hands. She worried that she would lose motor control of her fingers which, combined with the pain, would make resuming playing the flute impractical. With trombone, she could shift the emphasis from fingers to her right wrist.

Arthritis in itself is not reason enough to steer clear of music making. But, because its effects are so widely varied, there is no one-size-fits-all advice as to the best instrument or what you can realistically hope to play. Dr. Norris suggests you get an opinion from a physical therapist or other specialist in physical medicine or rehabilitation.

Multiple Sclerosis (MS). He gives the same advice for people suffering from multiple sclerosis. Like arthritis, this disease can limit your capacity to play an instrument, but—unlike arthritis—by it does so by robbing the joints of their sense of feeling. The effects can range from mild to disabling, resulting in varying degrees of spasticity, paralysis, stiffness, or weakness.

The National Multiple Sclerosis Society (NMSS), advises people with MS to make physical activity a regular part of life. The exercise recommended can include a broad range of activities—everything from t'ai chi or yoga to gardening, fishing, walking, or playing with a pet. Playing a musical instrument while not specifically mentioned, seems to fit nicely into this spectrum. The important thing is to understand your own limits and not push yourself to the fatigue point. Country singer Donna Fargo puts it more eloquently: "Having MS does not mean that your life is over. It does mean that you now have a new challenge. I encourage you to meet each day with a positive attitude. I'll keep singing, if you keep trying."

Lung Problems

Difficulty with breathing can limit any kind of physical activity. It can really get in the way of playing a wind instrument. We looked long and hard to find relationships between respiratory conditions and playing a wind instrument, without much success. Each case has to be considered on its own merits. Many amateur musicians with breathing ailments find a way around them. Peggy Saunders suffers from chronic asthma, yet has played clarinet regularly for years. She can't obviously play during an attack, but says playing doesn't worsen her condition, in general. An English expert, Dr. Richard Dryden, says that, within reason, nothing should prevent a person with asthma from playing a wind instrument, provided that they perceive the exercise as rewarding and not stressful. It may even be beneficial, he suggests, because playing involves conscious control over both inspiration and expiration. Dryden backs up this assertion with a 1994 study that found that teenage wind instrumentalists had significantly better "asthma health" than their non-playing peers and they perceived themselves better able to cope with the affliction.

The American Lung Association says that one of the best things you can do for yourself if you suffer shortness of breath from some lung diseases is to get some exercise or activity every day. Exercise that promotes stamina, such as walking and arm/leg movement, is recommended.

Playing an instrument isn't specifically named, but should be, we think, because it requires physical movement, and, in the case of wind instruments, breath control.

Asthma is, of course, just one of many respiratory disorders. The list is long, ranging from seasonal bouts of hayfever to chronic conditions of asthma or emphysema. Some, such as cancer, pneumonia, and tuberculosis, can even be life threatening. You can get specific advice on how your lung condition might affect your playing an instrument from consulting your physician, and general advice from the American Lung Association's Lung Line, 800-222-5864 (lungusa.org).

Understand Your Status—Know Your Options

We have talked about only a few of the many possibly disabling conditions that can get in the way of playing an instrument. What we want to highlight is that while these conditions affect what you can play, they don't automatically preclude you from playing. There are often ways to compensate. Some are as simple as listening to what your body is telling you and responding realistically. If a chronic condition fatigues you, choose the times when you feel more energy for playing. If you risk repetitive motion conditions such as carpal tunnel syndrome from working too long at a computer keyboard, seek out ways to vary your activity, improve your posture and use ergonomically appropriate equipment.

Technical devices may offer help, be they the right corrective eyewear or hearing aids to devices designed for special needs. Wearing a neck strap while playing clarinet, for example, relieves the right thumb of supporting the instrument, lessening the chance for damage to the thumb joint and wrist. Richard Norris suggests that instruments themselves can often be altered so that the holes are raised higher than normally, to better suit a player with less than average finger motion.

Music is too valuable a human experience to forsake for a wobbly excuse. Imagine how Beethoven's later life might have been improved if he had only had a hearing aid.

 Chapter 7

I Don't Have the Time

Nobody seems to have any free time, these days. Life seems as frantic as ever for us, even now, with our two children grown and gone from the house. Our household timetable is set by Lucie's schedule, since she's the one who works at a regular job outside the home. We're up at 5:34, finished with our breakfast by 6:05, back from our morning walk by 6:30. After 15 minutes of quiet meditation—the only quiet she will experience until the end of the day—Lucie packs up all her cares and woes and heads out to teach ESL (English as a second language) to 40 non-native students in three different schools. As with all conscientious teachers, the hours Lucie spends in the school represent only part of the time required to do her job well. Preparation takes up a lot of her time at home. Effecting communication between the parents of her students and the schools eats up even more. Most of her students' parents are immigrants with limited or no English themselves who depend on Lucie to help them communicate with the school authorities. With all this, she magically finds time for music, which at this time consist of a weekly trombone lesson, practicing, rehearsing and performing in a community band and a brass quintet.

Jerry's schedule is by comparison a breeze. After Lucie leaves at 7:00, he heads up to the home office to start his workday as architect and writer. The early start suits him, because he accomplishes his most productive work in the morning. He starts to sag in the early afternoon, so uses these hours for other errands and workouts at the YMCA.

As children we think we have forever. As adults we have learned how fragile life can be and we had better start right away and hope we have the time to accomplish the things we want to do. The only way to keep this thought from overwhelming us is to realize that the journey and every step along the way are precious.

Pat Onufrak

When he returns around 3:30 he puts in a few more hours of work or knocks off for the day, depending on his workload. This leaves a lot of discretionary time in the evenings and weekends to devote to music and other hobbies. He is not presently taking lessons, but practices almost every day to keep up with the demands of the groups he plays with. He has set another goal for this year: learning three separate Mozart concertos, one each for horn, clarinet, and bassoon.

How is your day structured? If you are self-employed you can set your own schedule, though many self-employed people end up working longer hours than people who work for an employer. But many of these, like Lucie, end up with little free time.

If you are one of these, you are not alone. Lack of time is the single biggest obstacle that stands between adults and music making. People we interviewed see time as an increasingly scarce commodity in their lives. They credit computers and other technological advances for making it possible for to produce more work faster, but, when all is said and done, doubt whether the progress has yielded them any more free time. Andrew Kimbrell bears this out in an article in the *Utne Reader*. He maintains that, in spite of technology, we are working harder than ever, and cites a poll in which 88 percent of workers said their jobs required longer hours and 68 percent complained of having to work faster.

People squeezed in the time trap have to parcel out their few hours of free time between families, community obligations, and keeping the house and car in working order. If there is any left, they are too tired to do anything more challenging than veging out in front of the TV or sitting at their home computer.

They may be spending much more time watching TV than they imagine and getting too little out of it, according to Robinson and Godbey, in *Time for Life,* a study of three decades of how Americans use time. According to the authors, Americans actually gained about 5 hours per week over the two decades between 1965 and 1985. And how did we spend this free time? Mostly watching television. The authors cite other studies that describe the effects of this use of leisure: deterioration of mood, decreased mental capabilities, decline in physical

Adult beginners are willing to spend time, money, and effort—often despite heavy demands on their schedule—in the belief that they can create something beautiful musically.

John Payne

fitness and increase in obesity.

People who spend much of their free time in front of a computer may be searching the Internet, writing e-mail, or just playing games. It's not so much what they are doing, as what they are not doing—exercising their bodies, interacting with others (other than on a virtual basis), creating something of beauty (unless they are writing or illustrating). If you are one of these, do you feel enriched when you leave your computer, or is it mostly a time to escape from the cares of the day and veg out?

We all need time to relax with an activity that puts as few demands as possible on our brain. And reaching for the TV remote certainly fills this need more easily than getting a sax out of the case, putting it together, wetting the reed, and practicing. And even if most of what's on TV makes us apathetic, stupid, weak, and fat, there are shows that are worthwhile. Nonetheless, Robinson and Godbey found that Americans reported getting less enjoyment out of TV than most other free-time activities. On a scale of 1-10, TV rated 7.8. Making music rated 9, ever so slightly behind sex, at 9.2.

What's Important?

How to organize your life to find more free time is a mainstay of self-help books and magazines these days, so we won't add to the clutter here. Suffice it to say that many of these sources agree that the first step is analyse how you spend your time in a typical day, then prioritize the activities. Ask yourself what music participation counts as. Is it recreation—and thereby in the same slot as watching TV? Or is it more like therapy, related to yoga or meditation? The second category seems more important. After all, you would probably get up from watching a TV program to get to an appointment with your therapist, but wouldn't likely spring from the therapist's couch to make it home in time for a TV show.

Decide what's important, then prioritize your activities.

If you conclude that you can enrich your life by getting actively into music, you need to make it high on your priority list. Work out how much time your participation will take each day or week. Consider the time required for:

❏ Lessons or other learning methods
❏ Practicing
❏ Playing in groups

How much time will all this require? Let's assume you are a normally busy adult and that you have a pretty realistic idea about where you want to go with music—somewhere between "by next year I'll be ready for a recital at the Met" and "by next year I'll be ready to play in front of my sister's family." Can you squeeze in twenty minutes in a day for five or six days a week? (less than the time you would spend watching a re-run). Twenty minutes won't get you to the same point in six weeks that an hour a day would, but twenty minutes of relaxed, focused practice will get you much further than an hour of time where part of your mind is still at work or centered on other problems.

Sandy Van der Kauter told of how she found time to practice cello when she worked as an attorney in Chicago. "I realized that if I waited until after work, I wouldn't do too well—there were other free-time things I wanted to, so I got up early before work. I found that if I could get up at 6, I could get up at 5. It was dark anyway, so what was another half hour?"

Finding Time

People asked how I found time to practice, but time expands when you're interested in something.
Michael Kimmelman, art critic
The New York Times

As an adult, you have more wiggle room in several matters connected with learning music than a child starting out. You may as well use this flexibility to the greatest advantage.

First, when setting up lessons, seek out a teacher or music school that is used to accommodating adult students. They are more likely to understand your scheduling hardships than teachers who deal primarily with school-age students. Lessons typically last an hour or half hour and run once a week. You can probably find a time after work or in the evening or weekend that will suit both you and your teacher. If your work schedule is too unpredictable for regular weekly lessons, consider lessons once every two weeks, once every three weeks, or as arranged on an *ad hoc* basis. If you opt for a learning method that doesn't require a teacher, such as self-teaching books, videos, or cassette tapes, you'll be free to structure your lesson time however you want to.

Then there is, um, practicing. The word itself may carry tainted baggage from your youth. Visions of mother standing guard, making sure you don't sneak out to play with your friends when you should be sitting at the upright struggling with "The Happy Farmer." Anyway, call it what you will, you can't learn to play without playing, so you'll need to schedule some time for it. How much and how

Find a teacher willing to accommodate your schedule.

often is where the flexibility comes in. Music teachers we talked to agree that a short, but frequent practice session is preferable to a rarer, but longer, one. The important thing is to practice enough to make progress and to *feel* that you are making progress. If you are starting from scratch, allot at least 20 solid minutes every day between lessons. When you get into the groove, you'll know how much you need and have a better idea of where to find the time.

Practicing alone is good for growing in technique, but may not be enough to keep your enthusiasm high. For that, you need the interaction with others. Playing in a group—a duo, quintet, band, or orchestra—is what keeps most amateur musicians going. You may begin very early in an ensemble, and there are plenty of groups that accept beginners. Or, wait until you have enough confidence to join an established group. In any case, start thinking now of how much time you might have available for group rehearsals.

Finding free time is one of the biggest hurdles for most adults who want to engage in music. The many amateurs we interviewed who find time to play, in spite of their busy professional lives, overwhelmingly concur that the quest is worth the effort.

Practicing alone is a good way to grow your technique, but you need to practice with others to get the most out of your musical development.

Horning In

 Chapter 8

The Dog Ate My Homework

By now we've hopefully knocked down the biggest hurdles keeping you out of music: age, lack of talent, physical disabilities, and time. In this chapter, we'll do battle with some of the less-often mentioned impediments. If any of them sound familiar, it's up to you to decide if they are real or an excuse on par with "the dog ate my homework?"

I'm Short on Patience

"I just don't have the patience for it," the reason many people give for not getting into, or back into, music prompts two questions:

> How much does it take?
> How much do you have?

Learning a new instrument takes a mountain of patience if you don't know an eighth note from a bank note. It takes less, maybe a hummock of patience, if you can read music. If you can read music and have ever played another instrument, learning a new one will be even easier. You'll be surprised at how many skills carry over to your new instrument. Achieving any competency still takes patience, though it depends on the instrument and what you aim to accomplish.

Assessing how much patience you have for such an endeavor isn't an exact science. Most of us have had to acquire new skills just to keep up with the rapidly changing pace of technology in the workplace.

Jerry exhibits next to zero patience for computers and their applications. Rather than welcome each new development, he tends to balk, holding out until the last minute to obtain new software and subject himself to a tedious, frustrating, and at times humiliating learning curve. Yet, he marvels at what he has added to his bag of cybernetic tricks over the past ten years. He has acquired and become at least somewhat competent with desktop publishing and graphic imaging software. As this is being written he is tearing out what little hair he has left, struggling to work out the kinks of a computer-interactive music accompaniment program (more about that in chapter 16).

You, too, have probably acquired new computer skills in the recent past which change the way you do things. How much patience did it take to acquire those new skills? We thought so. So don't sit there and tell us you don't have patience. Instead, consider how patience relates to learning.

First, everyone knows that people learn different things at different rates. You can be a whiz at math but an oaf at languages. But could you be a whiz at math and still get frustrated by not being able to count the rhythms in a measure of a particular piece of music? After all, aren't music and math supposed to be related aptitudes? Maybe. But a counselor at the Johnson O'Connor Research Foundation told us that psychologists now acknowledge many—not just one—math aptitudes. You can ace calculus but forget a phone number in the time between looking it up and dialing it.

Second, frustration is inevitable. You can expect to hit chuck holes at some point in the road with almost any musical instrument. But rather than chalking up your frustration to a lack of patience, find ways to minimize the frustration. Here are a few tips:

Don't let other frustrations interfere with your music.

❑ Pick an instrument with which you have a reasonable chance of success. If your finger dexterity is low, it will be easier to work the three valves of a trumpet than the many keys and holes of a sax. A trombone will be easier, still, since the slide is moved with wrist/arm motion, with minimal dependence on the fingers (you can get an idea of what's required for all of the major instruments in Part Three).

❑ Find a good mentor. Whether you rely on a knowledgeable friend or relative, or a professional teacher, seek a person who not only knows the instrument, but can support you, as an adult learner, throughout the ups and downs of the learning curve (more about finding a teacher in chapter 15).

❑ Set realistic goals. Hearing Haifetz play Mendelsohn's Violin Concerto may have attracted you to the violin and may even serve as a good model, but if you start out hell-bent to play it like Haifetz, you are probably setting yourself up for failure. Realize that you probably won't reach a level anywhere near the pros, but it doesn't matter if your goal is playing for pleasure. A simpatico mentor will understand this and help you set goals that

Practice only when you are in a positive mental state.

Pick an instrument that offers you a reasonable chance for success.

you can reach and feel good about.

❏ Find an outlet as quickly as possible. Amateur musicians who stay with it do so largely because of the support and satisfaction they get from playing with others of similar interests.

❏ Practice only when you are in a positive mental state. This is likely the toughest advice to follow for adults who have to squeeze their playing time in after a stressful day at work. Even so, tackling a frustrating activity when your mind is at peace will be less frustrating than at a time when you are stressed out.

Finally, give yourself permission to fail. Learning how to play an instrument will come with peaks and valleys. Unlike the pros who *have to* succeed, you don't. You can play or not play, and play at any level that satisfies you. Enjoy the peaks and shrug your shoulders at the valleys.

I Don't Have a Place to Practice

Lack of a practice space seldom means lack of physical space. It more often comes down to not having a place you can play without fear of disturbing or being disturbed by others. This is a valid concern. What comes out of your cello at the beginning may drive your cat from the room, while you (and probably even the cat) can live with that, you don't want it to upset members of your household or alienate your neighbors. And the idea of their hearing your every mistake can inhibit you from playing freely and openly.

There is usually a solution, but each case is different. In chapter 5 Joanne Bulley told about trying to practice her piano when her children were young. Her baby grand piano occupied a prominent and more-or-less fixed piece of real estate in the living room. As such, it was a part of the room, in the minds of the kids. So they had nothing to suggest that mom was off limits when she was playing the piano. Joanne toyed with the possibility of isolating the piano by surrounding it with shoji screens. She opted instead for changing the kids' attitudes in order to create a psychological barrier that went up at practice time.

The shoji screen fix might have worked just as well. While it wouldn't have isolated the sounds a whit, it would have defined a space that was off limits to the kids. Pianos tend to be large, stationary items hard to isolate. Finding a physical solution to the space problem for a smaller instrument is much easier. An unused room with a door is the first and most obvious answer. For pianists there is a fix that leaves the large instrument in place. Get an electronic piano and plug in the earphones when you are practicing.

A variety of devices are available to enable you to practice certain instruments. Drummers can play almost silently on practice pads. Practice mutes dampen the sound of brass instruments. Violinists can acquire solid-body violins that connect to earphones.

Sounds travel in all directions. Just as your sounds can disturb others within hearing range, their noises can be an obstacle to your concentration. The solutions are similar to those suggested for isolating them from your sounds: changing behavior, changing location, or practicing on an instrument using earphones. The behavioral approach might be as simple as negotiating: "I won't play *Lady of Spain* on my accordion while you are watching MTV if you won't pump up the decibels while I'm practicing." The location approach might entail not only finding a separate room, but a particular type of room. Sound reaches our ears by pressure waves through the air (airborne sound) and by vibrations induced into the structure directly. You can shut out most noise from other parts of the house by isolating yourself in a room as remote from the noise source as feasible and keeping the door closed. If you really want to minimize the outside noise, you can weather-strip the door and modify the walls to increase their sound absorption.

Pick a room above the fray, if possible. Tucked away in the basement may isolate you well enough from airborne noise, but will do nothing to quiet the thumping of feet on the floor above. Footfalls induce vibrations directly into the structure, which acts like the diaphragm of a speaker to broadcast the noise to the room below. An attic or upstairs bedroom puts you safely away from this problem.

If you play an acoustic piano, consider either getting a digital piano or other electronic keyboard that will allow you the option of playing it through earphones with the speakers turned off. Practicing in this mode not only prevents your sounds from escaping beyond your ears, but also keeps outside noise from interfering with your concentration. It also affords the kind of privacy that you may need in the beginning, if you are reluctant to expose others to your initial efforts. Wearing earphones might seem a bit claustrophobic at first, but you can probably get used to them.

You may have to be creative to find a quiet place to practice.

I Don't Want to Get Stuck with Classical Music

Heidi Scanlon, a Washington, DC web researcher and fitness trainer, has played piano since her youth. Beginning with classical, she went on to achieve competence in other genres. But whatever she played, she played from the written note. Even when called upon to improvise, she did so by memorizing a written-out arrangement. About a year and a half ago Heidi sought to broaden her reach and learn to play by ear. She felt she could best do it on an instrument other than piano, so as to avoid having to unlearn habits formed over many years. Country fiddling seemed just right, offering not only the chance to learn a new instrument, but a type of music that is learned almost exclusively away from the printed sheet. Neophytes typically link up with an experienced fiddler mentor who shows them the basics and teaches them a few tunes, which they learn by imitation. Eventually they gained enough skill and confidence to add the little stylistic flourishes that distinguish one fiddler from another. When last we talked, Heidi told us how much fun she was having fledging her wings at fiddling jams in the Washington, DC area.

Even though it uses the same instrument, fiddling just doesn't seem to have the same cachet as playing a violin. "Serious" violinists tend to think of fiddling as a more primitive form of violin playing, says Heidi. In fact, she adds, classical violin playing and fiddling come from two different traditions. Classical playing connotes playing from written music for the purpose of listening. Fiddling means playing by ear, largely for dancing. Besides, a classical violinist couldn't necessarily play a fiddle tune, without undoing a lot of habits, such as losing the vibrato, then learning to drone with one string while playing the melody with another.

Heidi shows that it is possible to shift between musical styles. If your view of the world of music was frozen in your youth, it can be thawed. Now that you don't have to please a parent or music teacher, you are free to approach music with a blank slate. Why not put this freedom to good use? The following table lists a few suggestions for how you can pump new life into an instrument resurrected from dormancy. Of course, if you are starting from scratch, you can begin in the third column.

Instrument	Early Experience	Possible New Directions
Piano	Lessons, scales, etudes, solos	Pop songs, jazz from fake books; new tonal combinations from digital piano or synthesizer
Violin, viola, cello	Lessons, scales, etudes, solos, playing in the school orchestra	Community orchestras; country fiddling; jazz violin; Klezmer fiddling
String bass	Lessons, scales, etudes, solos, playing in the school orchestra	Jazz from fake books; community orchestras; string ensembles; Dixieland bands; rock bands (switch to electric bass)
Cornet, trumpet, French horn, trombone, tuba	Lessons, scales, etudes, solos, playing in the school band or pep band	Jazz from fake books; community bands and orchestras; brass ensembles; oompah (German) bands; Dixieland bands
Clarinet, sax	Lessons, scales, etudes, solos, playing in the school orchestra	Jazz from fake books; community bands and orchestras; woodwind ensembles; Dixieland bands
Flute, oboe, bassoon	Lessons, scales, playing in the school band or orchestra	Community bands and orchestras; flute choirs; woodwind ensembles
Anything else	Unpleasant experience you are just as happy to forget	Learn any instrument that is new to you.

Second Movement:

GETTING THE RIGHT INSTRUMENT

Choosing an instrument can be hard or easy. Maybe you once heard Itzak Perlmann solo at a live concert and, overwhelmed by the beauty of the music, knew that the violin was the instrument for you. This kind of falling in love happens more often than you might imagine. Many of the people we interviewed described it, and all made it clear that this kind of strong response makes any other instrument second best. Go with it.

But if you are like most people, the choice isn't quite that easy. If you learned piano in your youth, you certainly don't want to waste the time and effort you put into it. The trouble is that right now, all you recall in connection to the word, piano, *is* the drudgery, when what you really want is music. Maybe you should switch to an instrument that doesn't exhaust you before you even begin.

This part of the book aims to help you make the right choice. We start out with Lucie's path from high school flute player to mid-life trombonist. The following five chapters explore the potentials offered by various instruments, according to the families by which they are usually grouped: percussion (chapter 10), strings (11), woodwinds (12), brass (13), and keyboards (14). We cover everything from woodwind recorders to synthesizers. Well, not everything, exactly. There are hundreds of instruments to choose from, many more than we could include with any details in this book. We chose to discuss the instruments we felt would offer the most potential to you as a beginning adult or as an adult who, having played an instrument earlier, would like to consider something new. If we left out harps, lutes, mandolins, and ukuleles from Chapter 11, it wasn't because we didn't think them worthy instruments. They are, and certainly have a niche in the world of music. It's just that we felt the niche wasn't quite big enough to make them good candidates for folks looking for the widest repertoire or the best candidates for playing in groups. If you have an interest in any of these, though, we encourage you to find out about them through other books, the Internet, or friends.

Chapter 9

Should a 45~Year~Old Woman Take Up the Trombone?

Lucie's first instrument was the flute--the family flute--the one her father played in college. She didn't especially want to play the flute. She wanted to play the harp, but for some reason her parents vetoed it. So the flute it was, and once reconciled to the idea, Lucie decided that the flute had the most beautiful sound in the world. She remembers the excitement of her first lessons, when Mr. Dearborn promised her that no woodwind player could ever get tuberculosis. It wasn't something that she'd ever worried about, but was still glad that something she enjoyed was somehow good for her.

     She remembers once taking her flute along on a family picnic by the Housatonic River. As she sat on a rock by the water and played, the sounds sparkled like the sun on the river.

     That joy was soon dashed by her fifth-grade music teacher, Mr. Merritt, who said two things that haunted her for years: "Follow the notes exactly, because the closer you come to what's written, the better you'll play," and "Now that you're getting better, you can start working hard for your first solo recital." That did it. Her fingers clamped down hard on the keys, and from that day on she held the flute in such a death grip that it was a wonder that any notes were able to escape. She continued to work hard, though it

I have learned that there lies dormant in the souls of all men a penchant for some particular musical instrument, and an unsuspected yearning to learn to play on it, that are bound to wake up and demand attention some day.

Mark Twain

---

never crossed her mind to explain to Mr. Merritt that she didn't want to play in a recital. She wanted to go back and make music with the Housatonic River.

Her sounds got more and more strangled, so it was probably just as well that she continued the family tradition and passed the flute on to her younger brother. He, too, eventually lost interest and returned it to Lucie. It followed her around from move to move during the next two decades, never getting out of the case.

Fast forward to the time our two children were in elementary and middle school. Max was taking trumpet. Cinda had begun clarinet, passed down from Jerry, who had not played it since high school. Jerry got his start on piano in his youth, played it professionally through college, and had kept his interest since then by playing it at home. With three of the four family members making music, Lucie began to see music as a way to bond the family and thought how nice it would be if the family could play together. For her part, she dusted off the long neglected family flute and started to play along with Jerry, reading from several music books of show tunes and standards he had accumulated over the years.

Max, Cinda, and Lucie joined the Marlborough, N.H. Town Band, a summer band designed to keep the kids playing during the summer. It also included a fair number of adults, many who were parents like Lucie, who wanted to encourage their children to do something they'd given up themselves. Jerry didn't play a band instrument at the time, but caught the fever, borrowed a baritone and joined the next summer.

It was fun. The music was easy, we were playing together as a family, and Lucie hadn't forgotten too many of the flute fingerings. The trouble was, she also hadn't forgotten her panicky habits from years ago. After a couple of summers she realized that while she still thought the flute had a beautiful sound, it was just not what she wanted to play.

Jerry's brother Russ is a professional trombonist. Lucie always loved to listen to him play. Here was an instrument whose tone was as mellow and rich as a flute's —but more so. It sounded the way a hot fudge sundae tastes.

That was the instrument for her, she decided, but

not without some trepidation. We hashed it out in conversations such as this:

Lucie: I've got to stick with flute. We can't afford a trombone.

Jerry: We don't have to buy one, at least not at first. We can rent one for $30 a month.

Lucie: But I don't know where to start.

Jerry: Why not start with a few lessons from Phil Crotto?

Lucie: But I'm too old to start on a new instrument.

Jerry: Come on, how old will you be if you don't start a new instrument?

Lucie: But I can't just cross over from flute to trombone.

Jerry: Why not?

Lucie: Because we can't afford a trombone!

She now realizes that her excuses were nothing more than flak thrown up to overcome the dread planted years ago by Mr. Merritt. Somehow, in the past few years, she has gotten through the dread and reached the point where she gets real comfort and enjoyment out of playing. She has played in the trombone section (has actually been the trombone section for some of the time) in the Westmoreland Town Band for the past seven years. Her confidence has grown to the point where she even experiences an occasional desire to grab the spotlight, when the band performs publicly. She may never want to play a recital, but loves it when the trombones get to honk!

Lucie gets much more out of the trombone than she ever did the flute.

Making the fundamental choices that affect your life is one of the nicest things about being an adult. In music, this means freedom to play what you want on the instrument you want to play it on—without the outside pressure of parents or peers. You can choose an instrument that you have always wanted to play. Lucie likes the tactile qualities of the trombone and she gets a thrill making brash glissandos (slides from one note to another)—something she certainly couldn't do on the flute. Your choice of instrument may be limited by your physical capabilities and the type of music you would like to play, as we'll see further on, but for the most part, the field is wide open. Here are some things to consider, if you haven't already made up your mind.

Should I Dust Off the Old Sax Or Try Something New?

If you are coming back to music you might have not considered the possibility of learning a new instrument. After all, wouldn't it be easier to resurrect the sax you played in your youth than start from scratch on a different one? The smell of the cork as you screw the mouthpiece on may trigger fond memories of the high school band. If you were good on your instrument, you don't want to waste all that learning. Besides, you don't particularly want to invest in a new instrument at a time when you are not convinced that you will continue—and a good one can cost plenty these days.

All of these are good reasons to pick up where you left off, even if that was years ago. But before you decide, consider these issues more carefully. As to kissing off the competence you once achieved, ask yourself how good you really were, anyway.

Taking up a new instrument might increase your chances of getting into a group. Or not.

Scott Swanson, an architect, played clarinet in elementary school through junior high. Like Lucie and many other kids starting out, he simply played the instrument his parents handed him. He says he was a mediocre player who always ended up way down in the section. So he sees no waste in switching to something new, which is exactly what he has done by recently taking up piano.

Another reason to consider a different instrument is to be able to fit into a particular group. Like Scott Swanson, Jerry also played clarinet in high school. Thirty years later he wound up in a small New Hampshire town that wasn't exactly jumping, musically. When he saw three of the family members trotting off to town band rehearsal each Tuesday evening in the summer, he wanted to share the experience. But, having passed on his old clarinet to Cinda, he didn't have a band instrument to play. He borrowed a baritone from the local elementary school, found it fairly easy to learn, and joined the band in the next summer. Like those frogs in the Kalahari Desert who complete their whole life cycle during the brief rainy period of a few weeks, this band folded at the end of the summer season. But this time his enthusiasm was piqued, he started scratching around to find other groups that continued through the rest of the year.

Happily, the Keene State College Concert Band took on up to a dozen or so community members each year to fill out the vacant spots left by students. Since the clarinet section was chronically short, he joined up and bought a new (used) clarinet. Two years later, there were suddenly no students to fill the bassoon section. Intrigued by this funny bedpost of an instrument, he borrowed one from the college and learned it well enough over the summer to play the second bassoon part in the band in the fall. He's still doing it 11 years later.

As far as wasting your "investment" of time and effort in learning your original instrument, very little of your investment is wasted. For starters, you probably had to learn to read music, something that you can use with any instrument. Coordinating your hands and/or mouth to manipulate the sounds of one instrument is a skill that will carry over to another. And finally, you don't have to abandon the first instrument, just because you learn a new one.

If, on the other hand, you loved playing that old sax, there is nothing written in stone preventing you from taking up where you left off. You'll probably be surprised how much you haven't lost and how quickly things start coming back. One word of advice, though: Time affects everything. The corks and pads on your sax may have gotten brittle. Pads that don't close tightly to the holes won't let you make the tone. Similarly, small cracks in wood instruments can affect their playability. If you intend using the same instrument, have it checked over by an expert and reconditioned to restore its original state.

Should I Limit Myself to Only One Instrument?

As an adult musician, you can do something you might never have dreamed of in your youth—take up more than one instrument at a time. If you played cornet in the school band, your course was charted by the needs of the cornet section. Now free of those constraints and the need to compete with your peers, you can diversify. Why not give other members of the brass family a try? The fingering is much the same for euphonium, tuba and French horn as for cornet. Except for tuba, they all read treble clef. The method of tone production is similar, as well, though the embouchure (shape and musculature of the mouth) required for one member of the brass family does not automatically carry over to others. A trumpet lip can be loosened up to play the larger mouthpiece of a euphonium or tuba with a little effort, but a tuba lip doesn't adapt as easily to playing trumpet or French horn.

Some instruments have definitely limited portability.

The woodwind family also has similarities that make it a family. Switching among clarinet, bass clarinet, or any of the saxes is relatively easy, because the fingerings are similar. The basic difference is the size of the instrument and, to a lesser extent, the embouchure (mouth position). Of course, moving from a single-reed instrument like the clarinet to a double reed, such as oboe or bassoon, is a different matter. Switching from a reed to a brass instrument is harder still, and vice versa. What about total crossover—say from an instrument you blow into to one you pluck, strike, or bow with your hands? Why not? You can try out several instruments before committing yourself to any one instrument. You can probably borrow them from a friend, local school, or by arranging with a music store (more about how to get hold of an instrument in the next five chapters).

Diversifying within one family of instruments or branching out to another group is rewarding in itself, but the biggest plus is the new doors you open. Just imagine how many more kinds of music you'll have access to and how you will increase your chances to play in groups.

Should I Go For an Instrument I Can Play Alone?

Some instruments are virtual one-man bands. Accordions, pianos, organs, and guitars often accompany other instruments or singers, but they are perfectly able to supply both the melody line and accompaniment to play alone. We'll call these "stand-alone" instruments. On the other hand, clarinets, horns, violins, and flutes, play only one note at a time. It can be a melody, to be accompanied by other instruments or one part of an accompaniment itself. In either case, they must play in an ensemble of some sort to achieve both melody and accompaniment. So we'll call this set "ensemble" instruments.

What does this have to do with your choice of an instrument? Simple: playing in the company of others may be the key to keeping you going, at least in the view of most of the amateur musicians we talked to.

Consider your own past. If you started out on piano, you probably dropped it when the lessons stopped. But if you played an ensemble instrument in your youth, you most likely played it in the school band or orchestra. The ensemble was your focus. It kept you going until you graduated and left the group.

Music teachers we talked to agree that participation with others is an important element to keeping going. John Payne, founder of the John Payne Music Center, a Brookline, Ma. organization that trains adults in jazz, believes playing in groups is so fundamental that he set up some 20 ensembles at the center and encourages students to get into one very shortly after beginning on an instrument.

So where does that leave you, if you want to maximize your chances of playing with others? Well, your worst choice might be a home organ. You can play the whole orchestra on one, for sure, and that is exactly what many home organists want to do. But isolated in a corner of your living room, you will have to provide your own drive without the sharing and input of others. A piano would be a better choice because it does have group-playing potential and the digital version is portable enough to be moved to other sites. A guitar, a stand-alone instrument, is better, still, because of its many group-playing possibilities. And any wind or stringed instrument will open the doors to playing in a community band, orchestra, or small ensemble.

How Can I Match My Instrument to My Musical Interest?

Instruments tend to have musical niches where they best fit. A tuba, for example, is at home in the back row of almost any band, laying down the bass notes. It is also a key player (make that "valve" player) of a brass quintet, where it even gets tossed an occasional solo line. Remember the chorus of Sousa's Stars and Stripes Forever that goes to the words, "be kind to your web footed friends, for a duck may be somebody's mother?" During the second time through the chorus the piccolo traditionally chirps out an intricate obligato that hovers above the melody. But when the Canadian Brass do it, the tuba plays the piccolo part. And, while it doesn't exactly sound like a lark chirping away, it gets all the notes. And we have noticed tubas taking the place of string basses in many of the jazz bands in our last few visits to the annual Montreal Jazz Festival. We've even started collecting CDs featuring tubas. One of these, Tubas from Hell, features Dave Gannet playing jazz tuba in surprising ways.

The tuba's escape from its traditional straitjacket is emblematic of a musical scene that is much freer today than ever before. The violin, the traditional linchpin of any orchestra or string quartet, reels out jazz in the hands of a Stephane Grappelli. Folk music would surely be worse off without country fiddling. Traditional instruments play non-traditional music. Instruments combine in unexpected ways. Entirely new sounds result from electronic instruments. The rules that govern which instrument can play which type of music are constantly being broken, or at least bent.

All this makes one wonder if there are any limits at all. We think so. Think for a moment of Samuel Barber's beautiful Adagio for Strings. This piece moves lyrically around until the climax, where the violins soar up to the summit, pulling the listener's soul up with it. Can you imagine this being played on bagpipes or accordion? While the possibilities are seemingly endless, many of the efforts to coax an instrument into a non-traditional mode stretch their fit just too far. Stephane Grappelli's jazz interpretations are technically flawless and musically well executed, but the violin has still to gain acceptance in the jazz world. The sound isn't quite a proper fit to some ears. And when the Canadian Brass has the tuba play the traditional piccolo part in Stars and Stripes, it's a new twist, but still a tour de force. The tuba's home is still at the bottom, where it is unexcelled at laying down the bass line.

None of our prejudices should prevent you from experimenting with your chosen instrument. It's exciting to explore new musical directions. But do so in full awareness of the instrument's usual niche and natural limitations. Consider the type or types of music you want to get into and learn why the instruments most commonly associated with this type of music occur most often. The sax is at home in jazz because of its variety of tonal qualities and capacity to be played in so many styles. Trombones work in Dixieland, thanks in part to their capability to glissando.

How Will My Physique Affect My Choice?

Learning a new instrument at mid life is hard enough. You don't need the added burdens of one for which you are not physically well suited. Each instrument makes certain demands on the body, which we describe in detail in the next five chapters. Here are some general things to think about in connection with selecting an instrument.

Body size. Your body size says more about your ability to carry a large instrument around than your ability to play it. Built like Arnold Schwarzenegger, you will have no trouble lugging an enormous string bass around, but that muscle bulk won't improve your chances of getting great music out of it. Long, nimble fingers will. Fingers are unimportant with trombones, however. Long arms and a supple right wrist for extending a trombone slide full out are desirable qualities. Large hands with long fingers are an asset for playing any keyboard, while small hands can easily get around on a flute, oboe, clarinet, or alto sax. Larger woodwinds, such as tenor saxes, bassoons, and bass clar-

There is no rule that says traditional instruments can't play non-traditional music.

inets, have holes and keys spaced farther apart, making them better suited to persons with long fingers and big hands. Except for trombones, which are operated by a slide, all brasses are played by depressing 3 or 4 valves, which are spaced to be comfortable to players, regardless of hand size. And, of course instruments that are struck , plucked, or bowed are equally accessible to people with various hand sizes.

Long arms are an asset for some woodwinds, especially oboes, English horns and bass clarinets.

Bones. How your bones connect can influence your choice of instruments. Stand relaxed with your arms hanging loosely at your sides. If your palms face inwards or slightly forward, you are built to play violin or viola, but may encounter strain when you rotate them 90 degrees to play a keyboard instrument. If your palms face to the rear, violin will be a strain for you, but a keyboard will be comfortable.

Mouth. Except for the woodwind recorder, that you simply blow into, all other wind instruments require a certain kind of mouth and teeth structure. Trumpets and French horns are the most demanding. If you don't have straight, symmetrical teeth, good gums, and a slight overbite, you will be at a disadvantage. Dentures will also be a problem. Low brass—trombones, euphoniums and tubas—are less demanding, and non-wind instruments are sure ways to get around any deficiency you may have with your mouth.

Lung capacity. Similarly, your lungs are only an issue if you want to play a wind instrument, and some are more demanding than others. Flutes and low brass offer less resistance than trumpets or clarinets. Because you have to blow more air into them, they are poorer candidates for anyone who is short winded or suffers from asthma.

Eyes and Ears. How well you see and hear affects your potential to play any instrument. That's why we discussed the consequences of diminished eyesight and hearing loss in detail in Chapter 6, and sensitivity to pitch and intensity in Chapter 5.

In the next five chapters we scan several instruments to help you find the best one to fit your physical circumstances, personality, musical preferences, and budget.

Chapter 10

Things That Go Bump in the Night (and Day)

Drums, the oldest, most primal instruments known to mankind, are the logical point of beginning for our tour of musical instruments. Our ancestors probably banged on things long before they learned how to blow, pluck, or bow them. Picture Ooga doing her spring cleaning of the cave. A huge pile of bones accumulated from a winter's worth of roasts sits stinking in one corner. She wants old Og to get rid of them, but he is asleep, so she hustles little Oggie to the odious chore, then ambles out to collect berries for lunch. Oggie starts piling his arms full of bones but overestimates his carrying capacity, dropping several. As they fall, they knock together making an interesting tone. Hmmm. He puts the armload down and hits two femurs together to get a mellow low tone, then gets a higher, klinkier, sound from two ribs. By the time Ooga returns from gathering berries, her young son has arranged eight bones in the dirt next to the fire and is happily banging out a Neanderthal version of *Louie, Louie*. The clattering rouses old Og, who says to Ooga, "Do my ears deceive me or did that silly kid just invent the marimba?"

Another reason for beginning with the percussion family is that drums are one of the hottest contenders for people who want to get into music but are leery about the baggage that comes with taking up a tonal instrument.

Another caveperson quite possibly invented the first drum by stretching an animal skin over some kind of frame. In any case, the two prototypes gave rise to two different branches of the percussion family. While all percus-

The drum is the very center of my personal life. Without the drum, I have no power. My calmness is shattered. I cannot interact. I cannot be in love. I cannot walk with my head upright.

Mickey Hart, *Drumming at the Edge of Magic*

sion are set into vibration by striking them with a tool or hand, those modeled on the marimba produce the different notes of the musical scale. Because they are tuned to specific pitches we'll call this branch "pitched percussion." The second branch consists of devices that produce a sound of indeterminate pitch when struck. It comprises not only drums of every variety but almost anything you can get strike to make a sound.

Percussion in Large Ensembles

Every Tuesday night for a full year Kathy Shaw drove her teenage daughter 18 miles to the weekly rehearsals of the Westmoreland, N.H. Town Band (WTB). Because of the distance, Kathy chose to wait out the two hours there rather than make another return trip. A captive audience of one, Kathy passed the time by writing letters from a seat in the rear of the cramped room, next to the bells player, Barbara Dunham.

One fall night as the band was just starting to rehearse pieces for its Christmas concert season, director Carlson Barret asked who would play the sleigh bells. Barbara Dunham answered that both she and the other percussionist had their hands full with other instruments.

Kathy mumbled from her seat, "Gee, even a dummy like me could do that," which prompted Barbara to shout out, "Hey Carlson, we have a volunteer.

Kathy, now backpedaling, said, "I can read music, but not percussion music."

Carlson replied, "All you need to do is count to four; can you do that?"

Kathy thought it over and agreed. She was spending the time there anyway, so why not do something useful? The initiation on sleigh bells quickly led to playing all of the other auxiliary items in the percussion section's grab bag: cymbals, tambourine, triangle and maracas. Before long she was on to one of the heavy hitters, the bass drum. Three years later, she switches from one noisemaker to another in clockwork precision, often juggling one in each hand simultaneously. Now a regular member of the WTB, she enjoys it for simple reasons: "I like being able to do something along with everybody else that doesn't really matter in the course of life--it's just simply fun."

Joining the percussion section of a community band or orchestra can well be the easiest way to get into music making if you are a beginner with anxiety about taking up a tonal instrument. Kathy became the third regular member of the band's percussion section, which usually swelled to four during the more active summer season. The major equipment in bands of this size typically includes a bass drum, one or two snares, and a glockenspiel, and a variety of accessories such as cymbals, wood blocks, and triangle. Specialty items are often obtained on an as-needed basis for particular music. When WTB performed *The Wabash Cannonball,* the director brought in a train whistle, which he played himself, to the disappointment of the percussion section.

The WTB, at a membership of between 25 and 35, gets by with three steady percussionists. If you end up in a band larger than this, your range of percussion instruments will include all of those listed for a town band, plus chimes, gongs, marimbas, xylophones, and timpani. The percussionists may start out by specializing on one instrument, as Kathy did on sleighbells, but tend to evolve into generalists capable of switching among any of the instruments in the section.

Pros: The percussion section of a band or orchestra offers several ways to beat out rhythm plus a few options for playing melody lines. It is very easy to start out and play the simplest instruments. If you are too short of time to get better by practicing at home, you can stay comfortably on a simple instrument. But there are also ample opportunities to grow, if you have the drive and time to practice.

Cons: If you get stuck in some slots, such as playing bass drum or cymbals, you may get bored. People whose primary need is to make a melody instead of playing a rhythm will probably be unfulfilled in the percussion section.

Physical requirements: Percussion instruments vary widely in difficulty, so demand different capabilities. All percussionists need a fair sense of rhythm. If you can't beat out a regular rhythm by tapping your foot, you probably aren't a good prospect. The easiest instruments in the section are those that are struck once intermittently (gongs) or at predictable paces, such as the bass drum. Almost anyone with one good arm should be able to play these. Next come the cymbals, which require two arms to clash them together, but little else other than knowing when to do it. Snare drums are more demanding. A player needs two very nimble, well-coordinated hands and a very good sense of rhythm to rip off rhythms at machine-gun speed with precision. Of the pitched percussion instruments, the glockenspiel is doubtless the easiest. Played with a mallet held in one hand, the instrument is seldom called on to play notes in very rapid order. Marimbas and xylophones are more demanding. They need two well-coordinated hands able to play rapid runs.

Is it for you? Rapping your fingers on the steering wheel to music of your car radio while waiting at a red light or tapping a pencil against your desk to music you hear over the office sound system are signs you have an affinity for rhythm. If you like the idea of providing the rhythm to other instruments that carry the melody, you may get great pleasure out of becoming part of a local ensemble's percussion section.

Getting an instrument: This is the best part. Bands and orchestras typically acquire their own percussion equipment. If you want to practice at home, as you should, you can do it on cheap, easily obtainable practice pads that won't disturb others.

Drum Sets

Drummers tend to be the brunt of jokes among musicians. It's grossly unfair to folks who prefer making rhythm to melody. The joke at left was probably invented by some jealous horn player. After all, most small jazz, pop, rock, country, and ethnic bands depend on rhythm. Nine times out of ten this boils down to a single person on a set of drums that includes a bass drum, a snare drum , a tom-tom, one or two cymbals, Hi-hat cymbals, and a cowbell. Drummers usually augment the basic "must-haves" with additional items geared to the type of music their group specializes in. A drummer in a combo that plays a lot of Latin or Afro-Cuban music, for example, might add several tom-toms, conga drums, and an assortment of hand-held

Q: What kind of people follow musicians around?

A: Drummers.

items such as claves and pair of maracas.

In short, a drum set is a compact version of all of the instruments that make up a percussion section in a larger ensemble. Recall that we claimed the bass drum was easy to play, but the snare was a real challenge. A drum set requires you to play these and other items simultaneously, and in synchronization with each other—a hefty charge. Gene Krupa and Buddy Rich inspired us with their technical mastery and infallible sense of rhythm. Joe Morello and Ed Thigpen showed us that drumming can also be subtle. At the other extreme, drummers in rock groups express the macho side of drumming, but always make it look like such work. Such disparate models prompt the question: What kind of person would want to take up a drum set? Simple. One who doesn't want to be simply a *member* of a percussion section, but wants to *be* the percussion section (any teenage boy, for example).

The basic equipment of a typical drum set. Almost all drummers augment the set with items useful to the type of music they play.

Pros: Having so many instruments at your disposal gives you unlimited possibility for invention. In a jazz group you'll probably get frequent opportunity to express your ideas. Good drummers are in demand.

Cons: Developing the skill to become a good jazz drummer (and you won't appeal to many groups if you fall short of this) is extremely demanding. You must not only start with exacting physical requirements but the stamina to learn to lay down precise patterns without rushing or slowing.

Drums make rhythm rather than melody, so are worthless outside of a group, which means you will be toting them from place to place. If the simplicity and small size of a piccolo make it a musician's dream to carry around, a drum set is a logistical nightmare. Figure on at least a half hour to dismantle the set and load it into the vehicle—which should be a van or wagon at the minimum)—and another half hour to take it out of the vehicle and set it up. Practicing next to sensitive neighbors is a surefire recipe for conflict, unless you practice on a set of practice pads.

Physical requirements: Don't even consider playing a drum set unless you have an excellent sense of rhythm and deft, well-coordinated hands and feet. To appraise this, try this simple test: Tap a steady beat of one, two, three, four, on a table or desk with your right hand. On every beat number three, tap your left hand. On every beat number one, tap your right foot. If you can do this at a steady rate without getting snarled up, you probably have the native talent to play a drum set. By the way, you should also be capable of lifting and maneuvering a load of equipment into and out of your vehicle.

Is it for you? Playing a set of drums in a combo may well be for you if you are more interested in making rhythm than tone or have doubts about your tonal capability. As the sole percussionist in an ensemble you will find endless opportunity to creatively express your ideas in combination with others. Be prepared, however, to accept the responsibility for setting down a reliable beat for the group.

There is mounting conviction that playing drums is a great way to relieve stress. Johnny Carson regularly played on his home drum set to relieve the pressures of his nightly television show.

Getting an instrument: New drum sets are priced according to the number of items in the set and the cachet of the brand. The most basic 5-piece set (bass, 2 toms, snare, hi-hat, cymbal) starts around $300. Expect a 5-piece set made by recognized national brands (Yamaha, Pearl, Ludwig, Gretsch) to cost at least double this amount. There's a lot of traffic in used drum sets, which you might find in the classifieds of your newspaper.

Tribal Drumming

The New Age movement of recent years has spawned interest in many things—crystals, pyramids, channeling, tarot cards, goddesses, healing, chants, trance, and dance.

Not all New Agers accept every expression of the move-ment, but all seem to rally around a general theme: life in the industrialized countries during the latter part of the 20th century somehow separated people from nature and the connection can only be re-established by seeking out and drawing upon practices that preceded the scientific age and Christian traditions. One such practice is tribal drumming, an expression that has attracted New Age practitioners in increasing numbers.

Drumming in "traditional" cultures accompanies ritual chants and ceremonies. The "new tribal drumming," according to Jeremy Youst, is borne out of "a tremendous impulse for people to come together." Youst is a therapist and leads a monthly sacred circle which includes tribal drumming. He adds that the beginning of a new millenni-um coincides with a need to create new forms in which to express what we don't get from our culture. The media, he argues, tries to separate and isolate people from each other. "In circling, we are all coming to the same place...there is no way you can get your mind to be the big boss, because in making music you are going into the right brain and it forces you to explore and express that other part of your-self that wants to come out, but has been repressed, by our culture. That high, that feeling of connection to a unity is the flame that draws us, like a campfire, out of the dark-ness. In sacred circle, what we have done is simply to attend to that flame. We come here like a church to create sacred space, a place to explore ourselves intentionally."

By now you probably suspect that there is some-thing different about tribal drumming in sacred circles than drumming in a jazz combo or town band. You suspect cor-rectly. Tribal drumming breaks away from the conven-tional drumming in an important way. Conventional drumming sets the rhythm for the music played by other instruments. The music itself is the goal. When everything clicks, the musical experience is satisfying to both players and audience. Under the best of conditions, the musical experience reaches a spiritual plane.

With tribal drumming, spirituality *is* the goal. Though it may back up chanting or dancing, these are not done to make a musical performance, but to provide a direct and primal avenue to spirituality.

Tribal drumming attracts people of all ages and

I would say that right now there is a tremendous impulse for peo-ple to come together... people are definitely getting interested in re-creating and co-creating new forms to express the thing that we don't receive out there in TV land and media-land, which is a con-tinual message of separation and isolation.

Jeremy Youst

"We come here like church to create sacred space, intentionally.
Jeremy Youst

Djembe drums from West Africa are favorites for tribal drumming. African drums are always played with the hands.

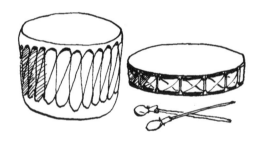

Native American drums used in tribal drumming are struck with sticks.

motivations. Men's drumming groups use it to release aggressions and other "male" emotions that they have difficulty expressing in other forms of social interaction. Women may use drumming to get in touch with the primal "goddess" within. Men and women alike often see drumming as a kind of therapy. As Jeremy Youst puts it, "When people take the risk, because of whatever reason--they have crashed and burned in their life, they're getting over some kind of substance abuse, addiction, or their husband has left them, when they go through to the other side, they realize that what's on the other side of the fear is love."

Pros: Tribal drumming lets you express your inner emotions through your hands, rather than simply being the rhythm accompaniment to a musical group. Practitioners claim it produces great spiritual and therapeutic benefits. It is also a way to communicate with other people. The instruments are simple and economical to obtain and carry around.

Cons: While you can approach learning a conventional instrument with a level of intensity consistent with your musical goals and available time, tribal drumming requires a commitment and dedication that goes beyond the merely casual.

Physical requirements: All you need is two hands capable of beating repeatedly on a drum head.

Is it for you? If spiritual enlightenment and expression of primal emotions are driving forces in your life, tribal drumming may be a facilitating process.

Getting an instrument: There are numerous types of ethnic drums that can be used for tribal drumming. The type you select should reflect the type of drumming and focus of the group you join. If your group leans toward African drumming, you might consider getting a djembe, an hourglass-shaped drum native to West Africa. According to African drumming specialist, Adam Moore Rugo, a good djembe should be heavy, without cracks that extend to the bearing edge of the head. The circle at the bearing edge should be planar, not uneven. The head skin should be intact, without holes or splits. A new instrument costs between $200 and $400.

Native American drumming may entail a variety of hand-held rattles, flutes, and mouthbows, in addition to drums. Drums, also come in many flavors of single- and double-sided types. There are Sioux drums, pow-wow drums, pueblo drums, earth drums, and others. All drums are played with beaters, rather than hands. Prices range according to size and type. Sioux drums start around $60 for a 9-inch diameter drum and range up to $400 for a 28-inch diameter model. Pow-wow drums start at 24 inches in diameter and extend up to 32 inches, for a cost range of $400—$600.

THE PERCUSSION CUPBOARD

Almost anything except a soft pillow can make a sound when struck. The range of instruments in both categories (pitched and unpitched percussion) is too large to describe here, but in the following section we give a thumbnail sketch of some of the ones you will most often encounter in large and small groups.

Pitched Percussion

Xylophones. Modern versions of the tuned bones our ancestors played, xylophones belong to the percussion family inasmuch as their sound comes from hardwood bars struck by mallets. The bars are tuned to the notes of the musical scale and arranged horizontally like a piano keyboard, with a 3 1/2-octave range. An array of hollow tubes mounted below the keyboard amplifies the tone of the bars.

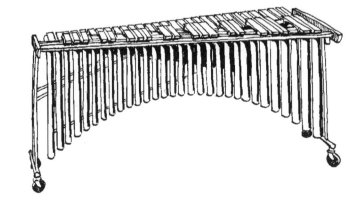

Xylophone. A marimba is similar in appearance.

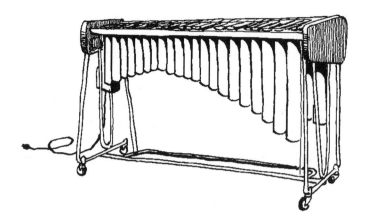

A vibraphone (or set of "vibes," as jazz musicians refer to it, consists of metal bars, and resonating tubes equipped with revolving disks, which vibrates the tone. The pedal bar below dampens the bars from vibrating.

The length of each "resonating" tube is matched to the frequency of the tone bar above it. Xylophones came to us via Africa and Latin America, where they are still played in indigenous music. In western music, xylophones are mostly accessory parts of the percussion sections of concert bands and orchestras.

Marimbas are similar to xylophones, but with a larger range (4 octaves) and a mellower, less brittle, tone. Marimbas are common in groups that play Latin music.

Vibraphones. Substitute metal for the wood bars of a marimba and add an electrical resonator and you have a vibraphone. The resonator consists of a series of discs mounted, one each, in the top of each resonator tube. An electric motor turns the discs, which cause the tone to pulsate in a vibrato (hence the name). A damper pedal enables the player to stop or sustain the sound. Known as "vibes" to jazz buffs, this instrument's forte is small combo jazz, made famous by the likes of Lionel Hampton, Milt (Bags) Jackson, and Gary Burton.

Glockenspiels and Celestas. Shrink the range and eliminate the resonator tubes and electric vibrato mechanism from a vibraphone and you have the makings of a glockenspiel or celesta. Glockenspiels (also called bell lyres, or bells) have the bars mounted either vertically, for

Glockenspiel, also known as bells

Tubular bells, or chimes

A tympanum, with a foot pedal to rapidly change the pitch of the membrane.

marching, or horizontally, for playing in a fixed position. Celestas look like toy pianos and contain their own hammers.

Chimes. Bands and orchestras sometimes play works requiring chimes (tubular bells), sets of hollow metal tubes suspended vertically from a frame.

Timpani. Large drums shaped like kettles (hence the alternate name, "kettle drums") consist of calfskin or plastic membranes stretched over a basin-shaped copper shell. Screws around the top edge tighten or loosen the membrane to change the pitch. The pitch can also be changed by a foot pedal. Larger bands and orchestras have two to five timpani, which one person plays with cloth mallets. You won't likely find timpani in smaller ensembles.

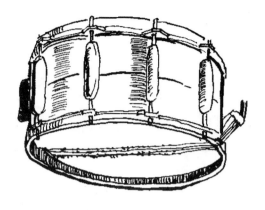

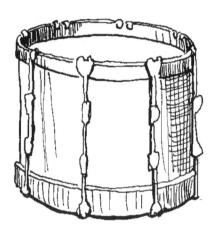

Snare drum (above) showing the wire snares strung across the bottom membrane. Tenor drum (below) has a lower pitch and no snares.

Unpitched Percussion

Snare Drums. The name comes from the array of 8-20 wire snares stretched across the bottom head, or diaphragm, that rattle when the top head is played. A lever makes it possible to loosened the snares, to make the drum sound more like other drums. But there is no real advantage to this if other specialized drums are at hand. The rattle produced by the snares has become a vital sound in marching bands, jazz, rock, and pop drumming. Wood drumsticks are the primary tool for playing snares. Wire brushes are used often in jazz when a softer, sustained sound is desired.

Tenor Drums. Whereas snare drums have head diameters longer than the depth (between heads), tenor drums reverse this relationship. The difference yields a deeper, mellower tone.

Tom-Toms. Tom-toms are double- or single-headed drums that never have snares. Even though tom-toms are classed as "unpitched" percussion, each drum does in fact have a tone, which can be higher or lower according to the drum size and the tension of the head. Drummers exploit this quality by having at least two, often more, tom-toms, each of a different pitch.

Bongos. Two small-diameter drums, each of a different pitch, fixed to each other by a connecting piece. Bongos are held between the knees and played with the hands in Afro-Cuban music.

Bass Drums. The papa bear of the drum family also comes with one or two heads. Its deep timbre varies from a barely perceptible thud to powerful, authoritative thump. Bass drums in large ensembles are played by a felt-tipped stick wielded by a member of the percussion section. The smaller bass drums used in combos are part of the drummer's set and are played by a foot pedal.

Cymbals. These are thin brass plates shaped like saucers are mounted on a rack to be played singly with a drumstick or are hand-held in pairs to be clashed together. The drum-set version of two opposing cymbals is called a hi-hat ("top hat" in British English), which is mounted on a rack and operated with a foot pedal.

Tamtams (Gongs). Large-diameter brass plates hung vertically from strings in a frame are played with a soft beater, whenever the music calls for special effects.

If you are a member of the percussion section of a band or orchestra, you will likely encounter various other odds and ends, such as **triangles, castanets, wood blocks, rattles, sleighbells, whips,** and even **train whistles**. Percussionists seldom get bored. **Djembes, sabars, kpanlogos, kutiro,** and **bougarabous** are but a few of the many ethnic drums played by hand in tribal drumming.

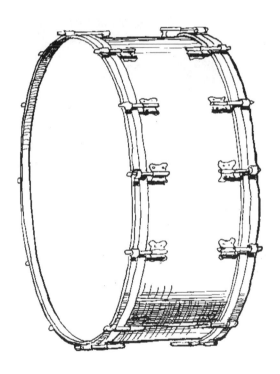

Bass drum, of the type used in bands and orchestras

A stationary cymbal (left) is played with drumsticks or brushes. Hi-hat cymbals (right) are always operated with a foot pedal.

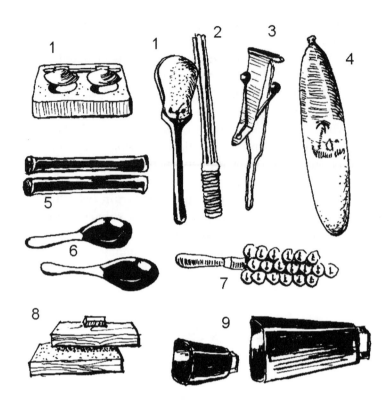

1 Castanets	2 Switch	3 Flexatone
4 Shaker	5 Claves	6 Maracas
7 Sleighbells	8 Sandblocks	9 Cowbells

Some of the auxiliary percussion used for special effects in a band or orchestra. The variety is almost endless, sometimes ranging to found items, such as tire rims and washboards. Jerry's band once used a cymbal struck with force, then dropped rapidly into a bucket of water to "douse" the sound.

Chapter 11

Things With Strings

The happy twanging of a banjo thumping out *Cripple Creek*. The somber, hypnotic, strains of an ensemble playing Samuel Barber's *Adagio for Strings*. Stringed instruments speak to every human emotion and embrace every musical genre. This chapter explores the family of instruments whose sound comes from strings vibrating from being bowed or plucked. The family is big. One member awaits you, whatever your musical preference and ability.

BOWED STRINGS

Bowed strings have been the heart of all orchestras from the chamber ensembles that entertained the nobility of the 17th and 18th centuries to the symphony orchestras of today. Three hundred years of history has yielded a vast repertoire of both ensemble and solo works for all four members of the string choir: the violin (soprano), viola (alto), cello (tenor), and double bass (bass).

The members of the viol family differ mainly in size and pitch range. Their basic shape and construction is similar: a long wooden neck extending out of a hollow wooden sounding box, with four strings stretched over the neck and box. Adjustable pegs at the top of the neck adjust the tension on the strings to set their pitch. The strings are occasionally plucked (pizzicato) but usually played by drawing a horsehair bow across them. Tiny teeth on the filaments of the horsehair excite the strings into vibration. To enable you to bow one string without touching the next one, there is a wooden plate, or bridge, between the strings and the belly, that has a curved top. The bridge also serves to conduct the vibrations of the strings into the soundbox to amplify the sound. Whew!

The bowed strings are similar, except in size. From left: violin, viola, cello, bass (double bass).

Violins and Violas

Played well, the violin is one of the most beautiful instruments to listen to. Played badly, it is one of the most excruciating. Not many adult beginners succeed to the former level, at least for classical violin music. "Those who do well are people who listened all their lives, but for some reason never got the chance or the environment to actually do something with it, and have finally gotten the nerve to do it," according to Bob Mark, treasurer and director of the chamber music program of the Upper Valley Music Center in Norwich, Vermont, an organization that brings together amateur string players in a variety of groups. Mark adds that once adults see what can happen in a sharing, non-competitive, non-threatening environment, they are inspired to action.

Unfortunately, if you learned early on to hate music you very likely learned to hate it through forced hours of practice on the violin. For boys, there was also the stigma of having to play an instrument that didn't seem quite right for a "real" male. How many boys who dropped the violin at the first opportunity might have continued, if they had had been given a chance to learn country fiddling instead of trying to imitate Yehudi Menuhin or Isaac Stern? Or had simply lived in the more accepting social climate of today?

Never mind. If you got off on the wrong foot with the violin in your youth or didn't get off at all, it's not too late. Admittedly, playing classical music well on the violin is hard. Learning how to coax musical tones out of a small wood box by scraping a horse-hair stick across its strings tests the mettle of even the most devoted young people who have their lives before them. Can you as an adult take on such a daunting challenge with any chance for success? Yes, say many string teachers. When a woman about to begin viola asked Salt Lake City violin and viola teacher Lorraine Larson what she could hope to accomplish, Lorraine answered, "I'm not going to try to make a virtuoso out of you, just do however much you want to." Lorraine says that violins and violas are both difficult to learn and play well, but are not beyond adult beginners. You may never reach the heights of Itzhak Perlman, but can certainly attain a level that will yield hours of satisfaction playing in a community orchestra, amateur string quartet, or even fiddling for a group of square dancers.

With violins in the starring role in most ensembles, violas often go unnoticed. Too bad, since the viola's tone is beautiful and sonorous. Tuned a perfect fifth below the violin, the viola is ideally positioned to sing the alto part in the string choir, much the same as the English horn does in the woodwinds. Yet, though it mostly supports the violins, the viola gets ample chance to shine on its own in small ensembles and has a variety of solo works to select from.

Violin or viola (slightly larger).

Q: What's the difference between a violin and a viola?
A: None. The violin just looks smaller because the violinist's head is so much bigger.

The way to happiness, I feel, is to strive for the reconciliation of human achievement with the healing forces of nature. There is just such an achieved reconciliation in a well-made violin.

Yehudi Menuhin

Pros: Playing a violin or viola opens the door to an enormous store of classical solo and ensemble music accumulated over 300 years. Outside the classical mode, violins are well-established in Gypsy, Celtic, Cajun, Klezmer, Country, and other folk music, and have even been used in jazz, thanks mostly to Stephane Grappeli's genius. Now they have even broken into the rock music scene, with the "turned on" violin—a solid wood model whose sound is amplified electronically, rather than by the resonating chamber of the box.

Cons: Violins and violas are not the easiest instruments to learn well from scratch (no pun intended). The difficulty stems in part from a neck so narrow as to make fingering the strings tricky and partly from the lack of frets to mark the position of one note from the next. Reading viola music requires learning the alto as well as treble clef—easy for beginners but sort of like learning to write with your other hand if you are used to reading treble and bass clefs. Good instruments are expensive.

Physical requirements: You need an extremely good sense of pitch, because with no frets, you must know exactly where to put your fingers on the strings to produce the intended pitch (a good teacher can help get you started by placing a tape temporarily on the neck to mark the correct finger placement). Turning your left wrist outward should be comfortable—persistent forcing will lead to injury. You'll need the same pitch sensitivity and wrist motor control to play viola, but slightly less finger dexterity, because of the viola's larger size, which also makes it a better bet for people with bigger hands or fingertips.

Is it for you? The violin is a sure ticket to getting into a community orchestra if you love classical orchestral and chamber music. The viola is an even surer bet, because good viola players are scarcer. Both instruments are also fundamental to string trios and quartets, though in a small ensemble each instrument plays a separate part, so it requires a bit of confidence. If your interests lie outside classical music, you have a world of folk music for violin; less for viola. In addition to excellent pitch sensitivity, you'll need good fine-motor control of your left hand and a dexterous right wrist to wield the bow.

Getting an instrument: Stringed instruments are far simpler in construction than wind instruments (not that they are simple to make). So, whereas all those keys and pads make it difficult to spot the defects of a clarinet or bassoon, you can see everything when you look at a violin or viola. If the body has a crack, it will be apparent. Check how precisely the peg holes are drilled. The black edging around the instrument should be real wood, inset, rather than simply painted on. The strings should be closely set to the fingerboard for a beginner. Strings set too high are harder to play. The real test comes with the tone. A good instrument played by an experienced player should sing with a sweet, full and pleasing tone throughout its range. To judge this, get the help of a knowledgeable violinist, because playing it is the only way to tell one instrument's quality from another. There are no objective hallmarks to look for. In general, age favors quality. Unlike instruments that have a lot of moving parts, such as pianos or wood-winds, bowed strings have few parts to wear out. Also, instruments made before the 1940s are made with better woods.

The cheapest new violins and violas, mass-produced in factories all over the world, cost as little as $350. Better-grade instruments are largely hand crafted in small shops, and start around $1,000, which is the price Lorraine Larson estimates you should figure on for a decent beginner-quality instrument. Bows vary widely in cost, from $150 on up. When buying a new violin/viola, make sure you understand whether the bow is included or what it costs, if not included.

Cellos

The warm, lyrical quality of a melody played on a cello is an emotional high. It's hard to see how anyone, regardless of their musical preferences, can listen to *The Swan* from *The Carnival of the Animals,* by Saint Saens, without being moved. Watching an artist like Yo Yo Ma or Mstislav Rostropovich elicit this response from this overgrown violin makes one believe that playing the cello is as satisfying to the musician as to the listener.

Cellos are pitched a full octave below violins, which enables them to play the tenor part of the string choir. Most cello music is written in the bass clef, but because the cello's range extends above the bass clef, music in the higher realms is often written in tenor clef. This can be initially confusing to anyone who is used to reading music in treble or bass clef. Cello construction is similar to other bowed strings, except for the addition of a long metal peg that sticks out the bottom of the soundbox and supports it off the floor. You play the cello sitting, with the instrument gripped between your knees.

Cellos come in four sizes: quarter, half, three-quarter, and full. The rule of thumb for determining the right size is to make sure the lowest peg is even with your left ear, when you are seated with the cello, holding the bow comfortably over the strings at a point between the fingerboard and bridge. Full-size cellos suit all but the smallest adults.

Cellist Yo Yo Ma constantly seeks ways to broaden the instrument's narrow image.

Pros: The strings on cellos are farther apart than on violins or violas, making fingering somewhat easier for people with larger hands. Cellos are much more comfortable to play than violins or violas. Instead of having to crank your head into an unnatural angle and twist your wrist, you sit comfortably with the instrument between your knees. Like violas, cellos are essential members of any orchestra and most string ensembles. Unlike violas, cellos also draw upon a heap of solo works that goes back at least 400 years.

Cons: Cellos are somewhat larger and less portable than violins or violas. As indispensable as cellos are to classical music, cellos have yet to break out of this mode. The only exception we are aware of is the minor excursion into the jazz world in the

1960s, where the Don Shirley Trio used a cello instead of a double bass. Instruments, even mediocre ones, are expensive.

   Physical requirements: Like other bowed strings, cellos don't have frets along the fingerboard to define one note from the next, relying instead on the player's judgment. To develop this judgment, you have to start with an excellent sense of pitch and invest some time and effort (tape can be applied to the fingerboard initially to mark the finger positions). You'll also need good left hand finger dexterity and a supple right wrist.

   Is it for you? It can be if you are seduced by the warm, liquid tone of a cello. As an adult beginner, you may never make a cello sing like Yo Yo Ma, but that's no reason to rule out this most mellow instrument. You should be able to make satisfying sounds in far shorter time than it will take on violin or viola. Cellos are good candidates for any adult beginner who wants to take up a bowed string.

   Getting an instrument: In general, what we said under "getting an instrument" for violins and violas also applies to cellos. Factory-made beginner-grade cellos start around $800 (Asian and some European brands). Domestic and European mid-quality models go for between $1,500 and $2,500.

Acoustic Basses

Acoustic basses are known in symphonic circles as "double basses," a clumsy term which evokes an image of some kind of Siamese twin. The "double" was traditionally needed, though, to differentiate the instrument from the cello, which played the bass part in small string ensembles. Outside the world of classical music, the instrument answers to many other names: bass, string bass, bass fiddle, bull fiddle, upright bass, doghouse bass, stand-up bass, and slapstick bass.

   Whatever you care to call it, this large, low-pitched acoustic instrument plays many roles. Orchestras usually include one or more basses. You even see an occasional bass in a concert band, but seldom in one that plays outdoors. There isn't much in the way of classical solo works for the bass, though Bach's *Bourrée* from his *Third Cello Suite* is often played on bass. Outside the classical setting acoustic basses have been an essential part of the rhythm section of country and folk groups, as well as jazz ensembles. But if you have heard Ray Brown make a bass talk in a jazz trio, you know that basses can rise to levels beyond simply laying down the bass line. Even so, acoustic basses are declining outside of classical music, being replaced by electric basses.

Acoustic basses are played standing or while perched on high stools. In classical music their strings are bowed or plucked. Plucking is the main—though not only—mode in other types of music.

Pros: If you learn to play an acoustic bass you should have little difficulty finding a place in an orchestra, chamber music ensemble, or an acoustic jazz or folk combo. Skill you acquire on acoustic bass can easily translate to an electric bass if you want to play with in a wired combo.

Cons: Unlike other strings, basses are rarely played solo, so without a group to play in you may soon lose interest. Their large size and wide string spacing makes acoustic basses fairly hard to play. Pressing the strings down is, in itself, hard work which exacts a toll on your fingertips. Their bulk makes acoustic basses logistical nightmares to transport. Don't even think of getting one if you don't have a wagon or van-sized vehicle. Acoustic basses are expensive.

Physical requirements:. Playing an acoustic bass demands a good sense of pitch, but slightly less than as a violin or viola. While you don't need the finger dexterity you would for a violin or viola, you do need strong, able fingers with tough skin. Large hands are an advantage. Moving the instrument around also favors a large, reasonably strong person.

Is it for you? The acoustic bass is a good string for a person who likes orchestral music and doesn't want to play solo parts. It's also a good entry point into traditional jazz and folk ensembles, where the chance for solos is slightly better.

PLUCKED STRINGS

Ancient images carved on urns from Persia and Greece show people plucking stringed instruments. Beginning with simple lyres and harps, they went on to play lutes, guitars, and zithers. By the fifteenth century, when someone figured out how to pluck the strings mechanically from a keyboard, the harpsichord was born. It blossomed in the baroque era, only to be eclipsed by the piano (pianoforte) in the 19th century. People continued plucking lutes, mandolins, and harps by hand. These instruments have survived to the present, though they are not as prevalent as banjos, guitars and basses. And though basses were covered under the *Bowed Strings* section, because they are primarily bowed in classical music, they also qualify as a plucked string, in the realms of jazz, rock, and folk music.

Acoustic Bass Guitars

Upright acoustic basses still hold their own in orchestras, but their limited portability has eroded their popularity in jazz ensembles. They have never penetrated the world of rock, due to their limited amplification potential. Two portable basses, shaped and held more or less like guitars answer the needs of these groups: acoustic bass guitars and solid body bass guitars.

Acoustic bass guitars resemble large guitars, except that they have four strings pitched much lower. It can be played unamplified, as with an acoustic guitar or be amplified by attaching a small magnetic pickup device to its belly. The pickup plugs into an amplifier which boosts the sound without distorting the instrument's tone.

Pros: Acoustic bass guitars are lightweight and very portable. They cost far less than uprights and are easier to finger. They can be played unamplified in acoustic groups for a sound resembling their larger cousins.

Cons: Amplification requires a magnetic pickup and amplifier, both additional costs to the basic instrument. Even with these, their amplification isn't enough to back up electric guitars in rock groups.

Physical requirements: You'll need good finger dexterity in both hands and tough skin on your left-hand

Acoustic bass guitars retain the mellow tone of acoustic upright basses, but with less depth. Fine for small, unamplified groups, they get lost in an electric combo.

fingers. If you select a fretless bass, you should have a good sense of pitch.

Is it for you? If your interests lean toward jazz or folk, with the intention of playing with acoustic groups, an acoustic bass guitar can provide a good alternative to an upright. If rock is your aim, a solid-body bass guitar is a better choice.

Getting an instrument: Acoustic bass guitars are somewhat rarer than solid-body basses, but are available in any music store that handles acoustic guitars. Costs are similar to acoustic guitars, starting around $300. Amplifiers, are additional (see data under the following category).

Solid-Body Bass Guitars (Electric Bass)

Patterned after the model built by Les Paul in 1941, the solid-body bass guitar is probably the most common bass in use today. Known more commonly as the "electric bass," this instrument is little more than four or more strings stretched over a slab of wood and a fretted (sometimes fretless) fingerboard, with a built-in magnetic pick-up. Unlike the acoustic bass and acoustic bass guitar, the solid-body bass cannot be played without an amp and can't be bowed. Nevertheless, it comes with pluses that have made it indispensable to virtually all rock groups and a growing number of folk and jazz ensembles. First, it is the cheapest of all basses to acquire, though you can spend endlessly on accessories such as amps, speakers, and sound-bending devices. Next, it can be played at volumes you feel, as well as hear. Because the body is solid, it can be any shape and take any kind of ornamentation, a feature rock groups exploit to create their identity. Another feature that rock groups like is the way the sound can be electronically contorted by adding a wah wah pedal, distortion pedal, echo or other device.

Pros: The instruments are highly portable and cost far less than upright acoustic basses. Their versatile sound capability can be constantly adjusted for volume or tonal characteristics. Easier to learn and play than acoustic upright basses, electric basses are fundamental to any rock band and are gaining in jazz and ethnic groups. They can be played through earphones, a boon for practicing without disturbing others.

Cons: Electric basses have a different tone than their hollow-body counterparts, though this is considered a plus in rock music. Having no acoustic soundboxes, they can only be played through electronic amplification. Though the instruments themselves are portable and relatively inexpensive, these advantages are offset by the extra cost and bulk of amplification and sound-tweaking equipment.

Physical requirements: As with any bass, good finger dexterity in both hands and tough skin on your left-hand fingers are necessary. If you select a fretless bass, you should have a good sense of pitch.

Is it for you? If rock or pop music is your main course, a solid-body bass is an absolute necessity. It is also a good bet for jazz, country, and certain types of ethnic music (Zydeco, Cajun).

Getting an instrument: Solid-body electric basses are sold in almost every kind of music store as well as numerous specialty music stores that cater to plucked strings or electronic instruments. Young rock musicians go through several instruments in the course of their sojourn, trading up or down, and leaving the vendors with a huge supply of used equipment. Costs of new instruments start at about $150. Amps with built-in speakers range from around $160 for a 25-amp unit to $500 for a 100-watt unit. Fender, Ampeg, and Peavey are established bass amplifiers.

A solid-body electric bass, with no hollow sound box to amplify its tone, depends totally on electric amplification. It has become the standard bass instrument for any wired rock group.

Acoustic Guitars

The classic, or Spanish, guitar is probably the most popular of all instruments—the one we have all had a fling with at one time or another. Jerry's was in the 1960s. Guitars were emblematic of the folk music revival of that time. He and other white, male college students spent hours listening and trying to imitate black blues singers such as Leadbelly or Blind Lemon Jefferson. But the main current, as far as guitars were concerned, was the social protest songs of Joan Baez, Pete Seeger, Woody Guthrie, and—lest we forget—Bob Dylan. To do Dylan right, you had to have—in addition to your guitar—a harmonica with a neck strap/rack. Of course, there were others who saw the guitar as a serious instrument, took lessons and practiced diligently, in hopes of one day playing like Andres Segovia.

Any instrument that can hypnotize an audience, whether playing Flamenco music, Mississippi Delta blues, or Bluegrass, must be versatile indeed. Even so, the guitar was largely ignored by other than folk musicians for much of its history. It owes its popularity today to the guitar luminaries of the past. Segovia, for classical guitar music; Carlos Montoya, Flamenco; Django Reinhardt and Charlie Christian, early jazz; and Barney Kessell, Charlie Byrd, and Wes Montgomery, modern jazz. Along the way there was also a string of country guitar pickers. Hank Williams, Roy Rogers, Chet Atkins come readily to mind.

Acoustic guitars can be played solo, accompanied or unaccompanied, or can, themselves, back up vocalists or other instruments. Guitars come in many varieties. The classic, or Spanish guitar has a hollow wood soundbox, a neck with a fretted fingerboard, and 6 or 12 strings, which can be plucked with the fingers and thumb or a pick. Guitar strings are either nylon or steel (preferred for blues playing). The Flamenco guitar, slightly smaller, gets a louder sound and comes with *golpe* plates to protect the soundboard from finger tapping. Resonator (Dobro) guitars, favored in blues music, get an even louder metallic sound via a resonating metal plate over the soundboard.

Pros: Guitars are lightweight, portable, and relatively inexpensive, with a sound that pleases. Like pianos, guitars can stand-alone or play in a group, be it around a campfire or in a concert hall. You can play some things on one after only a little training. For example, you can reach the "campfire" stage, just by learning to strum the most frequent chords of folk music. If you get beyond this level, you can draw from an enormous repertoire spanning folk, ethnic, jazz, and classical genres.

Cons: Learning guitar beyond the "campfire" level entails mastering more difficult chord fingerings, playing in different keys, and picking out melodies along with the chords, all of which requires substantial effort and diligence.

Physical requirements: Big hands with long fingers are an asset to a guitar player. Good left-hand finger

The hollow soundbox of the classical acoustic, or Spanish guitar produces a rich, mellow sound that blends with many kinds of music and enables the instrument to play alone or accompany other musicians.

dexterity is a must. Add good right-hand finger dexterity if you aim to do anything beyond strumming.

Is it for you? It is if you like guitar music, in any of its many varieties, and seek a portable instrument to accompany your voice, a vocal group, or other instruments, particularly in popular, folk, country, or ethnic music.

Getting an instrument: A quality guitar should be both beautiful and speak with a rich, clear tone that pleases the ear. Frets should be spaced accurately. To test for this, lightly touch a string exactly above the 12th fret while plucking it. Then press the string down at the same fret and pluck the string. The *harmonic* note produced in the first instance should be the same pitch as the one produced in the standard manner. Otherwise the frets are not located where they should be and you should reject the guitar. New classic guitars range from around $100 to $500 (Auburn, Ibanez, Alvarez, Yamaha). Used instruments not only cost less than new ones, but often sound better. Still, you should look for trouble spots. Frayed strings can be easily and cheaply replaced, but worn frets that cause a string to buzz are more of a chore. A warped neck is a serious enough defect to throw the instrument out of consideration. Also look carefully for structural damage that might be concealed by heavy re-varnishing. Find candidates in the classified ads of newspapers or in music stores that carry guitars.

Electric Guitars

Ahem. We come to the one instrument that probably raises the hackles of every lover of classical music, the one that can assault all the senses at once. The one that is so hard to relate to if you are not a kid, but the one you can't ignore, either. It transformed American pop culture of the latter half of the 20th century more than any other instrument (certainly more than the bassoon). The one indispensable item to rock and roll, the electric guitar has also become a staple of rhythm 'n blues and country music. But remember, as you grab for the doorknob to close yourself off from the blast of your teenager's latest CD, the electric guitar is not a creation of his/her generation. Long before these kids, Jimi Hendrix was tweaking establishment sen-

Solid-body electric guitars, available in many designs, have become the primary instrument of rock and are widely used in other genres, such as country & western, rhythm & blues.

sitivities with his irreverent distortions of the national anthem.

It is the solid-body electric guitar we are speaking of. As with acoustic basses, it has been possible to electronically amplify a classic (hollow-box) guitar by sticking a magnetic pickup on it since the early 1930s. But this often produced a nasty feedback. Les Paul found a way around the problem with his 1940 solid-body guitar he dubbed "The Log." The Les Paul guitar was produced commercially by the Fender Co. and later the Gibson Co. The electric solid-body guitar had an electronic tone quality that sounded in no way like its acoustic counterpart, but allowed infinite adjustment possibilities. The player could naturally play the instrument at any volume level. But that was only the beginning. The sound could also be sustained, bent, squealed, echoed, re-verbed, or buzzed—limited only by the player's imagination and budget, since these sound-tweaking capabilities can only be achieved through electronic add-on devices.

Pros: The electric guitar is a portable, relatively inexpensive and durable instrument, that is easy to learn at the most basic level. It is *the* lead instrument and chief accompaniment source for all electronic bands, including rock in all its varieties, rhythm 'n blues, and has been on the ascendancy into jazz for several years. You can play them through earphones (but who does?).

Cons: Solid-body electric guitars do not have the same tone as acoustic guitars (which is only a con if you expect them to). They can't play unplugged.

Physical requirements: Good left-hand finger dexterity is required to press the strings against the neck. The right hand strums the strings, which doesn't require much from the fingers, or plucks them with the fingers or a pick, which does require some finger dexterity.

Is it for you? If you are oriented toward electronic music and want to play any of the many varieties this mode offers, a solid-body electric guitar is a good entry point. But the field is crowded, so if you are looking for a sure slot in a group, be prepared for a lot of competition.

Getting an instrument: Electric guitars are very simple in construction, with minimal quality differences from one model to another. The guitar, itself will cost anywhere from $200-$800, with amplifiers/speakers running in the range of $200-$600, although dealers sell guitar-plus-amp packages starting as low as $250. Used instruments abound in guitar shops.

Banjos

The upper crust didn't think too highly of the banjo in the last century. An 1886 quote from the *Boston Daily Evening Voice* reported that banjos represented the depth of popular degradation—an instrument fit mainly for the jig-dancing lower classes of the community. This is too bad, considering the history of this noble folk instrument that began as a drum with strings overstretched, indigenous to Africa, the Far and Middle East for as far back as we can discern. The Moors brought instruments of this type to Europe when they conquered Spain in the 7th century. African slaves introduced banjos to the southern states in the 17th and 18th centuries. Soldiers returning from The Civil War spread them to the rest of the country. The "black" minstrels that very likely created the stereotyped image of banjos among white society in the U.S. were ironically not black at all, but white men in blackface.

Banjos caught on like wildfire with the public after the Civil War. By the 1880s, they were everywhere, banging out popular songs, marches, dances—even operatic overtures. Meanwhile, the instruments were evolving. Frets added to the fingerboard made them easier to play. Replacing the gut strings with steel made them louder. They got louder still with the addition of a metal tone ring. Banjo popularity got another boost following the First World War, when the American public turned inward, favoring home-grown artistic expression over foreign. The banjo fit this need perfectly and became an integral part of the budding jazz era. But its bright, happy sound came to an end when the stock market tumbled in 1929, collapsing the public's spirit with it. Interest revived, at least among folk music enthusiasts, in the 1960s, with the resurgence of Bluegrass music. You may remember the 1970s movie, *Deliverance,* which featured the song, *Dueling Banjos.* Recently, groups such as Bela Fleck & the Flecktones have moved the banjo back into jazz.

The two prevalent banjo types today are the 4-string, or plectrum, banjo, and the 5-string, or Bluegrass,

A five-string banjo

banjo. Plectrum banjos are usually strummed to accompany singers or other instruments. Bluegrass banjos are plucked with picks worn on the thumb, index, and third finger of the right hand.

Pros: Banjos are so much fun to play that it's hard to play anything but happy-sounding music on one. Any banjo rendition of Bluegrass, ragtime, or Dixieland, played well, seldom fails to stir an audience to exuberance. They are portable and usually loud enough to fill any hall without amplification, at least when they are playing with an acoustic group. If you attend any of the several banjo bash festivals that occur all over the U.S. each year, you can have loads of fun mingling with other enthusiasts and get pumped up on the latest banjo lore.

Cons: Banjos are limited to the genres already mentioned (though we recently heard an unlikely, but highly successful, marriage of banjo and clarinet on a Klezmer CD). Learning the classic picking technique comes only with a lot of effort.

Physical requirements: Very nimble fingers on both hands are an absolute necessity.

Is it for you? It is if you like the kinds of music banjos play well and seek something very different and with limited group-playing opportunities.

Getting an instrument: According to Gary H. Price, a banjo craftsman in Jones, OK., you should look for the following features in a banjo: a cast flange, a three-ply rim, a high-quality tone ring, tasteful and well executed decoration, and a tone that pleases the ear. Gibsons measure up, he says, but are more expensive than banjos made by smaller makers such as Price, Jim Grainger, Frank Neat, or Jimmy Cox. New instruments vary widely in cost, from around $300 to $5,000. Used banjos range upward from $200.

Chapter 12

Woodwinds: Pipes With Lots of Keys and Holes

The woodwinds get their name from the simple wood flutes of antiquity—pipes with a mouth hole to blow across. Someone along the way must have noticed that short flutes had higher pitches than long ones. But what to do if you wanted to play a tune that had more than one pitch? You could arm yourself with a whole set of flutes, each tuned to a specific pitch, and risk being laughed out of the cave when you couldn't change instruments fast enough and ended up dropping several into the fire. So maybe you went for strength in numbers and hired eight musicians for the gig. You gave each a specifically tuned flute and lined them up, ready to toot when it was time to play their specific note, in much the same way as a hand-bell chorus. This worked, but was cumbersome. Then an efficiency expert found a way to shorten the flute's sound-producing length without shortening its actual length. He cut holes into the tube, each placed so that the player could produce a whole scale simply by lifting successive fingers off the holes.

Meanwhile, another ancestor, perhaps in a different part of the world, had an inquiring mind and nothing better to do than slit hollow swamp grass and sit around all day blowing through the slits to make a buzzing sound. One day she happened to stick one of her grass reeds onto the end of a flute. When she blew on it an entirely different sound came out. Voila, the oboes and bassoons were born, or at least their ancestors, the shawms and curtals. Eventually somebody found that yet a different sound could be produced by using only one reed instead of two if it were fixed to a hollow mouthpiece of the proper shape.

All members of the woodwind family descended from hollow wood pipes with holes cut into them.

Clarinets and saxophones were the modern day legacy of this discovery.

The woodwinds we play today work in much the same way as their primitive forerunners—successively higher notes are sounded as the holes along their length are uncovered from bottom to top. But they play much easier and more in tune, thanks to generations of refinements in the placement and size of the holes and use of keys and pads to close off the holes that can't be reached with the fingers.

Recorders

The simplest woodwind instruments are recorders. If you are familiar with woodwind recorders, you may not take them completely seriously. The image that comes to mind may be your music teacher back in 3rd grade, trying to coax simple tunes out of you and your classmates as you blew into what seemed like plastic whistles with holes. Elementary school music teachers still favor recorders as a first instrument to get kids started on, which may account for their widespread use. An estimated 3.5 million plastic recorders are sold annually. Their appeal to teachers is their economy and simplicity. They require no embouchure, because you simply blow into the mouthpiece and let the sharp edge of the tone hole produce the tone. Also, with only seven holes topside and one thumb hole to worry about, recorders are the simplest woodwind to finger.

But recorders are not limited to kids. Many adult musicians take them seriously. Amateur recorder ensembles abound, drawing from a huge repertoire that goes back to the Renaissance. Fifteenth century instrument makers began making recorders in different lengths to enable them to be played in choirs of sopranos, altos, tenors, and basses. Bach, Handel, Purcell, Scarlatti, Telemann, Vivaldi and other baroque composers wrote a profusion of solo and ensemble works for recorders. Composers' infatuation with the recorder didn't survive into the classical and romantic eras, however. As the symphony orchestra developed, composers such as Mozart and Beethoven preferred the flute, which had a softer, more versatile tone quality.

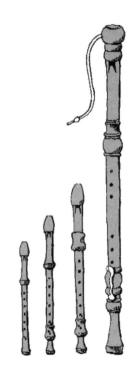

The four major members of the recorder family: soprano, alto, tenor, and bass (from left).

Today's recorder ensembles rely pretty much on the music of the baroque for their repertoire, earning them somewhat of a stuffy image among other musicians.

Pros: Recorders are compact and probably the most economical instrument to acquire. Easy to learn, they demand far less breath control than flutes. These pluses make them an excellent wind instrument to begin on, whether or not you go on to another wind instrument. The available repertoire is very large, if your tastes favor the music of the early Renaissance through the Baroque.

Cons: The lower octave of the soprano recorders and the entire range of altos, tenors and basses and basses, are too weak to compete with most other wind instruments. The high, shrill sound of soprano and sopranino recorders can be heard at some distance, so think twice if you have a sleeping baby or edgy neighbors. Another downside is the relatively narrow scope of music suited to traditional recorders.

Is it for you? Moderate finger agility and breath control are about the only demands recorders exact on your body. Alto, tenor, and bass recorders have a wider finger stretch than sopranos. If the recorder will be your only musical outlet, you should start out with a love of the music of the late renaissance and baroque eras.

Getting an instrument: A good plastic recorder, such as made by Aulos, Yamaha, and Zen-On, will serve well for traditional recorder fare or folk music. You can buy a plastic soprano recorder for less than $20, an alto for $30, a tenor for $65, and a bass for $250. Quality wood recorders made by Dolmetsch, Moeck, Mollenhauer, Küng or Roessler, come in a wide varieties of woods. Boxwood, pearwood, and maple are the most common, but you can also get exotic woods such as olivewood, ebony, and rosewood. Prices vary widely, depending on wood and quality. Current cost ranges are: $135—$400 for sopranos; $300—$750 for altos; $400—$1,000 for tenors, and $1,200—$2,500 for basses.

Flutes

Flutes, though a woodwind, are mostly made out of metal these days. The pedestrian models are made of brass, plated with a non-corrosive metal such as nickel or silver. Luxury models, as played by the likes of James Galway or Jean Pierre Rampal, are solid silver or gold. Whatever the metal, we expect a sweet, gentle sound from a flute, which has been both a blessing and a curse. Thanks to their sweetness, flutes, until recently, never strayed beyond the classical music realm. Then Herbie Mann came along and shook up the image by playing jazz flute. Ian Anderson, of the progressive rock group, Jethro Tull, took the flute into other new directions.

More recently, we have seen flutes claiming a prominent place in World Music. Their tone blends with almost any other instrument, so who knows where they will show up next? The possibilities expand even more when you consider that there is not just one flute, but a whole family. The most popular member, the treble flute, has a little brother, the piccolo, that plays an octave higher, and some siblings that play lower. There are two lower-pitched and larger members, the alto and bass flutes. Too long to play as a straight pipe, the bass flute bends back on itself in a U in order to place the holes where they can be reached, even with the help of keys. Though the alto and bass produce a beautiful, mellow, tone, it is too weak to be heard in most ensembles. Not surprisingly, these birds are rare.

The piccolo (above) is the highest voice of the flute family. It's use is limited mostly to bands, particularly in marches. The Soprano flute (below), is the most used member of the family, both as a solo and ensemble instrument.

Flute fingering is relatively easy to learn. Like all woodwinds, flutes have holes that must be opened and closed. Professionals prefer flutes that have some of the holes open, to be closed by their fingers. Beginners should opt for closed-hole flutes, where all holes are closed by pads that the fingers contact. But learning to produce a sustained tone without fainting is somewhat harder and requires a good deal of breath control. Developing an embouchure for flute playing is something most people can do, with a little effort.

Pros: Flutes are compact, versatile instruments that blend well with almost any other instrument (except maybe bagpipes). The flute repertoire is enormous, ranging from classical to modern. There are also numerous solo works, but to get the most out of a flute, you should also plan to join with others in a woodwind ensemble, orchestra, band, folk or jazz combo. The breath control needed for proper flute playing is said to promote health.

Cons: Poor breath control when playing a flute can make beginners dizzy and pose serious stress to players with shortness of breath or heart problems. Left-handed people may have a hard time adjusting to holding the instrument. Because of the high pitch, flutes are hard to practice without being heard in other rooms.

Is it for you? Straight teeth and the ability to control your lip muscles are a must. You can probably develop a flute embouchure if you can make a bottle sing by blowing across the top. Good lung capacity and breath control are also essential. Playing a flute requires good fine motor control, so flutes aren't a good bet for people with arthritic fingers or wrists.

Getting an instrument: Your first flute should be a C soprano flute. You can always add other members; a piccolo or alto flute, later. New student-grade flutes (Bundy, Conn, Vito) cost in the range of $350—$600. Mid-quality flutes range upward from around $800 (Selmer, Armstrong, Yamaha). Professional flutes range upward from around $2,000 (Haynes, Gemeinhardt, Amstrong). Used flutes are in abundance at music stores that sell to the school trade. You can probably pick up a playable one for a few hundred dollars. Make sure there are no air leaks at the pads. Test the seal by plugging the bottom end with a cork or having another person hold the palm of their hand over it tightly. With the mouthpiece removed and all pads closed, suck on the top end.

Clarinets

Clarinets as we know them today have been around since the early 1700s. Mozart loved the clarinet and wrote possibly the single best-known concerto for the clarinet, followed a short time later by a concerto by Carl Maria von Weber. By this time, clarinets were well established in the woodwind sections of symphony orchestras. Can you imagine *Peter and the Wolf* without the clarinet as the voice of the cat? With the rise of military and concert bands in the mid-nineteenth century, clarinets took the place of violins as the main solo voice in the treble range.

On the popular front, clarinets were one of the three lead instruments of the classical Dixieland combo along with a trumpet and trombone. They were alternates to saxes in the big bands of the swing era of the 1930s and 1940s, buoyed by the effervescent clarinet solos of Benny Goodman and Artie Shaw. Then, with the decline of big bands, clarinets sort of disappeared from jazz. Now they are once again on the rise, thanks to the efforts of one man: Richard Stoltzman. Stoltzman re-awakened the public's interest in the clarinet as Wynton Marsalis did for the trumpet A classically-trained musician, Stoltzman regularly performs everything from the most serious clarinet fare to the most *avant garde*. Don Byron, another cross-over clarinetist, has also helped the clarinet cause with his jazz and klezmer work.

Learning clarinet is probably slightly less taxing for an adult beginner than learning flute. Both embouchures require a bit of work to achieve, but the fingerings are similar. The main difference is that the clarinet won't leave you breathless. Instead of blowing across an open hole, you blow through a slit between the mouthpiece and the reed, which vibrates to produce the tone. With practice, you can learn to control the muscles of your lips and mouth to produce the pure tone of Richard Stoltzman, or say to hell with a classical tone and aim for the looser, laid back, tone of Dixieland jazz or Klezmer.

Clarinets come in several lengths, each with a different pitch. The B-flat soprano clarinet is the most commonly used in bands of all sorts. The A clarinet is pitched for orchestral use (though you should also have a B-flat clarinet if you play in an orchestra). E-flat sopranos, E-flat altos, and B-flat bass clarinets are common in larger concert bands. If you learn on a B-flat soprano, you can easily transfer your skills to any of the others with little difficulty. Music for all members of the family is written in the treble clef.

The two most-used members of the clarinet family. The b-flat soprano (left) is the standard instrument for all bands. It's counterpart for orchestras is pitched in the key of "A". The b-flat bass clarinet (right), a full octave lower than the soprano, is common in all concert bands.

Pros: After recorders, clarinets are probably the easiest woodwinds to learn. Versatile as solo or ensemble instruments, they draw from a wide musical storehouse from classical to modern. All members of the clarinet family are disassembled into sections, making them easy to carry from place to place.

Cons: Developing a classical (as opposed to jazz) clarinet embouchure takes work. Playing an instrument that buzzes a reed against your lower lip is not everyone's cup of tea. The time and effort required to get the instrument out of the case, put it together, and wet the reed makes a clarinet less convenient than non-reed instruments.

Is it for you? You should have straight teeth and a slight overbite (a definite underbite is a handicap), as well as good finger dexterity. You'll need better breath control than for a recorder, but not as much as for a flute. Clarinets play only one note at a time and often take the melody line in ensembles. You can lie low in the second or third clarinet section of a band, but if you aspire to the first section, be prepared to take the lead.

Getting an instrument: Clarinets range widely in quality and costs. For equal quality, the costs increase as you move down the family from soprano to bass. If you are called on to play an alto or bass clarinet in a band, expect the band to furnish the instrument. The tone you get depends more on your embouchure, the quality of the reed, and mouthpiece, than the material the instrument is made of, so plastic clarinets play almost as well as wood ones and will certainly get you by as a beginner. Plastic B-flat soprano clarinets as manufactured by Bundy, Vito, or Artley, run in the range of $300-$600. Soprano wood clarinets run in the range of $1,500-$3,000 (Selmer, Leblanc, Buffet). Because clarinets are so popular in school bands, music stores usually have a good supply of used ones, but do have any candidate checked out by a teacher or knowledgeable clarinetist before you ink the deal.

Saxophones

Chances are you have never heard of Sigurd Rascher or Alfred Galladoro, right? How about Paul Desmond, John

Coltrane, Charlie Parker or Stan Getz? We thought so. Most people familiar with instrumental music will recognize the latter group as giants of jazz. Rightly so, considering that the sax has become so inherently linked with jazz. Rascher and Galladoro are known only to aficionados of the classical saxophone. That there is a hefty pile of music for the serious saxophone says something about the versatility of this single reed instrument, which burst on the scene relatively recently in 1840, an invention of the Belgian, Adolphe Sax.

Saxes come in families, like many other instruments. The little sister at the top of the range is the B-flat soprano sax, followed by the E-flat alto, B-flat tenor, E-flat baritone, and B-flat bass. All saxes have a conical bore, but the soprano is the only one not curved into an "S" shape. The soprano sax flowered briefly in the 1930s, thanks to Sydney Bechet's introducing it into jazz. Then it faded. It's on the rise again, though. John Coltrane played his now famous rendition of *My Favorite Things* on a soprano sax in the 1960s. More recently, Paul Winter has played duets with whales and done some other new-age experiments using a soprano sax. These efforts aren't enough to dislodge altos and tenors from their secure place as the most-played members of the family and the ones you should consider if you are just starting out. Once you learn alto or tenor, you can easily play any other sax. The baritone, or "bari" sax is less common, but usually has a written part in most concert band arrangements and big bands and is always the fourth member of a sax quartet. Bass saxes are virtually obsolete.

Pros: Saxes are relatively easy to learn and play and probably offer more musical styles and tonal colors than any other instrument. The smaller saxes—soprano, alto, tenor—are very portable. Developing a sax embouchure is easier than for any other woodwind except the recorder, which of course doesn't require one. Saxes have a large repertoire of solo and small ensemble music and you'll find a saxophone section in any community band. As mentioned, saxes have become so tightly linked to jazz, that they belong in almost any size ensemble.

Cons: Outside of chamber music specifically written for the saxophone, there is little place for saxes in classical music, so you'll get nowhere hanging around

The b-flat soprano sax (left) has enjoyed a rebirth in recent years, thanks to the efforts of jazz artists such as Coleman Hawkins. The next lower sax family member is the e-flat alto (not shown), which, along with the b-flat tenor (right), are the most used saxes in bands of all types. The e-flat baritone, larger still, also has a place in bands, but the b-flat bass sax is virtually extinct.

chamber or symphony orchestras. Baritone saxes are very expensive and less portable.

Is it for you? A sax is a good choice for a beginning adult looking for a way to get into any kind of band. It's also a natural second instrument for a clarinetist who wants to broaden out into jazz or pop music. Sax playing requires good finger coordination. Straight teeth are an asset; an underbite is a handicap.

Getting an instrument: When beginning on the sax, start with an alto or tenor. You can easily transfer to a soprano and baritone later with no additional skills. Good student-quality altos (Bundy, Conn, Vito, Yamaha) cost in the neighborhood of $800-2,000. Higher quality instruments (Selmer, LeBlanc) range upward from $2,000. Tenors range between $1,500-$3,500. Saxes are ubiquitous in school bands, so you'll probably have a wide selection of used saxes in music stores. Get the help of a teacher or experienced saxophonist to check out any candidate.

Bassoons, Oboes, and English Horns

Jerry took up bassoon in 1990 and has been intrigued—at times overwhelmed—by it, ever since. At the best of times, he is playing the second, very lyrical movement of Mozart's *Bassoon Concerto,* the sustained tones rolling out of his soul and off each other like real maple syrup. At lesser times the reed squawks, the fingering seems impossible, and the tone sounds like a goose in bad trouble. Having at least dabbled with all of the wind instruments in varying degrees, he says that bassoons and their little sisters, oboes and English horns, are the hardest woodwinds to play well.

The infernal double reed is the nub of the problem. Whereas clarinets and saxophones use a single reed attached to a hollow mouthpiece, oboes and bassoons have no mouthpieces. Instead, there are two reeds bound together by thread and wire to form a shallow oval. The result is temperamental, requiring constant fussing with scrapers, reamers, and other specialized tools that must accompany the player at all times. Real oboists and bassoonists make their own reeds from cane blanks imported from Southern France. The craft, like fly tying, requires skill, patience,

Some people crave baseball...I find this unfathomable, but I can easily understand why a person could get excited about playing the bassoon.

Frank Zappa

Bassoonists are musicians who tell people they're tax accountants in real life.

Garrison Keillor

The German, or Heckel-system bassoon, is the instrument most used in North America.

and a lot of time. Not surprisingly, most bassoonists just buy their reeds from a music store or out of a catalog. Even these seldom play perfectly, as-is, and require some adjustment to play well.

Oboes and English horns are single lengths of hollow wooden tubes. Bassoons, if made straight, would stretch out to just over 8 feet long. To make them practical, they are split into two straight wood tubes connected at the bottom by a U-shaped metal tube. Another tube of smaller diameter connects the exit end of one tube with the reed. The arrangement of holes along the double tube has always been awkward for fingering. The first bassoons in the 1600s had a few extension keys to enable the player to close holes too far apart to reach. Over the next 200 years, bassoon makers tinkered, finding ways to add keys to improve playability. The present-day bassoons are fitted with an amazing assembly of keys that cross over or act off each other, some even activated by metal rods that pass through the wood tube to the other side. Rollers help the fingers move from one key to another. But, for all this, bassoons are still bastards to finger.

Much of the above also applies to oboes and English horns. Like bassoons, they are hard to play, but as smaller instruments, their difficulty comes from the embouchure and reed rather than fingering. English horns, slightly longer and lower oboes with rounded bells, are somewhat rare these days. A shame, considering their warm, mellow tone. The lyrical theme in the second movement of Dvořák's *New World Symphony* just has to be played on an English horn. In any case, English horns play exactly the same as oboes and are usually played by oboists, when the music calls for them.

Mitch Miller tried unsuccessfully to bring the oboe into popular music in the 1950s, but it didn't take, and none of the double reeds have yet cracked the world of jazz. Jerry is exploring jazz on the bassoon and can play a pretty convincing version of Miles Davis' *Round Midnight,* so he holds hope. People are more accepting today of experimentation and innovation. Who knows what the future holds for these tuxedo-class instruments?

Pros: Competent double-reed players are in demand in chamber groups, bands, and orchestras. A wide repertoire exists for solo and group playing, from the baroque to the present.

Cons: Double reeds are difficult to play well and are probably the most difficult wind instrument to learn. All are inconvenient to set up and put away. Reeds have to be soaked and the sections of the instrument assembled and disassembled. All require a well-developed embouchure. Bassoons are awkward to hold and finger. Good new instruments are very expensive, especially bassoons. Reeds are temperamental and require constant fussing over. Music for bassoons is often written in the tenor clef, unfamiliar to players of most other wind instruments. Bassoons do not project well outdoors. All double reed instruments are pretty much limited to classical music.

Is it for you? The need to continuously coddle a double reed may explain why there are so few oboists around. Add in the very high cost of instruments and the need to wrestle with awkward fingering, and you understand why bassoon players are also scarce. Nevertheless, if you have the interest and stamina to take on these built-in problems, you stand to get some real satisfaction from playing a double-reed instrument. You should have enough drive to get good, though. You can play comfortably in a section of several clarinets or saxes in a band with so-so capability, but will likely be the only player on your part on oboe or bassoon. Anything that comes out the end of your horn will stand out prominently for all to hear. You'll need to start with a good sense of pitch, extremely good control of mouth muscles and tongue, and good finger dexterity. Bassoons additionally favor big hands and good thumb dexterity.

Getting an instrument: All double reed instruments are expensive. The most economical plastic oboe (Artley) goes for around $1,300. Wood oboes cost between $1,400 and $4,200 (Buffet, Bulgheroni, Fox). The most economical bassoons are polypropylene plastic that sell for around $4,200 (Fox Renard). Maple bassoons range from $8,000 to $19,000 (Fox), or higher still for a German made Heckel bassoon. Your best bet when starting out is to borrow an instrument. If and when you decide to continue, you'll have a feel for what you want. Then you can look into getting a good used instrument or trading in your BMW to finance a new one.

Despite the rich, mellow alto voice of the English horn (left), it is rarely used. Its higher-pitched brother, the oboe (right) has a place in all orchestras and concert bands.

Woodwinds, Schmoodwinds—A Confusion of Materials

Except for saxophones, most of the instruments we now class as "woodwinds" started out made of wood. Brass has replaced wood for most flutes, though wood piccolos are still common. The basic models are brass plated with silver. Mid-range flutes come with silver-plated bodies and solid Sterling Silver head joint. The best flutes are made with solid Sterling Silver or 24-carat gold. Serious flutists claim flutes made of silver and gold really do play better than plated-brass flutes. And, for the step up in quality, they are willing to pay thousands of dollars more.

Wood remains the favored material for better quality clarinets, oboes and bassoons. Grenadilla, a tropical hardwood, stained black and rubbed to a dull sheen, is the preferred wood for clarinets and oboes. Bassoons are made of maple, usually stained a deep maroon, but sometimes left natural or stained a darker color.

Plastic, used for the more economical recorders since the early 1940s, is now used to make clarinets, oboes, and bassoons, though manufacturers call it by other names such as "composition" or "Resinite." Whatever you call it, a plastic material has some advantages and a disadvantage over real wood. On the plus side, it is much cheaper, because the material itself costs less and can be molded rather than machine worked. And even when formed by machine—as it is when used to make bassoons—it is less likely to split or deform, because of its greater dimensional stability. It doesn't shrink and swell with changes in temperature and humidity. Its only disadvantage is that the tone quality is slightly different than for a wood instrument, though the difference is hard to detect and certainly won't be noticeable by a beginner. The tone you get depends much more on what's above the body of the instrument—the mouthpiece, reed, your embouchure. For that reason, a plastic instrument may be a good choice for your first woodwind if your budget is tight.

The metal used in the keys of all woodwinds also shows much variety. Saxophones are made of brass and usually come with lacquered brass keys. Silver-plated saxes have silver or nickel-silver-plated keys (nickel-silver is not silver at all, but nickel and zinc). Economy-end flutes, clarinets, oboes and bassoons come with steel keys plated with silver, nickel, or nickel-silver. Mid-range instruments have silver-plated keys, while keys of the highest quality are solid Sterling Silver or gold.

 Chapter 13

Horns with Valves and Slides

Brass instruments were born long ago when stone age herdsmen hollowed out rams' horns, cut off the tips, and blew into the small ends to communicate with other herdsmen out of the range of speech. This much we know. Tracing the path from the simple ram's horn to the precise assembly of tubes and valves that makes up a modern trumpet involves a bit of conjecture. Here's our version of how it might have come about.

With the dawning of the bronze age the ram's horn became the model for a metal version, where the tube was elongated and flared. Someone noticed along the way that longer horns produced a lower pitch than shorter ones. Louder, too. When you blew raspberries through the longer models, the sound not only carried across the valley, but made the other shepherds jump. Such long horns were naturally hard to tote from place to place and a real burden on a horse. You couldn't transport them without dragging one end in the dirt, which inevitably dented the horn (interestingly, all the dented horns of today owe their heritage to that prototype dented horn). On one such trip, the horse stumbled, tripping over the straight horn and bending it into an L-shape. The rider dismounted and immediately blew into it to see if it still worked. Damn! He bent the horn further, into a U-shape, and it still played. Now it was only half as long, but much easier to carry. So he coiled the rest until he had a shape he could carry in one arm, without dragging.

And behold, skipping lightly over several intervening centuries of development, we have the wonderful brass instruments of today. A whole choir of horns from the trumpets and cornets singing the soprano voice, French horns picking out the alto, trombones and euphoniums taking the baritone part, and tubas handling the bass line.

As an adult beginner, if you learn a cornet or trumpet you can easily transfer your skills to play the lower-valved members, the euphonium and tuba. You can use the same basic embouchure on a trombone, but will have to learn slide positions. French horn playing requires a slightly different embouchure and fingering. If you start on one of the lower brasses, it's usually harder to develop an embouchure for the higher horns. So, for example, its easier for a trumpeter to switch to tuba than the reverse.

Trumpets and Cornets

Q: What's the difference between God and a trumpet player?

A: God doesn't think he can play the trumpet.

If there's a grain of truth in all humor, maybe the well-worn gag at left says something about the way trumpet players see themselves (bassoonists and clarinetists being naturally far humbler). In any case, God must have liked the trumpet or he wouldn't have had them wielded so frequently by angels in all those pictures. He also gave them ample opportunity to play on earth. Baroque composers such as Haydn wrote concertos for them. Classical and romantic era composers relied on their clarion tone to expand the tonal possibilities of the symphony orchestra. Bunny Berigan, Bix Beiderbecke, and Louis Armstrong made them indispensable to jazz in the 1920s. The big bands of the 30s and 40s made trumpets one of the three horn sections of their bands, along with saxes and trombones. In the 1940s, Dizzy Gillespie helped usher in bebop by inflating his cheeks to bullfrog proportions and blowing through a trumpet he had customized by bending the bell upwards. Miles Davis, Don Cherry, and others have made sure there is a place for a trumpet in small jazz combos ever since.

So what about cornets already, you ask. Cornets and trumpets look pretty much alike and are played in exactly the same way. The similarity ends there. Trumpets look like cornets that have been stretched out to make them longer, with a bore that is cylindrical except where it flares out at the bell. The shorter and squatter cornets have a mostly conical bore. The differences in shape yield different tone qualities. Trumpets were first used to play fanfares that announced important events. A brilliant, piercing tone suited them well for this task. Though the original long straight horn has been bent into a more compact shape and has had valves added to make it possible to play more notes, the brassy tone remains.

Cornets have a shorter history. They were spun off trumpets in the 19th century to provide an instrument that had a subtler, mellower tone. The bright, brassy tone of trumpets suited them well to orchestras, providing occasional powerful accents to the strings and woodwinds. But bands had no strings. Instead, the brass and woodwinds had to carry the melodic load. The mellower tone of cornets answered this need (though bands also use trumpets, which muddies an otherwise clear explanation, dammit). Anyway, if you can play one, you can play the other, and whatever tone you start with, you can alter by sticking the right mute into the bell. Straight mutes and cup mutes dampen the tone. Smartass trumpet players get the most fun of all out of "wah-wah" mutes, that they use to make the horn sound like a baby talking.

Coaxing a tone through the small aperture of a trumpet/cornet mouthpiece that won't send your pets running for cover requires a well-developed embouchure, which only comes with a lot of work. Once you get this kind of lip, you have to maintain it with regular playing. Many pros give it up when they reach a point when they feel their lip is slipping and they can no longer hit the higher notes without strain. That should not deter you from beginning these horns as an adult amateur, though. You may never be able to reach notes as high as Maynard Ferguson or Doc Severenson, but that still leaves a lot of territory in the lower octaves, where you can find ample satisfaction and fulfillment as a recreational player.

Pros: A trumpet or cornet is very portable; quick and easy to set up and take apart. The repertoire is enormous, spanning concert orchestral music from the baroque onward and concert and military band music from the 19th century to the present. Equally at home in the world of jazz, trumpets and cornets are found in many types of groups, from brass quintets to jazz bands to symphonic orchestras, town bands, and concert bands.

The longer, narrower shape that marks a trumpet (left) from a cornet (right) is apparent when they are placed side by side.

Cons: The time and effort needed to develop and maintain a capable embouchure may be more than you are willing to accept. It's hard to practice a trumpet quietly. Mutes help, but impede the airflow and alter the sound (you may find the answer to this problem with an electronic practice mute).

Is it for you? Straight teeth, un-scarred lips and healthy gums are necessary, along with a willingness to develop and maintain a trumpet embouchure. A good sensitivity to pitch is helpful. Because the trumpet/cornet often carries the melody line in bands and orchestras, you should have the confidence and boldness to take the lead when called upon. If you would be more comfortable hanging back than standing out, you might do better to consider an instrument that always plays a supporting role.

Trumpet players are believed to have rather large egos.

Getting an instrument: First decide between a trumpet or cornet, based on the type of music you want to play and the groups you aim to get into. Cornets are slightly easier to play for a beginner, so your best starting horn might be a standard B-flat cornet. Later, if you want to branch out, you can add a trumpet. Student-grade instruments achieve economy with looser fitting valves and a two-piece bell construction. Their sound and tone fall short of the intermediate or advanced models, but are okay to start on. New beginner cornets/trumpets cost in the range of $400-900 (Bach, Getzen, Holton). Intermediate/advanced instruments cost $1,000-$2,500 (Conn, King, Holton, Benge). You can probably get a good used trumpet/cornet for under $500, but don't put money down before having the horn checked out by an experienced player or teacher. Items to check include valves that leak or don't move easily, worn valves that have been restored by copper plating, damaged tubing and tuning slides that bind.

French Horns

The "French" part of French horns traces from their ancestors that were used on fox hunts in France, during the 17th century. It's an ill-deserved title so we'll simply refer to them henceforward as "horns." After all, the English, Germans, and Italians also contributed to their evolution, and valves were added by a Czech in 1814. Up to that time, the notes you could play were limited to the natural harmonic intervals on the horn, produced by tightening or loosening the embouchure. If you wanted to play in a different key, you had to fit on a length of tubing, or crook, to adjust the horn to play the intervals of that key. Horn players of the day must have looked like plumbers, toting around all those crooks.

> *Q: What's the difference between a French horn and a '57 Chevy?*
>
> *A: You can tune a '57 Chevy.*

Another refinement, along with valves, was the addition of a second set of tubing that made it easier to play the high notes. A thumb valve acted as a traffic manager to direct the airflow into either tubing section. Horns thus equipped are called "double" horns; those without are "single" horns. Unrolling all the twists and turns of a double horn would net you a conical tube 33 feet long.

A double French horn has two sets of tubing, which actually make it into two instruments, one pitched to the key of F, the other to B-flat. A thumb trigger acts as a traffic manager, toggling between the two. Uncoiled, the total length of the tubing rolls out to around 33 feet.

Few disagree that the horn is the most challenging brass instrument to play. Though horns have valves, they are almost incidental. Most of the skill required to get around on the infernal coil of tubing is in the lips. Good horn players have to develop and maintain not only superb embouchures but have very good ears to be able to place the note at the right pitch.

But, if you do achieve competence, the rewards are great. They begin with the satisfaction of producing a soothing tone. If a trumpet puts you in mind of satin, a horn is more akin to velvet. You can really feel the sound working its way through all that tubing and nudge your right hand on the way out the bell (unlike with other brass, the right hand is moved in and out of the bell to help control the tone and pitch). Composers from Bach to the modern period loved the horn and wrote numerous horn concertos (Mozart, Richard Strauss). Symphonies of the romantic period are full of Horn solos to die for (Beethoven, Brahms, Dvorak). In the 20th century, Richard Strauss used Horns to highlight his many tone poems. Horns are the indispensable fifth member of both woodwind quintets and brass quintets. French Horn clubs/societies have been established in Concord, MA, Lexington, KY, Los Angeles, CA, Spokane and Tacoma, WA., and Columbus, OH.

Pros: Horns offer the potential of a beautiful sound that blends with many other instruments. Vital members of chamber and symphony orchestras, military and concert bands, and chamber ensembles, horns also draw upon an extensive list of solo works. If you have the grit to become competent, you won't have to look far to find a group that will welcome you.

Cons: A very demanding embouchure makes the horn the hardest brass instrument to play. Good instruments are expensive. Horns have at this time not established a fit in musical genres outside of serious music.

Is it for you? You'll need almost perfect teeth and gums with no underbite, as well as excellent control of mouth and lip muscles, and an excellent sense of pitch. You should have a personality willing to take risks. Horns often stand out in group playing, and hitting the first note on target tests even seasoned hornists ("hornies"?) to the max.

Getting an instrument: Because horn playing is so hard, even with a good instrument, it makes no sense to handicap yourself with one that under-performs. Borrow or rent a good horn at the beginning, then, if you decide to continue, look for a good new or used horn. Most horn players settle on double horns because of their advantages in the higher range. Double horns cost between $1,500 and $5,000 (Conn, Besson, Yamaha). You'll be lucky to find a decent used double horn for less than $2,300. As with trumpet buying, get an expert's opinion of any horn you are considering. Some things to look out for include making sure all of the slides are easily removable; all solder joints should be firm; valves should work quickly and noiselessly; valve caps should be easy to remove; the bell on a screw-bell horn should come off easily, but not while you are playing. Finally, the fewer dents, the better.

Trombones

Slides are what set trombones apart from the other brass, enabling them to move smoothly from one note to another without making a jump. Trombonists in school bands exploit this feature to the max to bring trumpeters down a peg. Someone in the last century, probably a disgruntled trumpet player, tried to spoil the fun by making a trombone that could be played like "respectable" horns, by fixing the slide in place and adding valves. The valve trombone never really caught on, though, to the delight of real trombonists. Its shortfalls, they point out, are two: it can't gliss and has lousy intonation.

Sliding, or "glissing" around the scale is, of course, the hallmark of Dixieland jazz Still, it's not all they do (Lucie insists). The great band leaders/trombonists Tommy Dorsey and Glenn Miller coaxed a variety of expression out of their instruments when they soloed with their big bands in the 1930s and 1940s. Mainstream jazz artists such as J.J. Johnson have added their own nuances to the instrument to secure its place firmly in the world of jazz.

Trombones are, of course, a crucial part of the brass section of all concert and military bands. They even manage to sneak into symphony orchestras. While the

In high school, I saw trombone players described in a textbook as "The Clowns of the Orchestra" (indicating that the author found the image of grown men earning their living by sliding lubricated tubing back and forth, and leaving pools of spit in front of their chairs, pretty amusing).

Frank Zappa

The b-flat slide trombone hasn't changed appreciably in the last 200 years.

benefit is a well-needed shot of prestige, there are downsides. First, because the trombones are only called upon to play intermittently to provide punchy accents to the strings, they end up with a lot of spare time between passages—sometimes enough to finish a game of gin rummy. The other drawback of orchestral playing is that it doesn't take advantage of the trombone's full potential. If a trombonist ever did cut loose with a really soul-satisfying, down-and-dirty glissando, the conductor would drop his baton (or maybe throw it).

Pros: You don't need finger dexterity, as with other brass, so trombone would be a good choice for someone with a physical condition that limits the fine motor control of their fingers. Also, because the mouthpiece is bigger than that of a trumpet or French horn, the embouchure is looser and easier to acquire. Trombones draw upon a rich store of solo and ensemble music from the romantic period onward, which can be played in trombone and brass choirs, concert bands, brass bands, jazz ensembles and orchestras.

Cons: Because the notes are not fixed on the trombone as in the valved brass, you need an excellent sense of pitch to accurately produce the intended pitch.

Is it for you? A good ability to manipulate your right arm and wrist are essential (an arthritic right wrist or elbow would be painful with a trombone). Most of the time trombones in bands and orchestras play supporting roles to other instruments, but they occasionally take the lead, so the instrument is not a good bet for a "shrinking violet."

Getting an instrument: The heart of a trombone is, of course, its slide, which should be flawless and work effortlessly and smoothly. The tubing of the slides of economy level trombones has a seam. Better ones are seamless. You can likely pick up a good used trombone for less than $500, but have an expert check out the slide. New economy models start around $400 (Conn, Getzen, Besson) and range up to $3,500 (Benge, Bach, Yamaha, Willson).

Euphoniums and Baritones

Actually, euphoniums differ from baritones in ways other than the quip at left. Euphoniums' bore is wider, which gives them a deeper, less brassy tone quality. The wider bore also makes them bulkier and heavier; less convenient for marching. Both horns are the smaller siblings to the tuba and similar in every way except that they have shorter tubing and thus a higher pitch range.

Euphoniums, like other valved brass instruments, got hatched early in the 19th century and gradually found their way into European brass bands. They never did make it into orchestras, except for a handful of works by Holst, Strauss, and a few others. A body of solo works for the instrument issued forth during the 19th and 20th centuries. Euphonium soloists often play works written for the trombone or bassoon, which is possible because the ranges match. Outlets for euphoniums in group playing are pretty well restricted to military and concert bands, where, along with trombones, they play the tenor voice, similar to what a cello does in an orchestra. Unlike trombones, euphoniums have not yet become a part of jazz ensembles.

Pros: Euphoniums are likely the easiest of any brass instrument to learn, thanks mainly to the large mouthpiece. Their mellow tone makes them wonderful solo instruments as well as natural tenor voices for all kinds of bands and brass ensembles. Quartets of two euphoniums and two tubas are on the rise, and draw from a growing songlist arranged for this grouping.

Cons: Euphoniums are bulkier to carry around than cornets and trumpets, and more expensive to buy. Musical outlets are limited to solo, ensemble, and bands. Euphoniums are never seen with strings and have yet to crack the world of jazz, popular, and folk music.

Is it for you? A forgiving mouthpiece makes a euphonium both an easy instrument for a beginning brass player as well as a good downshifting instrument for a person who once played a trumpet or French horn, but no longer has the lip. Good wind power and breath control are necessary.

Getting an instrument: New student model euphoniums (Conn, Yamaha, King, Holton) run in the range of $1,900-$2,500. Professional instruments (Besson,

Q: What's the difference between a euphonium and a baritone?

A: About $50 an hour

A bell-forward baritone has the bell bent to project sideways for marching. Other models have bells oriented upward for playing inside.

Horns with Valves and Slides

Yamaha, Willson, Hirschbrunner) cost $3,000-$6,000. Music stores that serve schools usually stock used baritones in the range of $500-$800. But, as with all valved brass, the devil is in the valves, so make sure they work smoothly before buying.

Tubas and Sousaphones

The elephants of the brasses bellow with the best of them but can also purr like a kitten, A 500-pound kitten. The history of tubas follows much the same path as that of the euphonium. They share much the same type of music and musical outlets, with one exception: tubas are used in symphony orchestras; euphoniums are limited to bands. Richard Wagner liked them well enough to use them in the Funeral March of the opera, *Die Götterdämmerung*. Tubas play the main theme in Berlioz' *Symphonie Fantastique,* and tubas figure prominently in the *Tragic Overture* by Brahms. The Dixieland bands of yesteryear frequently used tubas to put down the bass line. The string bass edged tubas out of this function in the jazz groups of the 1930s-1980s. In the 1990s they began popping up again. And we have already mentioned, in chapter 9, how the Dirty Dozen Brass Band and others have blazed new trails for the tuba.

Tuba enthusiasts can also take nourishment and inspiration from joining *Tubists Universal Brotherhood Association* (T.U.B.A.), a growing organization with chapters in several cities. Another event staged in many cities at Christmastime is Tubachristmas®. Tubist Harvey Phillips conceived the idea in the 1970s and set it up as a nation-wide event. Imagine twenty or thirty tubas, baritones, and euphoniums playing Christmas carols in four-part harmony, like coordinated foghorns. Musicians, amateur and professional alike, are typically invited to a short rehearsal, followed by a concert in a shopping mall or other public place. Jerry has played his war-ravaged E-flat tuba in six events so far, having loads of fun each time while meeting low brass players from other places. Our most recent Tubachristmas®, performed in the atrium of the Keene State College student center, included 48 players from all six New England states plus New York.

Q: What is a tuba for?

A: A board 1 1/2" thick by 3 1/2" wide

The tuba is a large, bulky instrument that has to be played upright from a sitting position. That's fine for concerts, but lousy for carrying on horseback or marching. In 1849, an enterprising Viennese tinkerer named Stowasser figured out a way of reconfiguring the tubing so that it wrapped around, rather than sat in front of, the player. John Philip Sousa adapted the concept for the "sousaphone" he developed in the 20th century, and the instrument has become the standard of American marching bands since. Sousaphones don't have the mellow, deep tone of tubas, but project better laterally and can be carried over the shoulder.

Pros: Laying down the bass line for a large group is a satisfying experience. Tubas are welcome members of all manner of bands, some orchestras, and wind ensembles. Tubas are easy to learn and play, thanks to the a large-diameter, very forgiving mouthpiece. Tubas are easy second instruments for anyone who has played a trumpet or cornet.

Cons: Size can't be ignored. These behemoths are heavy, bulky, and hard to tote around. It's no coincidence that tuba players tend to be biggish males. Tubas don't have much of a life outside of group playing. Good tubas are costly. If you learned brass fingering positions from playing cornet or trumpet, you need to relearn the fingerings for the bass clef.

Is it for you? Big lips are an asset for tuba playing. A body type that leans toward the substantial will aid in holding a large, bulky instrument while playing. You can blow up several balloons with the air required to sustain whole notes in slow pieces, so good lungs are a plus. Working the valves calls for fair dexterity of the right hand fingers. In bands, tubas are seldom called on for solo passages, so are perfect instruments for shy persons (this is not the case with small ensembles, though, witness the tuba work in groups such as *The Canadian Brass*).

Getting an instrument: A new quality tuba can cost as much as a new car, and it won't even get you to the gig. So when beginning or considering switching to tuba, your best bet is to start out with one borrowed from a school or rented from a music store. The next step might be to seek out a used tuba. Music stores sometimes have them, but not in the abundance of other brass. You may

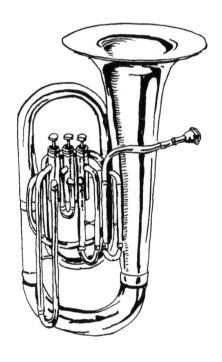

Tubas come in many shapes. The bell-upward model shown is the type most common in sit-down playing.

find candidates on the Internet, but won't know anything about their quality unless you have them shipped to you for trial. New tubas cost anywhere from $5,500 to $10,000 (Holton, King, Conn, Yamaha). Brass Sousaphones range between $4,000 and $7,000 (Conn, King). Fiberglass models don't have the tone of a brass Sousaphone, but are much less expensive, at around $2,500 (Yamaha). You'll be lucky to find a playable used tuba for under $1,000.

If It's Brass, Why Is It Silver?

You may have noticed a silver trumpet and wondered if it really was silver. The answer lies in the evolution of the family of horns we call "brass." Prototype brass instruments such as the serpent weren't even made of brass, but wood. But from the 19th century on, brass emerged as the material of choice for brass instruments, and for good reasons. Brass is a soft metal made from alloying copper, zinc, and bits of other metals to achieve various qualities. Malleable, brass could be heat-formed to yield the double-curved surfaces required for flared bells. Seams were easily sealed by soldering. The surface could be polished to a high sheen. And brass resisted corrosion.

Exposure to moisture and air caused a thin film of oxide to form, which protected the underlying metal but left the surface dull and tarnished, not bright and shiny as when new. The player could always restore the original bright luster by applying brass polish with enough elbow grease. Manufacturers solved the problem by applying a clear lacquer coating, which isolated the metal from the atmosphere. This method remains the standard finish for low to mid-quality instruments. Eventually, the lacquer itself wears off, starting at the locations most in contact with the player's skin. You can live with the spots or have the horn recoated.

But to get back to the original question, why are some brass instruments silver? They aren't. At least not all the way through. The base metal of all brass instruments is one of the three variety of brass: yellow brass, gold (red) brass, or nickel silver, actually an alloy of nickel and zinc. Silver is a denser metal than brass. When used to plate a brass trumpet or trombone, it changes the instrument's timbre, making it sound brighter, more brilliant. The higher quality brass instruments of today are silver plated. The highest quality ones are gold plated.

Chapter 14

Keyboard Kith and Kin

Two years before his death in 1980, jazz pianist Bill Evans appeared as a guest on *Piano Jazz,* a weekly feature on NPR hosted by pianist Marian McPartland.   Bill had played, for most of his short career, in small ensembles consisting of piano, bass, and drums. Bill was just as comfortable playing completely by himself.   When Marian asked him to compare playing solo to playing with a group, Bill said he preferred playing solo but didn't feel he had the dimension to really be a solo pianist, even though solo playing gave him the control of the nuances and rubatos (liberties with tempo). On the other hand, playing in a trio freed him from having to maintain a continuous bass line and keep the rhythm going.

Bill's answer summed up the essence of keyboards: they are both solo and ensemble instruments, allowing the player almost unlimited freedom to express musical ideas whether alone or in the company of others.

A violin defies you to produce a lovely sound, the trumpet can tear you up trying to play it, but the piano works right away—a child can do it.

Noah Adams
Piano Lessons

Acoustic Pianos

It takes an investment of both time and effort to get to the point where you can play anything of substance on a piano, but Noah Adams is right in one sense. When your finger hits a key, a tone sounds—a nice tone, right on pitch every time. You don't have to worry about a reed, mouthpiece, or having a good lip. For this wonderful state of affairs we have Bartolomeo Cristofori of Padua and sundry other inventors to thank. In 1709, Cristofori invented the mechanism that differentiated the piano from its forerunner, the harpsichord. Whereas the keys of a harpsichord plucked the strings, Cristofori's mechanism used felt-covered hammers to strike them. This wonderful advance made it possible to vary the volume from soft (*piano*) to loud (*forte*), hence the new name: *pianoforte*, which eventually became simply piano.

Pianos improved continually over the next two centuries, resulting in an acoustic instrument that is a marvel of mechanical genius. Its 88 keys span most of the range within our hearing. They connect to an intricate assembly of hammers, felt, and wire that work marvelously together. Noah Adams, in his book, *Piano Lessons,* credits the Steinway family with the lion's share of the refinements that we now take for granted. He tells of how Heinrich Steinweg, a cabinetmaker from Hamburg, Germany, came to the U.S. in 1850. Steinweg anglicized his surname to Steinway and set about with his three sons to build piano soundboards in Manhattan. The pianos he made on the side soon took over as his primary business and the Steinway name has since set the standard by which most other pianos are measured.

Console, or vertical, pianos are available in heights ranging from 43 to 46 inches.

By 1851, piano making by Steinway, Baldwin, Chickering and many other smaller makers had become big business in the United States. But making the grand piano accessible to the middle class meant finding a way to make it fit into rooms smaller than concert halls. The answer came by tipping the horizontal sounding board upright, saving enough floor space to make a "cabinet grand," or "upright piano" fit into any living room. Shrinking the upright to yield smaller, more economical pianos, spinets, made them even more available to the middle class in the post World War II years.

Naturally, shrinking the cabinet down to a height of as little as three feet didn't come without a noticeable sacrifice in tone quality. The popularity of spinets waned, and the term "spinet" is no longer used in the industry. Today, vertical soundboard pianos (now called vertical, console, or upright) get better tone than the older spinets and range between 43" and 46" in height. Grand pianos, still the paragon of tone quality, vary in size from 5-feet (baby grand) to 9-feet (concert grand).

Pros: Pianos are complete orchestras, capable of playing both the melody and accompaniment to music of almost any style and period. They draw from one of the richest stores of music of any instrument—everything from Bach to Scott Joplin to Chick Corea.

Cons: Acoustic pianos have well-established, but limited opportunities in groups, but the groups have to come to them, since they are not too portable. Good pianos are expensive and take up space—usually the better the piano, the bigger, and the more real estate you have to give up. The wood in pianos shrinks and swells with changes in the weather and season, and the tuning changes accordingly. Keeping them stable in hot-humid regions, such as most of the southeast U.S., usually means housing them in a room that is air-conditioned.

Is it for you? While pianos can back up other instruments, they are the perfect choice for the person who wants to *be* the orchestra rather than *a part* of the orchestra. Also, if you need to experiment with harmonies, the piano is what you want. If you think you may be "tone deaf" to some degree, the piano is a good choice, because the pitch of each note is fixed. Physical requirements include good motor control of the wrists and fingers and good coordination between both hands and your right foot. Naturally, your fingers should be small enough to fit the keys. Piano teacher Walt Sayre tells about a construction worker who wanted piano lessons, but doubted it would be possible. When Sayre said, 'What do you mean, you can't be taught? I can teach anybody to play something. Then he showed me his hands. They were the most immense hands I have ever seen. Each finger was larger than a piano key. He couldn't possibly play. I said, 'You're right, I couldn't possibly teach you piano."

Getting an instrument: Every piano has a unique personality—its own touch and tone. These qualities generally correspond to size and price. Grand pianos have bigger soundboards than uprights, and the difference is evident in the sound and response. Unfortunately, all grands are expensive, starting around

As the west was tamed and settled, the possession of a piano became the symbol of respectability and cultural achievement... young ladies applied themselves, as they did in Europe, to learning piano versions of the symphonies of Mozart and Beethoven, and the latest novelties of Felix Mendelssohn and Giovanni Bellini.

Yehudi Menuhin

Grand pianos range in size from the 9-foot concert models down to the 5-foot baby grand shown here.

$12,000 for a 5-foot baby grand to upwards of $70,000 for the largest Steinway or Baldwin. It's easy to see why most amateurs settle for something more modest. The best of today's consoles and uprights (Yamaha, Kawai) run in the neighborhood of $2,500 to $5,000. While their tone is superior to the spinets of prior years, it often falls short of the tone of some of the old parlor uprights. These are get-

Some pianists see themselves as a big fish in a small pond.

ting scarce these days, but you are quite likely to get one for under $500 if you can find one at all.

Never buy a used piano without first having it examined by a piano repairer/restorer. Pianos have many parts that wear out, break, or crack over time. An old upright may require as much or more in repairs as the purchase price.

Never buy *any* piano without first playing it. If you don't feel competent to judge its tone and action, take along an experienced pianist. Pianos vary in many ways, but the tone should please you over the whole range of the keyboard. The action should suit your touch preference, be it heavy or light. If you have weak fingers or any condition that impairs your fingers or wrists, get a piano with a loose, rather than stiff action.

Electronic Pianos

Acoustic pianos pretty much stay where you put them—no problem if you don't intend to play them away from home—but a big one if you do. If you don't take your own instrument, you put yourself in constant peril of playing on an instrument of unknown quality and tuning. Jerry remembers how this reality affected him when he played his first professional gigs in the 1950s, with *Gaylen Hansen's Music Makers* (the group would probably be called something like *Exploding Zucchini* today). As the only member of the group who didn't have to tote his instrument to the gig, Jerry looked on smugly as the others carried theirs out to the cars and tried to make them fit to leave room for the band. The rest of the band got their turn to smirk when the band was setting up, watching Jerry approach the piano, plunk his way up the keyboard to see which keys were to be avoided for being out of tune and which keys didn't play at all. The instrument he got stuck with was usually an old upright that had been pushed into a corner of a church social room or school gym and had endured endless assaults of kids rolling their knuckles up and down the black keys, or to team up to pound out *Heart and Soul*.

Salvation for pianists such as Jerry, who had to make the best of an unknown house piano, had been available since the early 1940s, if they were willing to play an instrument that didn't sound much like an acoustic piano. The first electric piano was invented by Harold Rhodes in the early 1940s. Rhodes wanted a small portable piano for entertaining wounded airmen in World War II. The piano he built from old pieces of B-17 bombers worked by hammers striking aluminum bars, or "tines," which were amplified by a vacuum-tube amplifier. Though the Rhodes had a unique sound, it did not pretend to sound like an acoustic piano. Rhodes sold his company to the Fender Co., whose instruments in the 1970s were popularized by artists such as Stevie Wonder, Herbie Hancock, and Chick Corea.

In the 1980s, an electronic piano was developed that sounded like its acoustic counterpart to all but the most picky piano purists . And, instead of a short keyboard with spring keys, like the Fender-Rhodes, the better digital pianos came with a full 88-key keyboard, each key weighted to feel like the mechanical action of the real thing. The whole instrument is small enough to carry from place to place and mount on a collapsible stand. All it needs to be in business is access to an electrical outlet and an amplifier, if you are playing outdoors or in a large space. For those who never intend to take their digital pianos off site, there are models built into cabinetry that look something

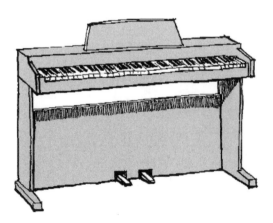

Digital pianos are mounted on permanent pedestals to more closely resemble their acoustic counterparts, or come as portable keyboards on a demountable base, for carrying to other sites.

like acoustic upright pianos.

Portability is only one of the pluses of digital pianos. Their solid-state digital electronics enables you to vary the volume not only by how hard you strike the note, but also with a volume control. You can even play them with earphones. You can shift the pitch a small amount to tune them to another instrument or by a quantum leap to transpose into a different key. You can even make them sound like an organ, vibraphone, harpsichord, or guitar. Some digitals allow splitting the keyboard, so you can, for example, play the melody in the upper portion with a vibraphone voice while playing a string bass in the lower section. There are other bells and whistles (almost literally), such as built-in recording devices and modulating wheels.

Pros: The pros cited for acoustic pianos also apply to digital pianos, plus they are portable, more economical, can be played at any volume and with earphones, can transpose and vary the pitch, and can be played in other voices in addition to piano voices. Many options are available, such as built-in recording capability and interconnectability with a computer (MIDI).

Cons: No electronic instrument can be played without a power source. The internal amplifier and speakers are sufficient for a room in a home but playing in a larger space or outdoors requires an auxiliary amplifier. Finally, while the touch and sound of quality digital pianos comes very close to that of a good acoustic piano, the match is not 100% exact.

Is it for you? It is if you seek the same kind of instrument as an acoustic piano, but want greater economy, portability, and versatility, with only a slight compromise to the sound match.

Getting an instrument: Full 88-key digital pianos come as keyboard-sized units to be mounted on a collapsible stand and as consoles, permanently mounted on a base to resemble an acoustic piano. Prices of new instruments as manufactured by Roland, Yamaha, Korg, Technics, and Kurzweil range from $1,500 to $3,000. As digitals become more popular, there is an increasing store of used instruments available. With so many features available, choosing the right digital can be confusing. Begin by deciding what features you want, whether you want a piece of furniture or a device that can be easily

Complacent writers turn into hacks. The piano gave me a sense of myself apart from being a critic.

Michael Kimmelman
Art critic, *The New York Times*

moved, then visit a few showrooms to try out several models. The sound and touch is not the same, from one digital piano to another.

Synthesizers

If digital pianos try to clone acoustical pianos by virtue of an 88-note weighted keyboard, piano-like tone, and in some models appearance, synthesizers resemble pianos only in the similarity of their keyboards. Their keyboards

A synthesizer is basically an electronic keyboard with numerous capabilities to create different tonal patterns.
Interconnectability with computers is a common feature, as well as built-in recording devices.

are typically spring-loaded rather than weighted and typically extend only 4 or 5 octaves. The distinctions are blurring, however, as digital pianos take on more of the features of synthesizers and vice versa. In any case, both are products of the computer age and, like all computer stuff, are changing far too rapidly for many of us to assimilate.

If there is a basic difference, it is in mission: digital pianos aim to substitute for acoustic pianos; synthesizers basically generate many types of sounds electronically. Musical tones are just the tip of the iceberg. Synthesizers also imitate ocean waves, spaceship landings, and dogs barking, Individual sounds are stored as "presets" in the synthesizer's computer memory. There may be hundreds of them—too many to access by separate buttons, so you call them up by entering a two-digit code. You use the sounds in the preset form or tweak them to create new sounds or combinations, then store those in the memory. Most synthesizers also sport joy sticks or wheels that raise or lower ("bend") the pitch of the note(s) you are playing and another wheel, the "mod wheel" that controls vibrato. Obviously, there are a lot of gimmicky sounds you might never use. Who would? Two types of users, presently: rock musicians and studio composers/arrangers/hobbyists.

Rock musicians draw upon the instrument's ability to synthesize unusual (read ear-punishing) sounds and ability to interconnect with all of the other devices that make up their electronic kit of parts. They often tote more than one synthesizer to a performance and mount them in vertical racks, each one set to a different sound.

Studio musicians, amateur to pro, also draw upon the versatility of synthesizers to generate infinite tonal possibilities and their interconnectability with other devices, but are not interested in using them for "real-time" performances. Instead, they use them as a MIDI device (see *What's a MIDI?*) to compose and arrange music, either for other instruments, or to be played solely on other electronic devices. As an arranging tool, a synthesizer can be used to input music directly into a computer memory, allowing it to be played back in a voice resembling an instrument.

Pros: Synthesizers have unmatched capacity for generating endless tonal combinations. They are portable and interface easily with other electronic sound media. They are indispensable if you want to interconnect your music output directly to other electronic devices, such as computers or drum machines.

Cons: As performance instruments, synthesizers are better suited to melodies or chords played with one hand than the two-handed performance mode typical of a piano, which is why they are so often used to play the lead in rock groups. If you expect to duplicate the sound of an acoustic instrument exactly with a synthesizer, you'll probably be disappointed. The piano sound may be convincing, but we have yet to hear a synthesized trumpet or violin that sounds like a real one. This is because synthesizers can imitate the constant tone quality (timbre) of another instrument fairly convincingly, but can't duplicate all of the nuances that come from a real player on that instrument. A

What the computer cannot do is breathe, as the notes on paper do not breathe. Life must be infused into them by the performer. The computer is like a mechanical player piano, with a broader range of colors perhaps, but able only to give back what has been fed into it. Moreover, the sound does not vibrate naturally, as does a column of air in a pipe; a loudspeaker is activated through direct electrical impulses. It is a sound without human warmth.

Curtis W. Davis

---

trumpet player creates subtle sound inflections in tonguing and vibrato, which may differ for each note played. Similarly, a violinist attacks (begins) each note a bit differently by the movement of the bow across the strings. These subtle inflections shape the sound of the note into something other than a tone that simply begins and ends, and since they vary with each player with each note, inflections are hard to ape electronically.

Finally, though the synthesizer may not cost much, the peripheral gear needed to round out the system—amps and sound modifying devices—can add up to much more than the initial outlay.

Is it for you? You should get one or more synthesizers if you want to play keyboard in a rock group. A synthesizer is also the thing if you are a computer nut whose musical interests lie in exploiting the possibilities of creating music through high-tech media. Naturally, you should be familiar with computer technology or have kids you can ask.

Getting an instrument: Synthesizers, themselves are not expensive, running in the range of $800 to $2,000. They seldom stand alone, however, but are one part of a system. If you aspire to performance use, your system will include amplifiers, speakers, and probably a variety of other devices that modify the sound. The same applies to studio use. Using a synthesizer for composing/arranging means connecting it to a computer and printer. You'll need software that may cost upwards of several hundred dollars, and will probably feel the need for adjunct devices, in time.

Organs

In his youth, Jerry often listened to the weekly broadcasts of the Mormon Tabernacle Choir from Temple Square in Salt Lake City. The choir was all right, but what caught his attention was the accompaniment, the great thundering pipes of the Tabernacle organ. On one visit to the Tabernacle, he saw it being played and was awed by the raw power at the hand of the organist, perched like a pilot in a plane in front of four keyboards with another one at his feet and surrounded by an array of stops.

Pipe organs are pretty much a thing of the past.

Having mostly vanished from theaters, the few remaining ones reside in older churches. Newer churches buy cheaper and smaller electronic organs that mimic the sound of pipe organs, in varying degrees of accuracy.

Jerry got his introduction to organ playing in his teens, when he was an organist for his church. He sat facing the two keyboards of the Hammond B3 organ, surrounded by stops and drawbars that you could arrange in endless combinations to produce different tonal combinations, some reminiscent of a haunted house. He thought it a shame all this was wasted on mere hymns.

Laurens Hammond introduced the Hammond Organ in 1935 and marketed it primarily to churches as the modern replacement to pipe organs. Though it didn't sound much like a real pipe organ, it met with success not only in churches over the next 40 years, but also in popular music and jazz. The result is a musical expression ranging from signature soap opera theme songs to Jimmy Smith's down-and-dirty jazz organ work. The guts of the Hammond Organ contained a series of "tone wheels" that revolved to generate the tone, which was then amplified by a vacuum tube amplifier. Tonal variation was achieved through a series of stops with pipe-organ designations, such as *diapason, bourdon, dulcet*, and a row of drawbars that could be pulled out to add harmonics (overtones) to the fundamental pitch in order to alter its tone quality. Percussive effects, vibrato, reverb were later added.

Still later, in the 1950s, Hammond came out with a smaller, much less

A console-model electronic organ, with two manuals (keyboards) and a full pedalboard.

costly, and simpler organ specifically targeted at the home market. The Hammond Chord Organ had one keyboard, on which the melody was played with the right hand. The left hand, meanwhile, pushed buttons arrayed to the left of the keyboard. Each button played a different chord. The company touted the Chord Organ as an instrument that anyone could play with very little effort.

Electronic organs of today use much the same highly sophisticated microprocessor technology as synthesizers to create numerous voices. There are models for every taste and budget. The smallest models, no larger than the smallest pianos, have only one keyboard and an abbreviated pedalboard. Manufacturers target the home market with these models and load them up with special effects such as built-in recorders, reverb, echo, rhythm sections and other gimmicks that serious organists would consider tacky. Moving up-market, you can choose between consoles equipped to sound like church organs and consoles modeled on the theater organs of the past. A mid-range organ such as the Allen P-2 contains two keyboards, a full pedalboard and more traditional organ effects. At the top of the heap are the huge 4-manual models such as the Allen MDS-81-S, intended for large auditoriums.

Pros: Organs, like pianos, play both melody and accompaniment. Their versatility in sound combinations suit them well to any type of music from Bach to popular music and jazz. They can be played soft or loud—even through earphones if you want to waste all that power.

Cons: Generally, organs are not instruments you can play with others, unless your goal is to become a church organist. Most organs are not portable. Coordinating both hands with both feet can be an obstacle to some people.

Is it for you? You obviously should like organ music and want to play all of the parts, though jazz organists often leave the backup work to the ensemble. You'll need good nimble fingers and coordination between them and your feet.

Getting an instrument: Begin by deciding the type of music you want to play and how much you are willing to spend. Prices vary widely, starting around $2,000 for the smallest "spinet" to $7,000 for a mid-range model, to $10,000 and up for a large theater model. You can save bundles by sacrificing the latest electronic gadgetry in favor of a used organ. Look for them in piano/organ retail outlets, the classified ads of newspapers, and over the Internet.

Accordions and Concertinas

The unkind slam at the left is indicative of the kind of abuse accordionists have had to endure in their struggle to convince "legitimate" musicians that a funny-looking squeezebox with a keyboard on one side and rows of little buttons on the other can produce something besides *Lady of Spain* and polka music. And to convince them that accordion players weren't all like Myron Floren blowing reedy bubbles for Lawrence Welk. Well, their efforts may be paying off. The accordion is enjoying a comeback, largely thanks to the popularity of Zydeco, Cajun, and other folk-based genres that employ accordions in prominent positions. Meanwhile, accordion makers have not stood still, either. While they still make the familiar mechanical/acoustic type, they have added electronic models using synthesizer technology to enable the accordion to interconnect with other electronic instruments.

Invented in Europe in the 1820s, acoustic accordions are essentially boxes of metal reeds that vibrate when air is squeezed through them as the player pumps the expandable bellows. The piano-like keys operated by the right hand play one note at a time, while buttons fingered by the left hand play bass notes or chords. Accordions typically have 3 1/2 octaves (41 keys) on the melody keyboard. On the chord side, low-end models come with as few as ten buttons, while the best ones sport upwards of 120.

Accordions have always been more popular in Europe than the U.S. Indeed, they have been fundamental to the folk traditions of many European countries. The polka music of Poland may be the best known, but accordions are also well rooted in Alpine Ländlermusik, Gypsy music, and Jewish Klezmer music. That the latter two genres were played by musicians who tended to wander from place to place no doubt helps explain the popularity of accordions in Europe.

Q: What's the definition of perfect pitch?

A: When you throw a banjo into a dumpster and hit an accordion dead center.

Electronic, or MIDI, accordions can be played as standard acoustic accordions or as controllers for other devices they are connected to. The connection can be a cable or wireless transmitter. Connected to a synthesizer (or "expander"), one accordion can be set up to play bass, chords, treble, and solo lines, to sound like a 5-piece band, with the accordion as one of the voices. If you stop pumping the bellows, only the other—electronically produced—voices will come through.

Accordions are just one of several 19th century instruments whose sound is produced by metal reeds set into vibration by air. Others include hurdy-gurdies, harmoniums, harmonicas, and concertinas. Concertinas, smaller cousins of accordions, use buttons on both sides instead of piano keys on the melody side. Button keys are about the only thing concertinas have in common with each other, though. They come in hexagonal, octagonal or square shapes. There are English and Anglo (or Anglo-German) key systems. Sizes range from small sopraninos to baritone models, with number and arrangement of buttons varying accordingly (accordionly?). The English concertina is preferred for song and dance accompaniment; the Anglo the choice of Irish musicians. Their appeal has varied from the European music halls at the turn of the century to Salvation Army street musicians. Concertinas have been mainstays of ethnic groups from wandering Gypsies to Irish folk dancers. Their popularity waned in the 20th century, until the folk music resurgence of the 1960s. Today you can hear them backing up Morris dancers and soloing in Cajun and Zydeco bands.

A piano-key accordion

Pros: Accordions and concertinas are highly portable instruments capable of several voices. They can play a solo line with other musicians doing the backup or provide their own accompaniment. Both instruments currently belong in many types of folk-music ensembles and are continually finding fits in other genres.

Cons: The recent resurgence of accordions and concertinas notwithstanding, the instruments still have an image problem. They have yet to crack the jazz world, in spite of the occasional jazz artist such as Art Van Damm in the 1950s. These instruments have met with even less acceptance in serious music (but, then, serious music itself is struggling these days).

Is it for you? Image aside, accordion and concertina players always look like they are having one hell of a good time, so if you bounce to Zydeco, Cajun, Gypsy, Klezmer, Irish jigs, or Polka music and like the sound of metal reeds, they might be a good choice. They're not easy to learn, though. Naturally, you will need good coordination of both hands and reasonable arm strength.

Getting an instrument: German accordions have a different tone quality than Italian ones, so if your music store has both types, have someone demonstrate the tonal difference so that you can decide which flavor you like. Accordions are complex, particularly the electronic models, so buying cheap may not be wise. Also, the low-end models have fewer chord/bass buttons, which seriously limits their scope of music. New acoustic accordions range upward from around $2,500. MIDI models start around $4,000. When considering a used accordion, check the bellows for wear and make sure the response of the piano keyboard is consistent and even. To do this press down three or four keys at a time while squeezing the bellows. If one or key sounds weaker than the next, all is not well. Also try out all of the buttons.

For concertinas, first become familiar with the types available, then select the type to best fit the genre of music you are most interested in. The Anglo system concertina is supposed to be easier to learn than the English. As with most instruments, you will benefit from having a knowledgeable player help you evaluate any candidate instrument you are considering. Wheatstone is said to be the best bet for used instruments, along with Jones, Crabb and Lachenal. Costs vary widely from $1,000 for a mid-range Lachenal to $3,000 for a first class treble Wheatstone English.

What's a MIDI?

The world of electronic music comes with a surfeit of acronyms and arcane terms. One of these, MIDI, crops up in any discussion of synthesizers, digital keyboards, or interactive media. MIDI is not a thing, nor an instrument, but a standard. It is short for *Musical Instrument Digital Interface*, an international standard instituted during the 1980s to provide a way to hook up electronic devices and ensure that data can be communicated between them. The MIDI standard has three parts: a communications protocol, a connector interface, and a distribution (file) format.

The MIDI standard is like a language that describes a sound in binary form. To sound a note in MIDI language you send a "note on" message, then assign a "velocity," which determines how loud it plays. Other MIDI messages include selecting which instrument to play, mixing sounds, and controlling other aspects of electronic musical instruments. MIDI is the primary source of music in popular PC games and CD-ROM entertainment titles. Thousands of MIDI files are available on the Internet for recreational use. We stumbled on an index of works by historical composers on a recent surf of the Internet, and were able to call up any of several hundred selections to play. But because the works were stored in MIDI format, they sound electronic, rather than orchestral (see "Cons" in the main article under "synthesizers").

When buffs use the term MIDI with no qualifier, they mean it to be an adjective that describes a controlling device with MIDI compatibility, such as a MIDI keyboard, MIDI accordion, or MIDI guitar. The term MIDI, used more casually, usually refers to an electronic keyboard such as a digital piano or synthesizer that has the capability to communicate with other electronic instruments or a computer.

Third Movement:

LEARNING MUSIC AS AN ADULT

It's a shame that our earliest exposures to learning music don't set us up for playing music after we grow up. An overworked, burned out, or insensitive elementary music teacher may have stopped your musical career in its tracks by criticising your earliest experiments on the recorder or sand blocks. If you did go on to play in the high school band, you may look back with fond memories of marching in the Memorial Day Parade or playing for the half-time shows at football games. Or maybe just playing around. You may even have taken your horn with you to college, where you played it for a year or two before putting it in the case.

For good.

No matter how much you got out of playing in your youth, it somehow wasn't enough to keep you going.

This disconnect can be laid at the steps of how schools approach music education, according to Dick Weisman, author of *Music Making in America*. School music programs are not designed to educate students to enjoy making music, he says, but to train large groups of students to perform for rituals such as Christmas concerts and parades. "The value of music for its own sake is simply not a part of the grand design."

Now, with memories of school music part of the past, you appreciate music for its own sake and want to participate in the process of creating it. Getting launched successfully as an adult will also require adjusting your attitude to appreciate the differences between learning as a young person and as an adult. It will also call for certain adjustments in your lifestyle to allow you to become involved. Now a different person, you know more about how you learn, and you can take charge of the process.

In this part book we'll explore these adjustments to help you find the best way for learning music, whether you choose to study with a teacher, teach yourself, or learn in a group.

Chapter 15

Finding and Working with a Compatible Teacher

Working with a teacher, mentor, coach—whatever you call a person who knows more about your instrument than you do—isn't the only way to learn how to make music on an unfamiliar instrument, but it's the surest, quickest way for most people. Even if you have time for only a few sessions, it may be enough to get you over the first hurdle. Once over the hurdle, you can opt to continue regular lessons, take occasional lessons, or continue with other approaches.

Naturally, you will expect your teacher to know the instrument. But the teacher who will help you most will also understand the differences between teaching adults and teaching children. Unfortunately, most music teachers are used to dealing with children or teenagers. "Many teachers refuse to acknowledge the emotional baggage that adult students carry with them and their need to learn in a different way than by using traditional methods," says Pat Onufrak, a flutist and adult piano student in McLean, VA. She adds that adults tend to accept poor treatment from a music teacher that they would never tolerate from any other adult in their life—even their boss. Instead of developing a student-teacher relationship on an adult level, they revert to acting like the timid child they were when they took music lessons long ago.

But don't avoid teachers just because they happen to teach children—unless they treat you as a kid. You're not one. A successful relationship with a music teacher depends on the teacher's willingness to accommodate the many ways in which you, as an adult learner, differ from a young person starting out. Here are a few:

You can experience the personal satisfaction and emotional release that comes from communicating and expressing oneself through music sooner than you might think—even if you are a complete beginner.

John Payne Music Center

"This is a treble clef. See, it looks like a snake. Have you ever seen a snake?"

❏ You talk as a grown-up, which enables you to communicate with a teacher on an adult level. Teachers who deal mainly with children often appreciate the difference.

❏ You have other well-developed skills that will give you a leg up over a child, who is learning everything else at the same time he or she is learning music. For example, finger coordination you have developed from typing on a keyboard should make it easier to learn any instrument with keys.

❏ Over the course of your adult life, you have heard a lot of music. The cumulative experience gives you an intuition of how music should sound. Children, lacking this built-in sense, won't as likely recognize a wrong note when they play it and will just keep on going.

❏ Your adult mind understands complexities and abstractions more readily than a child's, which makes it easier for the teacher to communicate ideas and helps you grasp them.

❏ On the flip side, you probably need more immediate gratification than a child. If you don't get it right after a few tries, you may get frustrated.

❏ Teachers are used to telling kids what they want and need. You are positioned to determine the content and direction of your lessons.

❏ Work and other obligations may demand more flexibility in scheduling your lessons and practicing than is true for a child.

Note that some of these are assets, others liabilities. The main thing is to be aware of how your age, life experience, work demands, and goals fit in with your musical aspirations, so you can chart a course for success.

Where to Look, What to Seek, What to Shun

Finding the right fit between you and a prospective teacher is critical to your chances for success. Peter Mose, a Toronto piano teacher who specializes in teaching adults, puts it thus: "I tell people that in essence, what they are choosing, or purchasing, with a teacher is a relationship, and the fit must be right for both parties, but especially for the student. A teacher must honor a student's goals, whether those goals are pointed toward *Home on the Range*, Billy Joel, George Gershwin, *Für Elise*, or the blues." Finding this special teacher, though, won't necessarily be easy. You'll probably turn up more leads in an urban area than in the boonies. The Boston yellow pages contain a full page of listings under "Music Instruction-Instrumental." A quick check of our own yellow pages turns up only four listings under the same category. Even so, the yellow pages probably aren't your best place to start looking. A better bet is your personal network. Friends and relatives who have taken lessons can not only suggest leads but will have first-hand information about the teachers. If you strike out here, you might check with the band or orchestra teacher of the local middle or high school. You should at the very least end up with some area teachers who teach kids. A telephone call will tell you if they also teach adults.

Tell your teacher your goals.

Your first conversation is the best opportunity to scope out your candidate teacher's approach. It's easier to steer clear of a dubious prospect than to back out once you have begun lessons. Have some specific questions to discuss at your first interview. You should come away from the conversation with much more than answers to your specific questions. The way the teacher answers your concerns tells you much about the more subtle ingredients needed for a good fit between your personalities. Here are some things you might want to include in the first conversation.

Begin by telling the teacher why you want lessons. What are your goals are and what do you want to achieve? Lucie has studied with three different teachers in the ten years she has played trombone. She wanted only the basics from her first teacher, so her questions in the interview were also basic: Do you teach adults? Are you free on Thursday afternoons? How much do you charge?

She sought out her second teacher later on when

she wanted to learn to improvise. The young man she found through a local music store played trumpet rather than trombone, but played in a jazz band and assured Lucie he could get her started on improvising. He couldn't, though. It was not his fault, since Lucie still had a shaky grasp on the basics (she had stopped working on scales and lip slurs when she quit her first series of lessons). This teacher helped her relax as she played and began to accept that even if technical perfection was beyond her, it was still worth striving for.

Lucie's present teacher, Walt Sayre, does play trombone—very well and in a wide variety of musical genres. By the time she linked up with him she had clear ideas of what she could accomplish on her own and specific areas where she felt a teacher could help her. She told him that her short-term goals were better intonation technique. She still wanted to eventually learn to improvise, so that she could play Dixieland or Klezmer music, but she now saw this as a long-term goal. She discussed these aims with Walt at the first lesson. He listened, told her that as an adult she was the boss, and that his role was as much coach as teacher. The fit has worked well so far.

If it sounds as if Lucie did a lot of bouncing around before finding a teacher that suited her own special circumstances, her quest isn't unique. Karen Jackson, the beginning fiddler from Chapter 4, thought she spotted a good deal when she saw an offer for a free, one-hour lesson for the first ten people to sign up. What it didn't say, was that the free lesson would be given to all ten takers at the same time. In any case, it didn't get her very far or lead to an arrangement for further lessons. She considered another teacher, but the distance she would have to go ruled this out. Still, she ended up with the name of a teacher closer to her home in Montpelier, Vt. It turned out that Sarah Blair was just what Karen wanted—someone who could teach her the art of Celtic fiddling. Sarah was not only a classically trained violinist, but one of the best Irish fiddlers in Vermont.

A final point. Look for a teacher who is a cheerleader. We know, you may cringe at the word, with its memories of high school pompom squads and relentless jingoism. Piano teacher Peter Mose used to. But not anymore. "Cheerleading may be easily half of my role as an independent teacher of adult piano students," he says. "Most of them, when it comes to music, are scared of their own shadows." Mose maintains that adults who have achieved a basic sense of competence in their careers and family life have forgotten what it was like to learn something new from ground zero. Because they feel so vulnerable undertaking musical study at this point in their lives, it is all the more important to have a mentor who understands their status and knows how to cheer them on.

Scheduling Lessons

If you are partly or fully retired, you will probably be able to work lessons into your schedule with little difficulty. For other adults, finding a time for lessons ranks among the chief roadblocks to starting into music. Teachers like to schedule their students at regular, predictable intervals, which works better for young beginners who have free time after school and on weekends than adults whose schedules are much more complicated and much less flexible. Some of the adults we interviewed were able to set up regular lesson times, but even then had to cancel out when contingencies came up. Others couldn't commit to traditional scheduling, so they found creative alternatives.

Taking cancellations. Karen Jackson had the time available for regular weekly fiddle lessons when she sought to sign up with Sara Blair. Unfortunately, Sarah's schedule was full at the time, leaving no slots for additional students. Instead, she offered Karen any vacancies that came up when regular students suddenly canceled out. This suited Karen, who ended up with about one lesson a month for four months, when a vacancy became available. Since that time she has been taking regular lessons on the fiddle in hourly sessions, one every two weeks. Teachers inevitably end up with cancellations they would rather see filled, but to put yourself in position to go in for a sudden lesson will require an extreme amount of flexibility on your part, as well as a workable arrangement with your teacher as to the content of the lessons. Still, it is a way around committing to regular lessons at a set time.

Stretch out the intervals. If weekly lessons are impossible because of your schedule or your lack of time

If your schedule prevents regular lessons, how about spacing them out?

---

to prepare, why not arrange for bi-weekly or even monthly lessons? Sure, you won't progress as fast, but you're not in a race. Not all teachers like bi-weekly lessons, though. Peter Mose refuses to take students on this basis for two reasons. First, it complicates his own lesson scheduling, now having to find a "twin" who can take the alternate slots. Second, if a student misses one lesson, he/she Mose won't see this student for a whole month—too long an interval for a beginner.

The important thing is to maintain a pace that keeps you interested and motivated, and one in which you won't lose the gains you have made. If the teacher is reluctant to reserve a slot for you on this basis and there are more than one in your family studying with the same teacher, you might arrange to switch slots.

Schedule irregularly. Your work schedule may fluctuate, leaving you more free time at some times than others. If you can predict these intervals with any certainty, you may be able to come up with a schedule that fits. Say you work for a monthly magazine that has a pressure time just before a deadline that occurs the last week of each month. You expect the next two weeks to be lighter. Why not tailor a schedule that allows you two weekly lessons followed by two weeks off?

Schedule *ad hoc*. If none of the above suggestions work for you , don't give up. You may be able to pop in for lessons at unspecified times by nothing more than a phone call to your teacher to arrange a mutually convenient time.

Getting the Most Out of Your Lessons

If arranging a time for lessons is hard, you want to make sure you get your time and money's worth. For that you'll need a positive attitude. What if your attitude has been tainted by negative early experiences with music lessons? Jerry remembers trudging off to Mrs. Tullis's for piano lessons every Thursday after school with the same enthusiasm he had for a trip to the dentist. But his dad assured him that the lessons were, like so many other things, "for his own good." The logic escaped him. He watched his dad play the piano from both the written sheet and by ear, all self taught. And what about musicians such as Louis Armstrong, who got famous without any formal training?

But it wasn't just the lessons. It was the torture of having to slave away practicing some stupid piece such as "Lilac Time" from John W. Schaum's piano method, while his friends were outside shooting each other up with home-made rubber guns and taking part in other creative activities.

These memories have made him a reluctant lesson taker as an adult. Your attitude may be similarly tainted by unpleasant memories. You'll have to tamp them back into your subconscious if you want to get a fresh start with any chance of success. But how?

Start by reviewing the ways in which your situation is different today. As a grown person you come to the lessons with your *own* motivation, which can be a combination of any of the many benefits of music making we have previously mentioned. Because you now see music making as a form of gratification—a diversion from your workday life—the lesson should become an integral part of the diversion. Of course it's always easier to look forward to a weekly lesson if you have had a good week to prepare than if you had no time to practice. Instead of being able to show off your progress to your teacher, you will arrive with a sense of dread at having to play. Discouraged, you'll wonder whether you are overcommitted, and whether you are wasting the time and money on lessons.

The very realization that it is *your* time and money can be a key to adjusting your attitude. You are now free to invest it or not, as you see fit, unlike when you took lessons as a child. Now in the driver's seat, you can chart your own course, one that a sympathetic teacher will support. You can help establish this kind of rapport by how you handle your time with the teacher.

For one thing, you don't need to spend every minute on the lesson content. Feel free to discuss aspects of your musical life, such as your goals, likes, dislikes, practice habits. Help your teacher to open up to you—as another adult—by asking similar questions of him or her. The chance to open up to another adult will probably be welcome to a teacher who deals mostly with younger persons and creates a relaxed atmosphere conducive to getting more out of the remaining "content" time. However, don't

I have taught quite a few former students who tooted their clarinets or flutes in the school band. Many had not played music in twenty years. After two or three beginning guitar lessons, they invariably came away astounded that they could sing and play a simple accompaniment to a song.

Dick Weissman
Music Making in America

Finding and Working With a Compatible Teacher   169 "con" the teacher by talking too much to conceal the fact that you are ill prepared. Just say so at the outset and find a way to use the time creatively.

Find out what you get the most out of in your practicing and steer your teacher in this direction. Your teacher may try to stick you with etudes and other method stuff intended to develop technique and ability. This works for some, quickly bores others. Ethan Winer, who started cello at 43, thinks you will progress faster by working on real pieces that you like for their own sake. He adds, "If you practice etudes for three years, all you have to show for your effort is, well, etudes. However, if you start now on a real concerto or sonata, you'll have learned to play a beautiful and meaningful piece of music for the same amount of effort."

Playing music can and should be an enjoyable, rewarding experience. Your teacher should be a person capable of helping you make it one. Finding and developing a good rapport with this person may not be easy, but it may spell the difference between your dropping out and getting launched on a path to success.

 Chapter 16

Can I Teach Myself?

Maybe you can't schedule lessons, however creatively you manipulate your time. Even if you arrange to take slots that suddenly open due to the cancellations of a teacher's regular students, you still have to be able to be available when they occur.

Or you might be wary of exposing your weaknesses to a teacher. Too much anxiety can keep you from playing as well before your teacher as you know you can when you are home alone. Fearing embarrassment from asking "dumb" questions, you won't openly communicate your concerns. Maybe you are just a quick learner who looks forward to taking on a new challenge with a minimum of outside help.

Whatever your reasons, you shouldn't give up on music just because you can't or don't want to engage a private teacher. Lessons may be the main road to music for young persons; they don't have to be for adults. There are more avenues for non-traditional music instruction than ever. Numerous workshops, institutes, and music camps offer short-term opportunities for learning in groups, as we'll see in the following chapter.

What You Can and Can't Learn on Your Own

If you can sing a song after hearing it a few times you have shown that you know how to learn to make music on your own—at least by imitation. Your ears heard a melody, sent it to some part of the brain that processed it and somehow sent the correct signals to your vocal chords to reproduce the sounds. You did it all by ear, without conscious

---

A hands-on learner defaults to the printed instructions only as a last resort.

thought. You could use this same approach to reproduce sounds you hear on instrument, but only after becoming familiar with the fingerings and other features necessary to play the instrument. These are skills you'll have to acquire from another source. Reading music is another skill that isn't innate—you have to learn it from somewhere.

You can acquire many of the skills required to make music by studying with a teacher, in a group learning setting, or working alone from instructional media. How much you can achieve on your own depends on you and what you aim to learn.

For starters, you can learn a lot of bad habits, and learn them well. Even so, Jerry likes the idea of learning on his own. A "hands-on" type of learner , he doesn't mind making mistakes along the way, as long as they aren't fatal. Ironically, though he writes how-to books, he seldom reads them to learn a new skill himself. Nor does he typically follow the step-by-step instructions for assembling a device. Instead, he finds a picture of the assembled item and tries to figure how the parts go together, defaulting to the instructions only when absolutely necessary. From the next room Lucie hears him cursing those 2-inch-thick computer manuals written by engineers who don't understand how the mind of the common person works (incidentally, would it be a great loss to mankind if they did away with the "help" button on the computer toolbar?). Jerry learns new software by having our son, Max, sit next to him, mute, except when asked a question. When Max gets frustrated at Jerry's repeated fumbling and grabs the mouse to show him the correct way, Jerry grabs it back, telling Max that he can only learn if he, not Max, does it.

He favors a similar method for learning music, though conceding that it's hard to find a sympathetic coach who will simply sit by your side until you ask something. So he uses a mixed approach, getting basic information from books or other outside sources, and asking for help from a live person when the written word or image won't suffice. For example, ten years ago, when he started bassoon, he got a few books out of the library on how to play the bassoon. Along with basic information about the instrument and fingering, they showed pictures of the bassoon embouchure, with written advice on how to form your lips and hold the reed. But he soon realized that this is one area where a book can't equal a real live person, and sought help from a bassoonist in the local college band. Watching her mouth as she played was sufficient to get him started. He has since picked up additional tips by playing with other bassoonists and attending the annual workshops. He has even resorted to taking a few lessons.

Which brings up another point about teaching yourself: Even with the best self-instruction program, your chances of success likely increase with the amount of outside help you get. The help doesn't have to come from a teacher. It can come from anyone who knows more than you do about the topic in question. But do make sure the person is qualified to give the *correct* information. If you ask your 14-year-old son who plays trumpet in the middle school band about how to form your embouchure, he'll probably show you how *he* does it, which may get you off on the wrong foot (or lip).

What's Available?

Self-instruction options abound. The teach-yourself-guitar books that have stood upright in racks at your local music store forever are still there, except now they probably sport a cassette tape or compact disk tucked in little pockets on the covers. CD-ROM disks, videos, and interactive computer software, round out the instructional materials for self teaching currently available. But finding the product that fits your needs and learning style may not be easy.

Books

Books of every sort come out by the thousands each year despite increasing competition from other media. Relatively cheap, self contained, and completely portable, books convey some kinds of information very well. They are good sources for learning *about* music and instruments and are even good sources for learning the basics of playing some instruments. They do better for instruments that have fixed pitch intervals, such as pianos and guitars, than for instruments without fixed pitch intervals (bowed strings, fretless electric basses). This may explain why there are so many teach-yourself books for piano and so few for wind and bowed string instruments. From a teach-yourself piano book, for example, you can learn how to read music and which written notes correspond to which keys on the keyboard. All that remains is to press down on the key to get a sound. And, sure, there are some subtleties involved for how you hold your fingers and wrists to attack the keys, but the notes always sound like a piano.

This isn't the case with a bowed string or wind instrument. A book could show you the approximate finger position for a particular note, but determining if it is flat, sharp, or on the mark is beyond the book's capability. The clarinet, a wind instrument, has a clear, fluid, bell-like sound that pleases the ear, when played well. Played by a beginner, it quacks like a duck. A book can tell you in words and pictures how to hold the clarinet mouthpiece in your mouth and what muscles to contract, but you can read until you are blue in the face and still not find out how it should sound or exactly what to do to get this sound. This is best demonstrated by a clarinetist, or, at least an instructional device capable of reproducing the sound faithfully.

So if your instrument is piano, guitar or banjo, you have a wide choice of teach-yourself books. The so-called "method" books you'll see for other instruments, often published in a series such as 1, 2, 3, ... or "beginner," intermediate," "advanced," are intended to be used with a teacher, not alone.

To get you started in the right direction if you know nothing about the instrument, a good how-to-play book will start at the very beginning and add information in digestible gulps that won't overwhelm you. At the same time, the information should be pithy enough to keep you interested. An example of this is *Mel Bay's Banjo Method.*

Mel Bay begins with a diagram of the banjo, with all the parts named, then moves on to the technique of playing the instrument. He doesn't try to convey every skill needed to play the banjo by the book alone. It is supplemented by a cassette disk, as are all of the better method books.

Books alone are seldom as effective as a real live teacher.

Music, in the end, is not eighth notes clinging to lines on a clef. It is sound heard with our ears and appreciated in the heart. No book, however well written, can convey this experience. Cassette tapes and compact disks can, which is why they increasingly accompany how-to books.

Instructional Videos

Whereas tapes and CDs give you actual sound examples and are tremendous assets for communicating musical ideas, videos add animated images to the sound for even greater usefulness. What they don't do, of course, is allow for any kind of interaction on your part. You play the video in your VCR, listen and watch, then try to apply the stuff to your own instrument. You can't ask the teacher any questions. Still, you can get much from videos. The blurb for a video for learning the fundamentals of the string bass, for example, claims to teach you the proper hand techniques for playing the instrument, how to stand, finger and hand exercises, and bow techniques. If it actually achieves only a few of these, it is probably worth the $20 or so it costs, and you can learn other aspects from other sources. But you may feel cheated if you invest more than this in a video that falls short of extravagant claims. We ran across one offer on the Internet that purports to teach a beginner to play piano by ear in 90 days with a package that includes a 2-hour video, 6 audio cassettes, and a 72-page workbook, all for the price of $199.95. Seems dubious.

A video will probably do a better job at showing you what can be done on an instrument than how to do it, and then only for a few instruments. We tracked down numerous videos for guitar—in rock, jazz, country styles. Piano, banjo, bass, and drums probably figure next in frequency. If you aspire to a bowed string, woodwind, or brass instrument, you may well come up empty, though we did find one jazz trumpet video.

In the end, you shouldn't expect much more than an introduction and inspiration from a video. Unless you start with knowledge of music and an ability to play another instrument, you will probably get much further with hands-on help from a live person than a product.

Interactive Computer Instruction

The potential for computers in music education is far greater than has been exploited so far. But this is rapidly changing. There are products available for anyone interested in music. The rank beginner can learn how to read music notation and basic musical theory with the help of a computer. Computer interactive software is increasingly available to teach you how to play an instrument. Unfortunately, it favors certain instruments over others (sorry wannabe bassoonists, better find a teacher).

To take advantage of this medium your computer will need a sound card and speakers, for starters. Other external devices such as a MIDI-compatible keyboard, a microphone, or a foot pedal, may be required, depending on the software.

Pianos are one of the instruments particularly suited to interactive computer learning, so it's not surprising that most of the self-teaching software available is for pianos. One such product, *Music Lab Melody* (Musicware, Inc.) is designed to teach you to read and write music, recognize the sounds of written notes and notate sounds that are heard. The goal is to be able to know how a written note will sound and be able to tap out the rhythm without counting. *Guido,* another program by the same company, seeks to teach intervals, pitch recognition, chords, and rhythm, with various interactive strategies. For example, it teaches intervals by playing two notes that define an interval. You click on the box on-screen to indicate what you think the interval is. The computer keeps score of your hits and misses. You can, as you progress, move on to more difficult levels and more complicated intervals.

Piano, a three-level course by Musicware, Inc., requires a computer with Pentium processor and a MIDI sound card, Windows95, a CD-ROM, and a MIDI piano keyboard. Course One begins with the fundamentals—the keyboard layout, fingering, basic rhythm patterns, time signatures, lengths of notes. Information is added step-by-step through eight units, with the student playing along and getting feedback.

What's it like to actually try to learn piano this way? If you are at home with computer technology and have been able to learn other things on your own, you might do well. For the rest of us, it can be frustrating, as it was for Noah Adams, host of National Public Radio's *All Things Considered,* when he tried to learn piano techniques from a course called *The Miracle Piano Teaching System.*

In his book, *Piano Lessons: Music, Love, & True Adventures,* Adams chronicles this saga of frustration from opening the boxes containing the keyboard, disks, and accessories, to finally giving up and putting everything back in the boxes and moving on to other methods of learning. After setting the system up, itself not without frustrations, he was annoyed to find that every time he turned on

I feel that what [the adult students] are here for is to get their hands on a real acoustic piano and feel the vibrations of the strings, through the keys. There is pleasure in that that you don't get from a computer.

Miriam Goder

the Miracle he had to listen to "Simple Gifts," played by piano, organ, then flutes and blaring trumpets. Clicking on "Begin Lessons," he was off and running, beginning with Beethoven's *Ode to Joy*. Tips for holding your fingers, posture, came up on the screen, followed by a picture of the keyboard and the first actual instruction. At one point a "Shooting Gallery" came on, with ducks flying slowly across a treble clef. If a duck flew on the C line, he was supposed to play a C as it went past. If he did, he was rewarded with a quack.

The concept of time was introduced with a metronome. When Adams played along in time with *Ode to Joy* he got a stroke "Nice going, Noah. There's much more to learn, but you can play your first song. You're a piano player!" So ended Lesson 1.

The program's quirks became increasingly annoying. The keyboard's keys were slick and too small. The sound didn't please. Still, Adams had fun switching voices from piano to harpsichord and organ. After many tedious lessons with the likes of *Mary Had a Little Lamb* he was able to play a song he liked, *Heart and Soul*, but not to the computer's satisfaction: "You mis-played the third note (C) in the second measure of the treble clef..."

He felt he was making progress a few months later, having learned about minor keys and accidentals and now was able to play *Dark Eyes*. But he ran into rough waters with a Beatles song, *Here, There, and Everywhere*. Unable to play it with the metronome, he defaulted to the "notes only" mode, which allowed him to play the piece at any speed, metronome be damned.

Adams slogged on, only to be stymied in Lesson 16 by Pachelbel's *Canon*, which was to be played with the built-in orchestral accompaniment. The sound of the orchestra froze him up and he sat mute. When the piece came to an end, the computer showed its disdain of his non-performance: "It was your turn to play the piece! You didn't play anything. Your overall performance was 0%. And your rhythm performance was 0%." Not too long after, he packed all the parts back into the boxes.

We, too, have had our frustrations with interactive computer music software. Jerry didn't know what to expect when he popped the program disk from the *SmartMusic Studio* (Coda Technology, Inc.) into his computer. The disk plays the accompaniment to various pieces of music while the user plays the melody line on the instrument. The user can adjust the pitch, volume, and tempo. Jerry noticed that one of the demo pieces was the Mozart *Clarinet Concerto,* a piece he had been working on. He selected the piece and played along. It worked well enough to attract him to the next level of involvement: ordering the special microphone and foot pedal. The microphone allows the computer to "hear" what you are playing and actually follow along as you speed or slow, much as you might expect from a good live accompanist. The pedal gives you a way to start and stop the program, such as restarting it after a cadenza.

Along with his order for the mic and pedal, Jerry ordered the full concerto, selecting from the list of over 4,000 musical entries, classical to jazz offered. If you opt for a classical piece, you play from a written score. With jazz you can improvise. The "play-along" concept isn't new—there have been cassette tapes and records out there

Learning music through interactive computer methods can be very frustrating.

for years. But where these chugged along at their own pace, allowing you to swim or—if you fell behind—sink, the idea behind *SmartMusic* is for it to actually follow the user. But it hasn't yet. Nor has Jerry succeeded in getting the pedal to work—this despite several queries to the company. He hasn't yet given up, because the program promises so much. Stay tuned.

Playing along to electronic accompaniment will never, of course, match the experience of playing with live people. And being tethered to your computer limits your mobility. But the electronic accompanist never finks out because of sickness, never hits wrong notes, and plays soft when you tell it to.

What Is Your Musical Learning Style?

You've made it through school, learned what you need to perform your job, and gained an incredible variety of knowledge and skills along the way. Though it's an amazing amount when you stop to think about it, you take most of it for granted. But you can appreciate the sheer volume of your intuitive knowledge by watching a five-year-old struggle with shoelaces (how impressed you are depends of course on whether you can manage your own shoelaces.)

Now that you're thinking of taking up a pursuit which will challenge you every bit as much as the bow knot does the kindergartener, you are probably wondering if it will be worth it in the long run. Before settling on a method of learning it might be useful to consider your learning style. It may not be the one your teachers used on you in school.

Educational psychologists divide learners into types, usually four, based on the work of Myers-Briggs and Kolb. The four types are usually numbered (as in McCarthy's 4-MAT system)—all much too arcane for our purposes. So we contrived our own completely non-scientific learning style test based on the work of these notable pioneers. Because it determines your learning style as it relates to music, it seemed natural to name the categories by musical keys. Circle your choices below to find out which "key" you are you in, then find your learning style in the following section.

	C	G	F-Sharp	E-Flat
Favorite drink	Wine made by a friend	Martini made by a friend	Beer	Anything
Keys on a key chain	All current keys plus key to last apartment	In order by size. Rough edges face same direction	In order chronologically or by use in job	Lost on two different chains
Computer hooked up by	A relative	You, following the steps in the manual	You, by trying to fit the results to the diagram	"Let's see what happens if we hook this jack in here"
You get into a cold lake by	Holding hands with someone and yelling "One, two, three!"	Wading in slowly by precise increments	Racing in and leaping with a big splash	Swinging from a rope
Overcame boredom in school by	Daydreaming	Doing other homework	Inventing ways to use the ruler to flip the eraser at the adjacent person	Asking smartass questions to heckle the teacher

If you are in the key of C, you can learn from group lessons, if you like and trust most of the people in the group. You are willing to wait for slower people to catch up with you, and aren't threatened by others in the group who learn faster than you. You can also learn from individual lessons, but make sure your teacher is compatible with your learning style. You will be much less successful working alone. Even getting started will challenge you so much that you will think of creative new excuses every day to put it off. Like other important parts of your life, you need human contact to make music.

A person whose learning style is in the key of G is a loner who can learn from a well-designed teach-yourself book or program. If you're in this group, you prefer self-instruction to a disorganized teacher. In group lessons you'll be annoyed by fellow students who come to class unprepared or who wanted to jump ahead. If you opt for a teacher, make sure he or she can give logical explanations, keep things in order, and follow the sequence in the book. Music for you is the sublime organization of chaos.

An F-sharp person is just the opposite—a "hands-on" person who doesn't follow the instructions in the manual. If you are one of these folks stuck with a music method book, you'll probably ignore the sequence of the lessons, preferring to check the book on a need-to-know basis while you experiment on your own to find the fingerings that work best for you. You'll probably take your instrument apart to see how it works. You can learn in group lessons, but you'll grump about every minute that isn't spent on music. You would do well with individual lessons at irregular intervals, that is, whenever you have questions you can't answer on your own. You make music the way some people climb mountains; you like the challenge.

Finally, if you're an E-flat learner, the best system is probably individual lessons or self-study combined with playing in a group. Any one system taken too long will leave you bored. You need variety and challenge and you like to take risks, so you may try for a recital or concert before you're really ready for it. You're likely to come in to a lesson not having practiced the assignment but having tried something completely different. Your teacher has to be comfortable with this, because you aren't likely to change at this point in your life. Music for you is a means of self-discovery.

Chapter 17

Learning in a Group

Jerry thought 35 bassoons playing four-part harmony sounded downright heavenly, but to Lucie it sounded like being caught in the low strings of a grand piano. The bassoon band is the culminating activity at Bassoon Day, an annual workshop at the University of New Hampshire. Though oboes are now diluting the event—now known as "Double-Reed Day"—it's okay, says Jerry. Bassoonists are a tolerant sort, and oboes need all the help they can get.

Janet Polk, a bassoon teacher and expert player, organized the event in 1992 to bring together bassoon aficionados and nurture the art of playing this odd instrument. Jerry has attended three so far and is constantly amazed to see people from far away show up, despite vigorous January weather. The event went on last year, in the midst of an ice storm severe enough to shut down the campus (luckily bassoons don't need to be plugged in). The 40 or so participants range from teenagers starting out on the instrument to adult amateurs. Morning sessions typically consist of an expert's presentation of some pithy, if esoteric, topic of interest to bassoonophiles. Contrabassoons, the granddaddies of the bassoon family, were the morning session fare of the first Bassoon Day Jerry attended. Bassoon guru Mark Popkin flew in from North Carolina to demonstrate the art of reed making at the following year's event. This year's event featured Alan Fox, president of Fox Products Corporation, the biggest bassoon maker in the world. Fox showed a fascinating video that traced the process of bassoon making, from maple blocks curing in stacks to precision instruments.

During the two-hour break at noon, participants can have lunch, play in small groups, or visit vendor's booths, then return for an afternoon recital featuring bassoons alone, with each other, and with other instruments. The bassoon band caps the day, giving everyone a chance to play.

Bassoon Day is a wonderful group-learning experience, yet no one actually learns how to play a bassoon at this event. That's not its purpose. If you play a somewhat esoteric instrument such as the bassoon, simply coming together with several others of your flock is, in itself, a spark that fires you up and makes you want to keep going on your instrument. There are many other settings of more than a day's length, that offer opportunities to learn or improve your musical skills in the company of others. Some of these are abroad, combining a vacation with playing your instrument.

Imagine an eight-day cruise of the Greek Islands, starting in Venice and ending in Istanbul with stops at Katakolon, Sevastopol, Odessa, Constanta. Aboard ship, you'd practice chamber music, coaxed by a professional musician, with opportunities to perform with other musicians. At other times, you would relax, dance in the aisles and on the isles. Or, how about spending a week honing your musical skills while enjoying the local cuisine and wines, sightseeing, and beachcombing at Mallorca or Provence? These are but two of many ads for music workshop/vacations we ran across in a recent edition of the newsletter, *Music for the Love of It*. All you need is the dough (the European events cost anywhere from $500 to $2,500) and enough ability and confidence to qualify you as an "experienced amateur."

But what if you are not an experienced amateur or don't have the time or money to trot off to Europe? Take heart. Group-learning sites abound. Let's visit a few.

Getting Into Jazz at the John Payne Music Center

"Beginners Wanted—guitar, piano, voice, bass, drums, flute, sax, clarinet lessons in jazz, rock, classical pop, folk, or whatever you'd like," begins one of the promotional flyers for the John Payne Music Center (JPMC). Now in its 20th year, the JPMC gets adults going in music in a non-traditional, supportive, relaxed, environment—a converted

A music vacation cruise is one way to combine a vacation with a group-learning experience.

warehouse in Brookline Village, just outside Boston. No starched, white formality here. On the day we visited the center we were met by John Payne himself, in jeans and denim shirt. He took us to one of the small studios, furnished with a set of drums and a Fender-Rhodes electric piano whose keys had obviously played many a jazz riff.

John described himself as a "seat-of-the-pants" guy who grew up around a banjo-playing dad. John played clarinet and guitar in his youth, but had no formal training outside of a few lessons and playing in the school band. At 20, he took up the sax, and picked up flute a year later. These are his mainstays today and what he teaches at the center, along with his original instrument, the clarinet. Other teachers come on board as independent contractors, as required by the constantly changing number of students and instrumental mix. The students today are definitely older, on average, than in the beginning, says John. "We don't discriminate on the basis of age. We have, sometimes, ten-year-olds playing in the same groups as 60-year-olds."

Rich Cole, a Boston-area attorney who has argued before the U.S. Supreme Court, is one of JPMC's adult beginners and success stories. Before beginning on sax at the JPMC in 1980, Cole's musical background consisted solely of a bit of kazoo playing. He joined one of the jazz ensembles and saxophone choirs early on, then switched to the JPMC rock ensemble, where he says, "You're able to live out your fantasies at low cost—to be able to blow a horn and belt out a tune vocally on stage is an extraordinary experience. And it's an incredible stress reducer. I can go in the JPMC with very low energy and annoyed at the world and by the end of the ensemble I'm all pumped up."

The JPMC rock ensemble is only one of 20 different ensembles that form the basic approach of the center: learning by playing in groups. While many students at the center have private instruction, they are encouraged to join an ensemble as soon as possible. Most of the ensembles were jazz groups when we visited the center, typically a piano-bass-drums rhythm section, 3 to 4 horns, and occasionally vocalists. Miriam Hyman, the office administrator, said the mix was evolving to include Klezmer, Latin, world music and other genres. One of the larger groups is the sax choir, which plays a wide variety of 20th century music, from jazz to rock to John Lennon. John Payne says it is mind boggling to see what twenty people, many in their 40s and 50s can do. "On a bad night they are very enthusiastic and fun to watch; on a good night they sound like pros."

Jamming at the Vermont Jazz Center

Attila Zoller, a Hungarian guitarist who had played with Stan Getz, Lee Konitz, and Benny Goodman, came to Newfane, Vermont with the unlikely dream of making the Green Mountains a mecca for jazz. He fulfilled the dream by starting a summer music program in 1975. The Vermont Jazz Center (VJC) started out as a summer event in a local school, with outside artists brought in to attract participants. The program succeeded over the next twenty years, when Zoller became increasingly ill. Before he died in 1997, he passed the baton to another immigrant, Eugene Uman, a jazz pianist from Colombia who, having graduated from the jazz program at Queens College in New York, established his teaching credentials at Boston's Berkeley

School of Music and the New England Conservatory.

Uman set about to make the organization financially solid and find a permanent home to enable it to augment the summer workshop with year-round instruction in jazz. Now installed in a former factory building five miles outside Brattleboro, the VJC had 20 students during its last semester, about a third of which were high-school age, the rest older. Students come for hour-long lessons, some once a week; others once every two weeks. All students come with some training, even if it's only the most basic music theory they might have picked up from a piano teacher, according to Uman.

Jazz improvisation is the core of the curriculum at the VJC. As with the John Payne Music Center, the goal is to be able to play in a group. Two 5-piece adult jazz ensembles currently meet, one Monday night, one Tuesday. A student group meets on Friday. Things really cook with the Wednesday Night jam session.

The high point of the year comes in August with the annual summer workshop. John Abercrombie, Shiela Jordan, Bobby Sanabria and Jimmy Heath are some of the jazz musicians of national renown that have enhanced past workshops. Daytime activities include seminars in theory and improvisation, style, composition, individual and master classes. In the evenings, the Vermont hills reverberate with the sounds of the jam sessions and student concerts.

Never forget that music is much too important to be left entirely in the hands of professionals.

Robert Fulghum
Maybe (Maybe Not)

Classical Music in the Green Mountains

Jazz isn't the goal of every amateur musician, and it may not be yours. For amateur musicians who live in Southern Vermont and New Hampshire along the Connecticut River there's an outfit 60 miles up U.S. 91 from the Vermont Jazz Center that focuses on classical and chamber music. Unlike the Vermont Jazz Center, The Upper Valley Music Center (UVMC) has no permanent home. Instead, its activities take place in the homes of its members and a few area school classrooms. Even without real estate of its own, the organization performs valuable services, bringing novice and expert musicians together, as well as helping members find the right teacher, playing partner, and ensemble. Meanwhile, it has become a clearinghouse for information through its directory and newsletter. The founders, Bob Mark and Louis Cornell are trying to fill a need no one knew existed. Cornell, an amateur violist, sheep farmer, and retired professor of English, describes the UVMC as more like a music school than anything else, but without a paid faculty. Mark, a former music teacher, considers the lack of a permanent home a minor inconvenience. "There are more important things to raise money for, like feeding the hungry and the homeless," he says.

UVMC offers programs for both children and adults. The adult programs run two months on, one month off. One of the programs is an orchestra that meets Wednesday nights at a local school. Several chamber groups get together for rehearsals in private homes. When we spoke with Bob Mark, he said there were currently eight such groups, mostly quartets and trios of stringed instruments with occasional clarinets, oboes, and bassoons. Some players are beginners. Most have some experience, with abilities clustering in the neighborhood of 2 to 3 on a scale of 1 to 5, according to Mark. The emphasis is always on playing for its own sake, rather than preparing for a performance, he says. "When you perform you have to learn everything, then spend all of the rest of the time learning how to perform, and learning how to perform when you are an amateur is a very difficult thing, because it takes you into a realm that demands that you have proficiency far beyond the level of amateur playing."

Washington, DC—a Place to Battle Butterflies...

Learning how to perform before others is exactly the point of the Adult Music Student Forum (AMSF), an organization that gives its members the chance to overcome the fear of playing in front of others by providing performance settings in phased levels of difficulty.

Four recital series give members, from beginners on, opportunities to share their enthusiasm and experience, trade ideas, and grow their confidence while nurturing their art. The first two series are for members with limited experience. The A series is for beginners; the B series for the next level. Given in private homes, these recitals are informal. To keep the intimidation level low, the audience is limited to other participants. For members with intermediate or advanced ability, there are "Cadenza Recitals," also in private homes, but allowing outsiders to join the audience, as space permits. All members perform in formal recitals open to the public on Sunday afternoons.

AMSF was founded ten years ago by Matt Harre to serve adult piano students in the Washington, DC area. Pianists are still in the majority, but other instrumentalists continue to join the organization. One of these is returning cellist Chris Herman. Trained as an attorney, Chris came to Washington in 1979 to work for the Environmental Protection Agency. The cello playing that he got so much out of in his youth gave way to more active recreation and the instrument gathered dust for the better part of the next 20 years. But when work and family circumstances eventually put the squeeze on him, Chris realized that "suddenly there wasn't any more time for bike rides." He saw resurrecting his cello as something that would provide substitute—if not highly active—recreation in the snatches of time he had available. He knew that he would have to address both long-standing technical problems and the anxiety of performing in public. Chris saw a newspaper item about AMSF, decided it was just what he needed, and joined up.

It worked. After two years with the organization, Chris says that AMFS's graduated approach to playing in public in "bite-size digestible chunks" has bolstered his confidence. Now he actually looks forward to playing in public.

An ample slate of special events supplements AMSF's student recitals. Among those listed recently over the AMSF Internet website were lectures on avoiding and treating practice injuries, memorization, and performing for pleasure. Workshops listed included a focus on Chopin, a woodwind ensemble, and the Alexander Technique. Recitals and events are listed in the organization's newsletter, *Keynotes.*

The Adult Music Student Form is important to me because it gives me the opportunity to share the musical experience (and its trials and tribulations) with others.

Pat Onufrak

...or Take Fiddling Classes

Heidi Scanlon, the emerging country fiddler from chapter 8, is another AMFS member who joined to gain experience playing in public. She concurs with Chris Herman that the phased recital approach is a great way to learn how to perform. "If you play enough for other people," she says, "it's no longer a big deal. AMFS served Heidi and other amateurs well as a facilitator for various levels of performing. It wasn't set up, however, to teach country fiddling. For that, Heidi had to search elsewhere. The nation's capital is known for many things to many people. Who would have imagined it to be a nexus of fiddling? It is, says Heidi. The suburb of Takoma Park, just north of the city is a hotbed of "Old Time" fiddling, a style rooted in the folk traditions of the Appalachian foothills not too far away.

A query through her Compuserve music forum turned up several candidate fiddling teachers, one of which was Andrea Hoag. Well known in the Washington area for her violin prowess, Hoag is also a master of Scandinavian fiddling. She teaches fiddling classes of four to ten adults in five-week cycles. Most of the newcomers are adults 35 to 55 years old, says Heidi Scanlon. Abilities vary. About one in five once played classical violin, but most have never even touched the violin. Some can't even read music, she adds, but it doesn't matter. Fiddling is an art form traditionally played by ear and that's the way Andrea Hoag teaches it.

She starts with the most fundamental basic: attitude. Because mastering the fiddle is difficult, you have to be a lot more generous with yourself than you might be accustomed to. As Heidi puts it, "You can't be a perfectionist and be a beginning violin player, because you just can't do it right the first time." Even so warned, many drop out soon after beginning. Some just don't have the time. Others simply get frustrated by how long it takes to get anywhere on the instrument and at "seeing their cats run out of the room" every time they play. Ms. Hoag keeps the numbers of each class stable by moving novice students into more advanced groups, as needed. The intermixing helps the beginners, but not necessarily the experienced ones, says Heidi, who herself, seeks to improve her skills by playing with better fiddlers.

Heidi finds them at monthly "slow jams," get-togethers of fiddlers and friends that give inexpert players the opportunity to hear others play and join in as they are able. While not disparaging her mostly solo piano efforts, she is thrilled by the chance to match her playing to that of other people instead of making music by herself.

Picking Banjo in Chicago

If folk music is your aim and you live in the Chicago area, you have a choice of group learning sites. Two of these are the Old Town School of Folk Music, a large school, and the Jones Family Music School, a small one.

Frank Hamilton founded The Old Town School in the folk music boom of the late 1950s, on the premise that everyone can learn, play, and enjoy music in a supportive environment, regardless of skill or ambition. The school flourished in the 1960s, but hit a wall in the 1970s, when music went electric. The renaissance of acoustic and world music in the 1980s gave all folk music new life. Today, the school offers individual and group classes to around 4,000 students in banjo, guitar, fiddle, mandolin, ukulele, flute, whistle, dijeridoo, harmonica, dance, and percussion. The 1950s concept of "folk" has been broadened to include gospel, Celtic, folk-punk, Native American, and Chinese music. The school has meanwhile expanded into a second location, a 33,000-square-foot former Chicago library building, remodeled to include a performance hall, retail shop, cafe, and classrooms.

Be generous with yourself when taking up a difficult instrument.

Twenty miles to the west of Chicago lies the suburb of Lombard, where Tom Jones, wife Anne, and daughter Cathy teach some 40, mostly adult students, how to play folk music, from their picturesque Tudor/Arts & Crafts-style house. The Jones Family Music School offers private lessons or group classes in the evenings.

Novices stand to gain more in a group than experienced players.

Saturday mornings finds all corners of the house occupied. The living room is the frequent site of jam sessions, sing-a-rounds, workshops, and house concerts. Adults who want to learn lap dulcimer or banjo, but who can't get to the house, can still learn from the Joneses by attending the evening classes they teach at DuPage Junior College or classes offered as part of the local public school district's adult education series.

Learning Latin by the Bay

Group-learning opportunities span interest areas of incredible diversity. Imagine playing your flute, violin, cello, guitar, or bass in an ensemble whose focus is Latin music—specifically, Cuban charanga. You can, if you play one of these instruments at an intermediate level and live near San Francisco. The Flamenco-Latin Ensembles are representative of several groups and workshops that students at the Community Music Center San Francisco are urged to play in. The center operates from its headquarters in a Victorian building in San Francisco's historic Mission District and a branch in the Richmond District. The operational premise is that music is a life-enhancing activity that no one should be deprived of because of age, ethnic background, or income level. The diversity in clientele is matched by the variety of musical pursuits. If Latin doesn't bang your bongo, you can opt for Chinese Folkloric Music, blues, classical, or jazz styles. The center offers classes and private lessons in all of the major band and orchestra instruments, with several not-so-major ones thrown in, such as koto, conga drums, butterfly harp, and hammer dulcimer.

Finding a Group-Learning Site Near You

The organizations described so far are representative of the many opportunities scattered around the U.S. for learning almost any kind of music in a group setting. Finding one that suits your interests and personality will depend on where you are and what you want. If you live in a metropolitan area, your choices are likely to be much greater than in the sticks. Ironically, you'll likely find more group-learning opportunities for Bluegrass banjo in Chicago than in rural Kentucky. But don't despair until you have done at least a bit of creative searching. Following are some suggestions.

Personal Network. People you know are the obvious and easy place to start. Do you have any friends or relatives who have been involved in a class or workshop? If not, how about asking your child's band or orchestra teacher for suggestions.

The Yellow Pages. You can also turn up leads from the phone book's yellow pages under headings such as "Music Instruction-Instrumental." It will be up to you to check them out, since they won't differentiate between group and individual instruction.

Community Education Programs. Local school districts often offer night classes for the public in subjects ranging from cooking with insects to desktop publishing. Music and dance classes figure in as staples. The continuing education programs of community colleges also offer courses of particular interest to the general public.

Music Stores. If you want to take up the sax, you'll likely find the latest scuttlebutt at a music store that sells saxophones. If it doesn't have a bulletin board listing local classes and workshops, ask the clerks.

The Internet. Heidi Scanlon found the teacher who instructs her fiddling class through a musical chat group on Compuserve. In addition to chat groups, you can turn up leads under topic searches. Start with a keyword search for the instrument you are interested in. You'll probably end up with links to other sites. Check also under terms such as "music camps," "music classes," "community music centers," and "music instruction."

If your time permits only a week or so of concentrated instruction, consider attending one of the many music camps and retreats described in chapter 19 and listed in the "Resources" section of the Appendix. Attendees at these events always come home with their musical batteries charged.

Finale:

WHERE DO I GO
FROM HERE?

Keeping your weight down after you have reached your target level is just as important to a successful weight-loss program as the method you use to shed the weight. Maintaining the new level over time can prove a greater challenge than the starving or physical torture you endured to slim down.

It's much the same with music. After struggling to get launched you'll reach the point where you can put the mechanics of making music in the back of your mind and just enjoy the experience of playing. For a time it will be enough to bask in the moment, enjoying the fruits of your labors. Enjoy. But music making is like a flame. If it is not fueled, it will expire. Keeping it alive requires conscious effort and a sense of purpose. You have to constantly ask yourself what you want from music and, how you can get it, and how much of your life you want it to occupy.

The answers to these questions can give you a sense of direction that will ensure that making music will bring you moments of joy on a regular basis and enrich your life for years to come. We end our book with some tips to help you find outlets for your music and offer some ways to keep the flame burning.

Chapter 18

Finding Outlets

There's no shortcut to developing skill on an instrument. To develop your technique or work up a piece, you need a certain amount of practicing by yourself. But playing the musical hermit exclusively isn't enough to keep most amateur musicians going. They need the satisfaction that comes from sharing their art with others. Outlets take many forms. You might find sufficient fuel for your musical engine by playing the accompaniment on the piano or guitar for occasional sing-alongs with friends or in church. If you play a wind or stringed instrument, you might find a spot in a community band or orchestra. One thing can lead to another, and before long, you can become involved as much as you want with music. Consider the following example.

All of the adult students I have taught really hit it for a minute or two then decide that it's too hard. But I'm convinced that is due to the lack of an outlet. It's fun to learn how to play, but no fun to just sit in the closet and practice if you don't have an outlet.

Dave Blackinton, Director of Bands, Brigham Young University

Backing Into Music

Gordon Bennet, a consulting software engineer in the Rochester, New York area, played his trombone from the fourth grade through his second year in college, when—like so many of us—career and other life changes competed for his time and attention. Something had to give, and it was the horn, which went back into the case where it lay undisturbed for the next 16 years. One day he mentioned to his pastor that he had once played trombone. The pastor said he played trumpet himself and had been thinking about forming a brass quartet to play Christmas carols in church. Gordon was game, and they set about to find two more members to round out the quartet.

A short time later Gordon was dropping his kids off with Holly, the woman who watched them before and after school. They got to talking about plans for the approaching Christmas holidays. Holly's ears perked up when Gordon told her about the quartet and how it had opened the door for his comeback to music. Holly said she, too, played trombone and was a member of the community band. Why not come and try out a rehearsal?, she asked. Gordon replied that he wasn't quite ready for that yet, but he and his wife Carol, a dormant bassoonist, might consider it an option for the future. The seed now planted took root under Holly's gentle persuasion during the next few months. Gordon and Carol went to the band's next concert. They were hooked.

But there was a hitch. Carol didn't have a bassoon. The one she had last played belonged to the high school. Even used bassoons cost several thousand dollars. So instead of buying one, Gordon rented a bassoon and surprised Carol with it on Mother's Day. By the next fall, the couple were at the starting gate for the band's concert season.

Six years later, the Bennets are regular members of the Honeoye Falls Community Concert Band. Gordon's association with the band was a point of entry into other groups. One of these is a swing band, formed for a benefit concert to help sponsor the high school jazz ensemble's trip to Lincoln Center. The swing band continued after the fundraiser, and went on to play for wedding receptions, summer concerts in the village park gazebo, and a dinner in a hangar at the National Warplane Museum. Now involved with two bands, Gordon continued to widen his musical circle. Some fellow trombonists invited Gordon to sit in on rehearsals for the trombone quintet they belonged to, then welcomed him as a permanent member when one of the regular members left.

Gordon's trombone quintet has reached the point where it gets paid for some gigs. Gordon wouldn't mind eventually "gigging around semi-professionally," although this isn't his goal. "My wife and I have both rediscovered how much fun it is to play our instruments, to be in a band, and to just associate with other musicians," he says. "Music is an important part of our lives, and our kids have picked up on our enthusiasm." That said, he just wants to keep on enjoying playing and improving: "...the main thing is to keep it fun."

Bands and orchestras are but a few of the outlets available for adult amateurs. There are many other types of ensembles, ranging in size from duets on up. To finding one that fits, start with a realistic appraisal of your ability, then do a little creative searching. Like getting the perfect job, locating an apt musical is largely a matter of being at the right place at the right time.

How to Find an Outlet

John Payne believes an outlet is so important that he encourages beginning students to get into one of the John Payne Music Center's ensembles as early as possible. If, like most beginners, you aren't fortunate enough to hone your craft in a setting such as this, you'll have to find your own outlets. Before you leap at the chance to join the first group that will take you, consider that you stand to gain more from playing with musicians better than yourself than with those not as good. But therein lies a dilemma. As Ethan Winer, a late-start cellist puts it, "When you are just starting out, the only people you can get to play with you are other beginners, and you end up reinforcing each other's bad habits." He recommends that if you, as a beginner, can't find more advanced players to play with, you might look for other beginners who are as dedicated as you are, so you won't outgrow them. Or, seek out a community band or orchestra, even if you feel insecure. Just play the passages you you are able to. Lay out when you come to harder passages or play them softly. "Nobody will mind if you can't play everything perfectly, as long as you don't wreck it for the others by playing out of tune too loudly," he adds.

Locating a community band or orchestra near you should be fairly easy if you live in a small town or rural area. While they aren't likely listed in the yellow pages, community ensembles are generally well known in the areas in which they publicly perform. If you don't know anyone in a group, ask around among local music teachers. They may even know of specialized ensembles, such as flute choirs, or accordion bands within driving distance.

Finding a suitable ensemble in a larger urban area may take a bit more work. Again, start with music teachers and any personal acquaintances that may be in the know. If you come up empty, search the Net. *The Cycle of Fifths and Community Music Mailing List* (both listed in the Appendix) are website links to community bands and orchestras all over the world. *The Association of Concert Bands* and *National Band Association* are umbrella associations that maintain lists of active local groups.

Locating a community band or orchestra tends to be easier in rural than urban areas.

Joining an Established Group

People get into groups in many ways. Some find slots, even without intending to. Remember how Kathy Shaw got pulled into the percussion section of the Westmoreland Town Band simply because she drove her daughter to rehearsals and happened to be there when the director needed someone to play sleighbells.

Being invited is, of course, the nicest way to get into an existing ensemble. But it depends as much on being at the right place at the right time as on your capability. More likely, you will have to seek out a group and ask about joining. Community bands and orchestras depend on unpaid volunteers for their existence, but that doesn't necessarily mean they take all comers. Ensembles need to maintain a certain balance of parts, so you may be out of luck if the band you want to play sax in is already flush with saxes. Some groups set minimum standards for ability and require assurance in the form of an audition, cassette tape, or personal recommendation by a teacher or other member of the ensemble.

You can quickly scope out these preliminary questions with a phone call to the director. If the prospect seems likely, your next step might be to sit in on a few rehearsals before committing yourself as a regular member. You'll discover things from the business side of the music stand that you never noticed from the audience. The fit may not be right, for any of several reasons. Maybe the wisecracks of the guy who plays first trumpet have gotten tiresome. Or the conductor doesn't demand enough in the way of quality playing—or is too demanding. Your schedule might not allow you to be available for regular weekly rehearsals or performances during the busy time of year. Maybe you will get bored by the type of music in the group's repertoire, finding it unchallenging. Just as likely, it may be too challenging. As a newcomer, you pretty much have to accept the music, personalities, and dynamics of the group. You have to decide whether the group's pluses exceed its minuses and whether you have more to gain by tolerating the shortcomings for the chance to play

If your group contains only beginners, you might simply reinforce each other's bad habits.

and develop your ability, or by holding out for something better.

But the Band Doesn't Use Pianos

Keyboard instruments have an advantage over winds and strings, in that they provide both the melody line and accompaniment, thus eliminating the need for other players. You can play any of the thousands pieces of sheet music written for piano or improvise by ear, using no written music. Completely by yourself.

And thus the flip side: The opportunities to play with others are much fewer. "There are always people who need good accompanists," says flutist/pianist Pat Onufrak, "but sometimes the music is not as fulfilling for the accompanist. In flute literature, there are some true flute and piano duets, but the piano parts are really tough, so that sort of leaves out the less advanced players." So how can a keyboardist get social? Here are a few suggestions:

Make yourself available as an accompanist. Church, school, and community groups always need pianists to back up singers or instrumentalists for shows and amateur productions. It will take a fair amount of technique to accompany singers in the realms of popular or show music, but playing hymns in church is among the simplest tasks.

Consider chamber music. The flute-piano duets Pat Onufrak speaks of are only a few of the many types of chamber music that include the piano as one of the instruments. Ensemble music is available in styles from the baroque to modern for piano four-hands (two people playing a duet on the same piano), two pianos, and trios, quartets, and quintets using pianos.

Learn to play from "fake books." Whereas piano sheet music and piano music in song books are typically written with every note indicated, sometimes it also contains symbols above the staff that name the chord. This allows you to play the music from the notes written on the staff or just follow the written melody line and use the chord symbols to create your own accompaniment. For example, if you were playing *Mary Had a Little Lamb* in the key of C in this mode, you would follow the written

Being invited is the nicest way to get into an existing ensemble.

As a newcomer, you pretty much have to accept the music and dynamics of the group as it is.

melody line with your right hand, and use the chord symbols to suggest how your left hand would create a chord accompaniment. A "C" would appear above the staff at the first bar, along with the word, "Mary." You would continue playing this chord through "had, a little lamb." With the beginning of the second "little," a new chord, G7 appears.

Fake books are written entirely in this manner. Because they take up far less space, hundreds of songs can be crammed into a single book. Fake books are available containing popular songs, jazz, folk, and Broadway show music. Once you get the hang of playing in this mode, you will be positioned to play in jazz bands and various pop singing groups, or even informal sing-alongs.

So don't give up on piano as a social instrument. As Pat Onufrak says, "When friends are gathering together to sing or entertain each other, piano and guitar are much more useful than woodwinds, strings or brass."

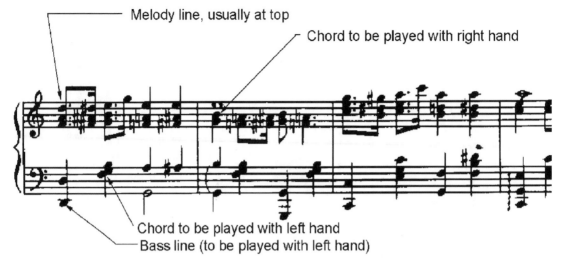

Standard Arrangement for Keyboard

Typical Fake Book Arrangement

Standard notation (above) spells out everything, limiting interpretation to phrasing, dynamics (volume changes), and tempo. Fake books (below) contain only the melody line and chord names. It's up to the player to construct the chords and interpretation.

Forming Your Own Ensemble

We were talking about the Canadian Brass on one of our walks one day. Lucie remarked that this group sounded as if they were having a lot of fun doing what they do so well

"Why don't we form a brass quintet?" Jerry asked, pointing out that we already had the two bottom instruments, Lucie's trombone and Jerry's tuba. He suggested a couple of candidates for the remaining instruments, trumpets and French horn. Frank, a long-time friend who played several instruments, would be a natural for French horn. Floyd, who had taught our son trumpet, might agree to take on trumpet 1. Jeff, who played trumpet in the town band, would be a good candidate for trumpet 2.

"Oh no," said Lucie. "Since I'm obviously the weak link, the only way I'll be a part of this is if we level the playing field."

"First off," Jerry replied, "you're not the weak link you think you are. But even if you were, just what do you propose to level the playing field?"

"Simple," she said. "You should play an instrument that gives you a real challenge—French horn, for example."

Jerry pointed out that among the various instruments he plays, the French horn is conspicuously absent for good reason: it's beastly difficult to play. It requires a near perfect ear to discern the correct pitch of each note in your head before you play it and a well-developed lip to enable you to play it on pitch. Even starting out with a pretty good ear, Jerry certainly had no horn-grade lip, being basically a reed guy, at home on clarinet and bassoon. He played tuba thanks only to the fact that its large mouthpiece requires only a loose embouchure. Besides, he didn't have a horn, and even used ones cost plenty.

So he agreed.

Frank, Jerry's original choice for horn, also played tuba, so this would be his slot. Frank jumped at the chance, even offering Jerry the use of his horn. Unfortunately it wasn't the best of instruments. Suffice it to say that if playing a quality new horn is like driving a Lexus, playing Frank's was more akin to a '58 Dodge Dart. Nonetheless, equipped with a fingering chart and book about horn playing, Jerry set out to develop as much competence as he could in a short time.

Floyd and Jeff also eagerly jumped on board. We ordered some pieces from the Internet and we were set for our first rehearsal, on a January afternoon.

We got through the pieces pretty well, but it was painfully obvious to Jerry that Lucie had picked the right handicap for him. He could hit most of the notes in the bottom register, but anything higher was a total loss. By late

Having others to play with is very nice on piano, absolutely crucial with fiddle. One of the reasons I'm not discouraged is because I play with other beginners, so I know it's not just me, that it is, in fact, a difficult instrument.

Heidi Scanlon

spring his range increased to about an octave and a half—nowhere near the horn's capability, but enough to play all but the highest notes in the pieces we had in our repertoire, which by now consisted of three pieces we got through mail order: Gershwin's *Bess, You Is My Woman, Now;* Debussy's *The Girl with the Flaxen Hair;* and three rags by Scott Joplin. The first two are beautiful, lyrical ballads which seemed simple, if judged only from the lack of rapid passages. But we soon discovered how hard it is to make a slow-moving ballad sound like music. The Joplin rags promised lighthearted fun, but were full of tricky, syncopated rhythms that demanded precision.

Still, the group liked the pieces well enough to want to learn them, though we put *Bess* on the back burner until which time as Jerry could reach its high notes. The group also agreed that the song list would be eclectic, composed of both serious and light pieces from the Baroque to the present. In this spirit, we subsequently added a march, several serious pieces from the 18th century, and *Tin Roof Blues.* Lucie particularly liked the latter, with it's down-and-dirty trombone smears.

By the second or third rehearsal we all felt we needed a name. Though we admired nationally famous groups such as the Canadian Brass and Empire Brass, we wanted a name that was friendlier, less pompous. Most of Jerry's suggestions—"Brass Monkey," for example — met with groans. In the end, we settled on "Otter Brook Brass," which tied us geographically to a nearby stream and evoked the playful nature of otters.

Otter Brook Brass played its first gig at a country inn on a gray, sleety February afternoon, just over a year from the date of our first rehearsal. We had expected to play in a corner of the dining room, as a sort of background to the late lunch diners. Instead, we were ushered into a side room, containing some 30 chairs arranged for a recital. Fifteen were occupied by the friendly audience, most of them senior citizens. We started into our first number, a fanfare-type piece from the baroque era, then followed with the traditional hymn, *Amazing Grace.* The small room created an intimate relationship between us and the audience, which we exploited by talking informally between numbers, telling bits of trivia about our various instruments and introducing the next piece.

We had prepared an eclectic play list of ten pieces drawn from opera, marches, ragtime, and the impressionist period. The program would, we thought, surely fill the hour. By our fourth piece, the Toreador song from *Carmen,* it was obvious that we had underestimated, even with our schmoozing with the audience between numbers. We managed to filled the last twenty minutes by playing two pieces that we hadn't rehearsed, and repeating the rousing march, *Barnum and Bailey's Favorite.* The audience didn't seem to mind.

After we had packed our horns in their cases, we retired to the dining room, where we savored a fine meal, spiced with the satisfaction of a successful debut.

If you want to form your own small ensemble, be prepared to take the initiative to attract others of like mind and compatible personality. People you already know or know of will be the best prospects. If you come up short, consider advertising for other members. You can get free advertising by posting notices in places likely to be seen by prospects. For example, If we had wanted to find members for our brass quintet in this way, we might have posted notices in the music store in Keene, the music department bulletin board of Keene State College, and at the Keene Institute of Music and Related Arts. We could also have put out the word with a few music teachers. When you find candidates, the fun starts. Now you have to turn an assemblage of disparate people into a tightly knit musical group that can hang together over time. It won't be easy. The ups and downs we have gone through with Otter Brook Brass have taught us a few lessons about getting a small ensemble off and running. Here are a few. They don't need to all be decided at the outset, but the earlier you fix the basic goals and policies, the better your chances of success.

Play together to test the musical fit. It's hard to find several people of nearly equal musical expertise, but there's a limit to how wide the gap can be. The weaker player or players in a lopsided group can learn from playing next to stronger players, but can be intimidated when the stronger players want to play music to match their talents. If the others are forced to play less challenging fare, they may get bored and lose interest in the group. Organize your first session along the lines of a test run to give all players ample opportunity to see whether the fit is right,

Even a bad performance can inspire the amateur listener. The greatest musicians make it easier. They are welcoming, enveloping, demanding, sometimes wielding an almost erotic energy, turning a vast public into avid amateurs. Lovers all.

Edward Rothstein

before commitments are made.

The personality fit is just as important as the musical fit. You can get some sense of whether you all are on the same wavelength at the first play-in. Unfortunately the little differences that can grate over time, may not be apparent at first, when everybody is out to please. Once you lock yourselves into a relationship, you are stuck making the best of it, and will have to use the same strategies for resolving difference as in any relationship. Open communication, sensitivity, and tolerance will all come in handy.

Choose members for your ensemble who will likely agree on the type of music to be played.

Agree on the music. Floyd, the first trumpet in Otter Brook Brass, likes brass music from the baroque. Frank, the tubist, would probably like to see us play more oompah. The rest of us hedge toward more modern fare, recognizing that this covers territory from Scott Joplin rags to Debussy. Our repertoire, consequently, is a mixed bag containing something for everyone. Everybody is happy, at least some of the time, and audiences like variety. We couldn't have held together without this kind of musical consensus, though.

Decide whether you will play for yourselves, others, or both. You'll probably start out as a rehearsal group. For a time, learning to play pieces without colliding in a musical train wreck will be the main charge. It may even be enough to keep you interested. However, most groups evolve to a point where they want to share their music with an audience. Talk about your goals at an early date—will the emphasis be rehearsing to perform, or playing only for yourselves? Realize that your goals may change as your group develops.

Forge a gig policy. Even if you agree that some of your playing will be in public performances, you still need a meeting of the minds on the ground rules. Will you get paid or play for free? Otter Brook generally does not charge to play for charities or non-profit events, but does for businesses (though, considering the money we have made this way, it's probably in our best interests to keep our day jobs). Also, you should work out the types of events you aim to play for. Weddings, church services, shopping malls, village greens, senior centers—all potential venues—offer a different kind of relationship between the performer and audience and call for different types of music and programs.

Determine an organizational structure. Duos or trios can function quite adequately on a completely democratic level, with decisions made by consensus and a minimal amount of musical direction, which can be shared. This kind of loose organization gets increasingly hard to follow, the bigger the ensemble. The result can be chaos, bad feelings, and inefficient use of rehearsal time. There are ways around it, but you may have to be creative to find just the right mix. For example, a group of five or more players needs, at a minimum, someone to lead the group, even if this task is reduced to kicking off each piece and making sure everyone stops together. It may need stronger leadership to help the group get beyond just playing notes to actually making music. In Otter Brook Brass we share the kick-off/cut-off responsibilities. So far, they have been determined by who brought that particular piece to the group, or who happens to have the lead-in part. Broader musical leadership is also shared, successfully, so far.

Some groups work well by concensus. Others need a strong leader.

Set policies for nuts and bolts. Keeping a musical group together is a constant challenge. Particularly if it is composed of disparate players with various occupations who live some distance away. Working out the times and location of rehearsals is the first logistical priority. Then come the questions of who will select music to be played, how will it be acquired. Who will be responsible for arranging gigs? How will communication be handled between members? Will one person be responsible, a committee, or a telephone tree system? Will you use phone or e-mail? Finally, what kind of arrangement will there be for discussing issues that come up—informally at rehearsals or at special "threshing sessions?"

Other Opportunities

In chapter 4 we told about the high Karen Jackson gets at the Saturday afternoon fiddle jams, when fiddlers, pipers, and harpists get hopping on an Irish jig. Another budding fiddler, Heidi Scanlon (chapter 17), gives her bow a work-out at monthly get-togethers of fiddlers and friends in the Washington, DC area. These "slow jams" give inexpert players the opportunity to hear others play and join in as they are able. And if you happen to play fiddle and don't live in Montpelier, Vt. or Washington, DC, you can probably turn up another fiddle fest site with a little sniffing around. What about other instruments?

Remember when we told about what it's like to play a tuba in a room with twenty or thirty other tubas, baritones, and euphoniums in the annual Tubachristmases© staged in public places all over the U.S.? Well, there are also banjo rallies sponsored by the American Banjo Fraternity. If recorder is your instrument, you might get invigorated by spending a week in coached rehearsals, master classes, and dance at the Canto Antiguo Early Music Workshop in Ojai, California, in July. Jazz buffs can attend daily combo classes, learn theory and improvisation, and jazz history at the Bud Shank Jazz Workshop in Port Townsend, Washington. Aspiring string player? How does a week-long music camp event with the name, "Chamber Music for Fun" sound? It invites string players of every proficiency level to learn to play the literature in a relaxed environment in Twin Lake, MN. If you can get to Las Vegas for a week in September, you can play flute by day and black jack by night at the Las Vegas Adult Band Camp.

These are but a few of the numerous workshops, summer music camps, and seminars that regularly take place at various sites around the world, each geared to a particular instrument, type of music, or type of group. You can find out about events of interest to you by connecting to the appropriate grapevine. Find out whether there is a local or national organization geared to your instrument or musical bent. We list several in the Appendix. For example, if banjo is your instrument, you might link up with the Fretted Instrument Guild of America. For French horn aficionados, there is the International Horn Society. Organizations such as the International Concertina Association bear witness to the fact that no instrument is so esoteric as to not warrant some kind of larger group. If you are looking for ways to connect with larger ensembles, check with the Association of Concert Bands or National

Band Association. Many of these associations regularly publish items of interest over the Internet or in newsletters. Getting into the right stream will put you in contact with groups in your area and keep you informed about lore pertaining to your instrument and upcoming national events.

The Internet has become a vast clearinghouse for associations of all types. Indeed, some organizations exist only through the communication channels of this medium. The Cycle of Fifths, for example, is a web-ring listing of community music groups around the world, including choirs, theater groups, bands and orchestras.

Attending events such as these gives you a chance to meet other amateurs, some better than you, some worse. The chance to charge your musical battery in the company of others of similar interest is both a lot of fun and a sure way to keep your music alive.

Chapter 19

What Next?

According to Albert Schweitzer, there are two means for refuge from the miseries of life: music and cats. As owners of two cats we're not sure about the latter, but firmly believe in the universal power of music. It can charm, regardless of the source. The Serbian tyrant Slobodon Milosevic reportedly knocks out a mean tune on the piano. Late one evening in 1995, while attending the Bosnia peace talks at a military base in Dayton, Ohio, Milosevic wandered into the officers' mess. With military personnel and hangers-on milling around, Milosevic sat at the piano. Within two hours he had the crowd eating out of his hand. In view of subsequent events in Serbia, it may have been the last time anyone ate out of his hand (or would want to).

Nobody cares if you can't dance well. Just get up and dance.

Dave Barry

Other well-known—and better respected—personalities express themselves through music. Humorist Dave Barry plays rock guitar. When Albert Einstein wasn't pondering concepts that would blow the minds of lesser folks, he played violin. Woody Allen's main sideline is Dixieland clarinet. And, lest we forget, there's Bill and his sax.

All of these celebrities, of course, achieved their fame for something other than their music—just as well for the most part. Yet music was central to their lives. Because it wasn't their career, they didn't feel compelled to excel at it. Einstein, according to Yehudi Menuhin, "played the fiddle well enough to take part in chamber music at home, but luckily he never dreamed of a concert career." Woody Allen owes his fame to his genius as a comedy writer/actor/director—not to his clarinet playing.

If you read Dave Barry's humor column, you can't miss his frequent references to rock music: "'Varlet and the Squeaking Codpieces,' wouldn't that be a great name for a rock group?" Barry began playing rock guitar in a garage band while in high school. Like thousands of others, the group folded when its members went their separate ways. Barry's interest never waned, though, and found a vent in 1992, when he formed a rock group with fourteen other writers of national repute—including Stephen King, Amy Tan, and Matt Groening—and went on tour. The "Rock Bottom Remainders" barnstormed the East Coast for two weeks in a bus, staying up late, eating junk food, and wreaking havoc with the classics of rock 'n' roll. A hilarious book, *Mid-Life Confidential* (Plume, 1995) chronicles the group's genesis and tour, with each of the writers contributing a different chapter.

Playing music should be, among other things, fun.

Why Am I Doing This, Anyway?

The Rock Bottom Remainders came into being mainly to have fun. The members, all secure in their careers (or as secure as any writer can be) thought it would be amusing to re-enact a part of their past and play in a rock group.

The key word here is "play"—the kind of free, unstructured play children engage in before adults give them single-purpose toys or habituate them to passive entertainment. Why shouldn't we adults get the same kind of joy out of playing music?

We should. Playing music should be simple, rewarding fun. Okay, learning how to make music rather than just produce notes takes a certain amount of dedicated effort. But it shouldn't always be work. That's what professional musicians get paid for. We amateurs get our reward in the pleasure of the experience of playing and the sharing of our music with others. With the experience itself the goal, we don't feel obligated to come up to the standards of the pros. Give yourself permission to make mistakes, even to flop occasionally. Keep a light-hearted attitude toward your playing, even at the risk of being regarded as a dilettante. To be called a dilettante might ruin an aspiring professional, but shouldn't affect you, because you can choose to play or not play, without worrying about your music having to put bread on the table.

At some point, most adults struggling to learn a new or different instrument realize that the road to proficiency is anything but smooth. It's full of twists and turns, is steep at times, flat at others. When you hit the bumps you may forget the smooth, downhill stretches you have already traveled and wonder why you are putting yourself through this. These are the times you will be most tempted to put your horn back in the case for good.

When amateur musicians get together, they talk about music. When professional musicians get together, they talk about money.

Overheard somewhere

Don't.

Find a way around your impasse. All adult amateurs face frustrations. Gordon Bennett, the consulting software engineer from Rochester, New York, admits to continual frustration over his lack of improvement (perceived and real) and the lack of time to practice as much as he wants to. Rehearsal and performance dates of the groups he plays with have to be constantly re-scheduled, because, like Gordon, the members have busy lives.

Heidi Scanlon, the Washington, DC web researcher, faces frustrations of a different sort. An accomplished pianist, Heidi is learning folk fiddling, starting from ground zero. She is constantly reminded of the duality of being able to produce music competently on one instrument while struggling for each minor success on the other. "The music just doesn't sound as pretty as I would like it to," she says. Flutist Pat Onufrak (chapter 15) reports a similar frustration in trying to learn piano.

Yet, these folks struggle on to find that the rewards are worth the struggle. Gordon Bennet is exhilarated by the achievement of transforming a piece of music he can barely read into one that he can perform in public. He feels incredibly elated performing in a group where, suddenly, all of the director's comments from the rehearsals seem to gel, and a group of individuals suddenly become a single entity that makes beautiful music. Just as important to him is the cameraderie he enjoys with the other musicians, who he claims are some of the best people he knows.

Heidi Scanlon also gets a charge out of working through something difficult and winning. "I get a certain type of emotional intensity from facing a challenge that is both physical and mental, that engages me head to toe," she says.

To Pat Onufrak, making music is a way to complete the experience of music. Yet, listening to a recording of great music is not enough. She wants a closer relationship with the music that can only come through playing it herself.

Interviews with these and other amateurs have helped us answer the questions that nag every musician who plays for the joy of it: why am I doing this?, what do I want to achieve?, and how can I keep enthused? We hope the suggestions that emerged out these conversations will help keep you on track with your musical future.

What Do I Want to Achieve?

When I did finally manage to produce something resembling music, it was uneven; it rode upon a dubious tempo and was entirely unburdened by the imperatives of dynamics and proper rhythm. Nevertheless, I was beside myself with glee. It was enough.

Melanie Rehak

Jerry's father handed him down his own well-worn metal clarinet when Jerry was in the fifth grade. After his dad showed him how to put it together, put the reed on and finger it, he sent Jerry off to learn the rest by playing in the elementary school orchestra. Jerry took this in stride, not thinking much about what the instrument might mean to him in later life. He became seriously interested in the clarinet in high school, got a better instrument, took some lessons, and even planned on majoring in music in college. But soon realized he was swimming upstream. His friends, all engineering bound, constantly reminded him that opting for a music major would most likely lead to becoming a public school music teacher, with the incipient low income potential and low esteem this profession promised at the time. Jerry's dad, a school art teacher, also tried to dissuade him from a career in music, even though music was an important part of his dad's life.

The constant drip on the stone finally eroded Jerry's resolve, and he chose architecture, a field he felt would allow some artistic expression while offering a chance for reasonable financial rewards (though he now says this was naive). The clarinet went on the shelf. When he took it out 30 years later it was for a specific purpose, to play in the Keene State College Concert Band. The experience opened other doors. He has since taken up other instruments and gone on to play in a variety of other groups.

Jerry knew what he wanted to achieve when he resurrected his clarinet: an ability that would permit him to play in the college band. The question might not be so simply answered for you. It might help to think of it as coming up with a mission statement. Answering the following questions might help get you going:

1. Can you keep your enthusiasm and commitment by playing alone, or will you need the sharing of musical experience that comes from playing with others?
2. What types of groups do you want to join?
3. How good do you need to be to get into them?
4. How can you best develop this capability—private lessons, self-teaching, group learning, a combination of these?
5. How long do you think it will take you to reach this point?

What type of group do you want to get into, anyway?

---

6. How much time are you willing to spend each week on music, practicing and playing in groups?
7. After you reach your minimum level of proficiency, will you be content to hold steady or do you need to continue forging ahead?

How Can I Keep My Music Alive?

If you are like most people acquiring a new skill, you'll probably struggle hard at first, then come to a magical point where you feel good about what you can do and how far you have come. Unfortunately, the euphoria won't last. You'll bog down when you hit the "purple barrier." That's the point where you pedal harder and harder to gain less and less. In economics it's the law of diminishing returns. The quantum leaps you made at first have now become progressively smaller jumps. Your discouragement may lead you to play less, which will itself reinforce the downward cycle until you are tempted to pack the damn thing back into the case for good and have done with this silly escapade.

The euphoria of your initial success may not last.

Can you prevent this from happening? Yes, says William Leland, a music educator and editor of *Muzine,* an online magazine for amateurs. Leland recommends that you start out with a realistic attitude. Realize that what you are about to embark on isn't easy and the path is littered with tedium and frustration. Specifically:

❑ **Set realistic goals.** Anticipate that you will have let-downs and periods of low motivation and plan your progress accordingly. If you are starting out on trumpet, don't aim for mastery of Haydn's trumpet concerto in nine months. Settle for a simple arrangement of a tune you like. You'll keep your steam better by attacking new pieces of gradually-increasing difficulty than by banging your head against too-difficult pieces. Jerry's goal this year is to learn all three movements of the Mozart *Clarinet Concerto.* He may or may not perform the piece, but the satisfaction of having mastered it will be enough to keep his enthusiasm alive.

- ❑ **Commit yourself in time.** Promise yourself that you won't quit when you hit the first wall. Instead, you'll stick with it for a period of time beyond this. Then describe your commitment to a supportive person and and ask him or her to cheer you on (kick your butt, if necessary) until you reach the end date.

- ❑ **Find someone to play with.** Playing with others offers satisfaction from a shared experience as well as provides a support group. You can reap these benefits from a group as small as one other person, with which you play duets, to as large as a community band or orchestra (as discussed in more detail in previous chapters).

Your chances of success will be greater if you have a person who will support your musical endeavors.

- ❑ **Listen to music.** If you want to write science fiction, you have to read the works of others in this genre. Similarly, becoming a sensitive musician—even at the amateur level—requires familiarity with the world of music. Listen to recorded music. Go to concerts—not just those of pros, but local amateur musicians as well. You'll not only play better for it, but hear things you never did before you began playing yourself.

As to the last point, both of us now notice the bassoons and trombones when we hear a band or orchestra in ways we never did before we started playing these instruments ourselves. Put another way, playing music yourself makes you a better listener. Rather than passively hearing the sounds, taking them for granted, you become involved with the production of the sounds, creating them in yourself. Three other tips might help you keep motivated:

- ❑ **Vary the menu.** If you find yourself wondering if you have to play those damn scales forever, you don't. Getting bored by what you are playing is a sure recipe for losing interest. Scrap the offending fare and replace it with something that interests you, even if it doesn't hold the same promise for improving your technique. Check the Internet to see what sheet music is available for your instrument. You'll be surprised at the variety. A good teacher will understand that you need a change and support you in this move.

Listen to music.

❑ **Switch instruments.** After six months on the trumpet, you hit the wall. You realize that no matter how hard you work, you'll never develop a lip capable of reaching the high notes. The six months of time and effort are not wasted. You can easily transfer your skills to another brass instrument with a less demanding embouchure, such as a euphonium or tuba. Even if you switch instruments outside the brass family, you take with you all of the other skills you have acquired about reading and interpreting music. What do you have to lose?

❑ **Attend workshops, seminars, and music camps.** In Chapter 17 Jerry told about how attending the annual bassoon day at the University of New Hampshire was a great way to learn in the setting of a group. These kinds of get-togethers also provide fuel for the attendees' enthusiasm. Where else can you rub shoulders with forty or fifty other bassoonists in the same place? The realization that you are not the only person with a weird instrument fires you up and makes you want to

One way to keep from getting bored is to switch instruments.

continue. There are workshops, seminars, and music camps all over for every type of music from bluegrass to jazz to chamber music. And we cease to be amazed at the instruments they cater to. If banjo is your instrument, for example, you could get your battery charged up by attending rallies of the American Banjo Fraternity. The 1998 rally in Lewiston, Pennsylvania, celebrated the organization's golden anniversary, by honoring the music and instruments of Fred Bacon.

Not all of these suggestions will appeal to you. All amateurs who continue to grow and take pleasure from music find some combination that gives them the push they need to keep their spark alive. And in keeping it alive, it keeps them alive by fulfilling two important needs of the soul. As Yehudi Menuhin states them, "From the very beginning of human life, one of the purposes of music has been to give us pleasure. The other is to tell us the truth."

Find someone to play with.

What Next?

Appendices

Bibliography

Adams, Noah, *Piano Lessons: Music, Love & True
Adventures.* New York: Delta, 1996

Arnsdell, Gary, *Music For Life: Aspects Of Creative
Music Therapy With Adult Clients.* London and
Bristol, Pennsylvania: Jessica Kingsley
Publishers, 1995.

Ben-Tovim, Atarah; Boyd, Douglas, *You Can Make
Music.* London: Victor Gollancz, 1986.

Booth, Wayne C., *For the Love of It: Amateuring and Its
Rivals.* Chicago: University of Chicago Press,
1999.

Boyle, J. David, and Radocy, Rudolf E., *Measurement
and Evaluation of Musical Experiences.* New
York: Schirmer Books, 1987

Bruser, Madeline, *The Art of Practicing: A Guide to
Making Music from the Heart.* New York: Bell
Tower, 1997.

Fisk, Nicholas, *Making Music.* Boston: Crescendo
Publishing Co., 1966.

Judy, Stephanie, *Music for the Joy of It: Enhancing
Creativity, Skills, and Musical Confidence.* Los
Angeles: Jeremy P. Tarcher, Inc., 1990.

Katsch, Shelley; Merle-Fishman, Carol, *The Music Within
You: How You Can Enhance Your Creativity,
Communication and Confidence Through Music.*
New York: Fireside, 1985.

Menuhin, Yehudi, and Davis, Curtis W., *The Music of*

Man: Exploring the Miracle of Music and its Influence Throughout the Ages. New York: Fireside, 1979.

Newsome, David R. and Barbara Sprague, *Making Money Teaching Music.* Cincinnati: Writers Digest Books, 1995.

Nicholls, Geoff, *The Drum Book: A History of the Rock Drum Kit.* San Francisco: Miller Freeman Books, 1997.

Norris, Richard, M.D., *The Musician's Survival Manual: A Guide to Preventing and Treating Injuries in Instrumentalists.* St. Louis: International Conference of Symphony and Opera Musicians (ICSOM).

Théberge, Paul, *Any Sound You Can Imagine: Making Music/Consuming Technology.* Hanover, NH: Wesleyan University Press, 1997.

Weissman, Dick, *Music Making in America.* New York: Frederick Ungar Publishing Co., 1982

Werner, Kenny, *Effortless Mastery: Liberating the Master Musician Within.* New Albany, Indiana: Jamey Aebersold Jazz, Inc. 1996.

Whitener, Scott, *A Complete Guide to Brass: Instruments and Pedagogy.* New York: Schirmer Books, 1990.

Wilson, Frank R., *Tone Deaf & All Thumbs: An Invitation to Music-Making.* New York: Vintage Books, 1986.

Glossary

A

Accordion: A hand-held instrument consisting of a piano keyboard mounted to a set of folding bellows, which when pushed or pulled, draws air over metal reeds inside, which produce the sound. A series of buttons on the opposite side control bass notes and chords.

Acoustic guitar: (see "Guitar")

Acoustic: As used in this book, the term refers to instruments whose sound is produced by a physical body set into vibration-- such as a reed, membrane, or lips--and not dependent on electronic means.

Aptitude: A natural, or innate talent or ability.

B

Banjo: A plucked stringed instrument consisting of 4 or 5 strings stretched over a solid neck and hollow sounding box. A membrane is stretched over the top side of the box. It is open at the back.

Baritone: A brass instrument similar to a euphonium, but with a smaller bore and brassier tone quality.

Bass clef: The sign at the beginning of the staff that indicates the pitches of the staff, from the lowest line, G 11 notes below middle C on the piano, to the highest line, A, 2 notes below middle C.

Bass drum: The largest unpitched drum, double- or single-sided, played by a hand-held , felt-tipped stick in large ensembles and a foot pedal in small ensembles (assuming the bass drum is part of the drum set).

Bass: 1) The low range of musical tonality; also the lowest members of a particular musical family. 2) The lowest stringed instrument, consisting of 4 strings stretched over a solid neck and sounding box, a hollow box in acoustic basses; a solid piece of wood in electric basses. There are two varieties of acoustic basses. The upright version, also called bull fiddle, bass viol, double bass and and string bass, stands on the floor. A portable version is hand held and resembles a large guitar.

Bassoon: The bass member of the double-reed woodwinds, consisting of a long tube bent back on itself in five sections.

Bells: (see "Glockenspiel")

Belly: The top surface of the sounding box of a bowed instrument.

Bluegrass: A type of folk

music of the Southern Appalachians rooted in the traditions of the British Isles.

Bore: The hollow channel inside woodwind and brass instruments, which can remain the same diameter throughout its length (cylindrical) or gradually get larger toward the exit end, similar to a funnel (conical, or tapered).

Braille music: Music notated by impressing the symbols into the sheet, to make it accessible to blind persons.

Brass: A malleable, non-corrosive metal used as the base metal for certain wind instruments, and the name of the family of wind instruments operated by valves or slides.

Bridge: 1) The wood support for the strings at their lower end on bowed string instruments. 2) A slang term for the middle part of a popular song.

Bull fiddle: (see "Acoustic Bass")

C

Cajun: A style of music indigenous to the people of Southern Louisiana who trace their roots to the Acadians of Nova Scotia. Many of the songs are meant for dancing and have words in French Creole.

Castanets: Two round pieces of hardwood, hollowed in the center, clicked together for percussive effects typical of Latin music.

Celesta: A set of tuned steel bars played mechanically by hammers activated by a piano keyboard. The instrument is mounted in a cabinet that resembles a miniature piano.

Cello: The tenor voice of the bowed strings, consisting of 4 strings stretched over a hollow wood box.

Chimes: Sets of hollow metal tubes suspended vertically by strings in a frame and played by striking with a mallet.

Clarinet: A woodwind instrument whose tone is produced by air vibrating a single reed against a hollow mouthpiece. Pitch is varied by opening and closing holes along its bore, some of which are covered by pads.

Classical music: In strict usage, the term refers to the written performance music of Europe during the latter 1700s, early 1800s. In this book, classical music means any type of "serious" written music, as opposed to folk, jazz, country & western, rock, and other popular genres.

Concertina: A small, hexagonal, accordion.

Cornet: The soprano member of the brass family, consisting of a bent, conical metal tube, three valves, and a mouthpiece.

Cymbal: A thin, saucer-shaped brass plate played by tapping with a drum stick or clashing together with opposing cymbal.

D

Digital piano: An instrument with a piano keyboard, whose sound is produced through digital electronic technology.

Dobro: A type of guitar with a metal plate over the soundboard to produce the louder, more metallic sound desired in blues.

Drum set: Various drums arranged to be played by one person. A basic set, or kit, contains a bass, snare, tenor, and cymbals.

Duration: The time lapse, or length, of a musical tone or space (rest) between tones.

E

Embouchure: Literally, the French word for "mouth position." Musically, it refers to the shape of the lips required to produce a tone on a particular instrument. The term "lip" is used as a slang expression for embouchure.

English horn: An alto double reed woodwind similar to the oboe, except that it is slightly longer and pitched a fifth lower.

Ethnic drumming: (see "Tribal Drumming").

Euphonium: A brass instrument similar to a tuba, but smaller and higher pitched.

F

Fake book: A book containing songs notated by their melody lines in the treble clef, with the names of the chords to be played indicated above the clef by a symbol.

Fiddle: A violin used for improvised traditional folk music, as opposed to written music.

Fifth: An interval of 7 semitones, or half notes, such as from C to G or G to D.

Fingerboard: The top surface of the neck of a stringed instrument to which the strings are pressed.

Fingering: The finger positions required on the strings, valves, or keys of an instrument to obtain a certain pitch.

Flute: A hollow metal pipe with holes along its length, some covered by pads, and open at the bottom. Tone is produced at the top by blowing across a hole in the mouthpiece into the sharp edge of the hole.

Fourth: An interval of 5 semitones, or half notes, such as from C to F.

French horn: A brass instrument with a long, conical bore wound into a spiral and ending in a funnel-shaped mouthpiece. Modern horns have three valves, usually rotary in type.

Fret: A horizontal ridge on the neck of a fretted string, such as a guitar, ukulele, banjo, or lute, which acts as a stop when the player's finger presses the string into the space between two frets, fixing the pitch in predictable intervals (as opposed to bowed strings which, without frets, require the play-er's judgment to find the right position).

G

Gig: Slang expression for musical engagement, paid or unpaid.

Gliss: Slang for "glissan-do."

Glissando: Passing from one note to another gradually, rather than abruptly, as done by a slide trombone.

Glockenspiel: A vertically arrayed set of tuned steel bars played with hard-tipped mallets.

Golpe plates: Metal plates over the soundboards of flamenco guitars to protect the soundboards from finger tapping.

Gong: (see "Tamtam")

Guitar: A plucked string instrument consisting of 6 strings stretched over a solid neck and sounding board. In acoustic guitars, the sounding board is a hollow wood box. It is a solid piece of wood in electric guitars.

H

Helicon: A circular tuba invented by Stowasser in

Vienna in 1849 and the forerunner of the sousaphone.

Hertz: A measurement of the frequency of sound waves. One hertz equals one cycle per second.

Horn: Used casually to refer to any member of the brass instruments, or specifically, to refer to the French horn.

Hz: Abbreviation for "hertz."

I

Improvise: To play loosely around a melodic line without playing the line precisely, but staying within the chord structure. Improvisation is the basis of all jazz music and important in other non-written genres, such as folk.

Intensity: The loudness of a sound, measured in *sones*. Relative loudness is measured in *decibels*.

J

Jazz: A type of free-flowing music blending music indigenous to the New World with that of Africa, depending heavily on individual improvisation.

K

Kettle drums: (see "Timpani")

Keyboard: The portion of an instrument containing strings or keys struck or plucked by the fingers; also, an instrument operated by a piano-like keyboard.

Klezmer: A type of music, largely improvised, played by Jewish musicians in the Ghettoes of European Cities. Klezmer music has enjoyed a revival in the U.S. in recent years, thanks to groups such as the New York Klezmorim.

L

Lip: A slang expression used to mean "embouchure."

Lyre: (see "Glockenspiel")

M

Marimba: A horizontal keyboard consisting of tuned hardwood bars with a set of hollow tubes mounted below to amplify the sound. Marimbas are played with felt-tipped mallets.

Mentor: Anyone--a professional teacher, or

accomplished acquaintance--who can coach you in some part of your musical development.

Method book: An instructional book intended to teach how to play an instrument.

MIDI device: An electronic musical instrument such as a digital piano with the capability to communicate with other electronic instruments or a computer.

MIDI: An acronym that stands for *Musical Instrument Digital Interface*, an international standard instituted during the 1980s to provide data linkage between electronic devices. When the term MIDI is used alone, it usually refers to a MIDI device.

O

Oboe: The soprano member of the double-reed woodwinds, consisting of a conical-bore tube in three sections with holes and keys.

Octave: An interval from a given note to its next higher multiple, such as middle C (256 cps) to the C above middle C (512 cps).

Organ: An instrument the player operates by a piano keyboard and a separate array of foot pedals. Stops above the keyboard permit various sound combinations. Classical pipe organs produce sound by controlling airflow through pipes of various lengths. Electronic organs imitate the sound of pipe organs through electronic means.

P

Peg: The wooden pin which fits into a hole at the top of the neck of a stringed instrument, to which the strings are attached. Tightening or loosening the peg changes the pitch of the string.

Percussion: The family of instruments which make sounds when certain components are set into vibration by being struck, or plucked. The family includes tonal, or pitched, instruments, such as the piano or marimba, and non-pitched instruments, such as snare drums.

Perfect pitch: The ability to recognize the pitch of a tone with no help from a reference.

Piano: Short for "pianoforte," the original

name of the present 88-key acoustic instrument played by fingers striking keys which activate a mechanical assembly (action), ending in felt-tipped hammers that strike the strings, setting them into vibration.

Pitch: The perceived highness or lowness of a sound, resulting from the number of vibrations over a given time period. Pitch is measured in terms of frequency, in units called *hertz,* where one hertz equals one cycle per second.

Pitched percussion: Instruments of the percussion family that have tones of specific pitches, such as pianos, marimbas, and timpani.

Plectrum: A small piece of horn, tortoise shell, or other material used to pluck certain stringed instruments. Also, an alternate name of a 4-string banjo.

Presbycusis: Hearing loss associated with aging.

R

Recorder: A hollow wood pipe with holes along its length and open at the bottom end. The tone is produced at the top by blowing into a slit in the shaped wood mouthpiece. The air

strikes a sharpened blade which produces a whistle-like tone.

Recorder: A type of flute with open finger holes along its length. Tone is produced when air blown through a slot in the mouthpiece strikes a sharp edge that creates a whistle-like tone.

Reed: A thin piece of wood or metal set into vibration by air moving over it to produce a tone. Wood reeds for wind instruments are tapered. Metal organ and accordion reeds are not.

Relative pitch: The ability to recognize the pitch of one tone from another reference tone. For example, if someone plays a C and tells you what it is, then plays a second, different tone, you will be able to name it from its relationship to the C.

Rhythm: The organization of time in music, primarily the relative lengths of the sounds and silences.

Rub-board: A washboard, consisting of a piece of corrugated metal in a wood frame, adapted for playing as a rhythm instrument by rubbing with thimbles or spoons.

S

SATB: Vocal music consisting of four parts: soprano, alto, tenor, and bass.

Saxophone: A single reed keyed instrument with a conical bore, shaped in a straight line (soprano saxophone) or bent back on itself (alto, tenor, baritone, bass).

Second: An interval of 2 semitones, or half notes, such as from C to D.

Seventh: An interval of 10 semitones, or half notes, such as from C to B-flat (a major seventh is an interval of 11 semitones, such as from C to B).

Sixth: An interval of 9 semitones, or half notes, such as from C to A.

Sleighbells: Sets of small, spherical bells mounted on straps and jingled by hand.

Snare drum: A double-headed drum proportioned such that the head diameter is greater than the depth between heads. Wire snares stretched across the bottom head rattle against the head when the top head is played, causing the distinctive snare drum sound.

Sousaphone: A circular variation of the tuba, whose shape was adapted by John Philip Sousa to make an instrument that could be carried when marching.

Staff: A group of 5 horizontal lines across the page. Each line and intervening space represents a particular pitch, as determined by the range assigned to the staff by the clef (see "treble clef" and "bass clef").

String bass: (see "Acoustic Bass")

String: A length of steel wire or animal gut that, when set into vibration, makes the musical sound of the "string" family of instruments, as well as pianos.

Synthesizer: A device that creates various combinations of sound electronically. Modern synthesizers are operated by piano keyboards and often have built-in recording/playback features.

T

Talent: As used in this book, talent is the ability to do something, resulting from applying one's natural aptitude.

Tamtam: A large-diameter thin brass plate hung vertically from strings in a frame and played with a soft beater.

Tenor drum: A double-headed drum proportioned such that the head diameter is less than the depth between heads.

Third: An interval of 4 semitones, or half notes, such as from C to E.

Timbre: The quality of tone that makes one instrument's tone sound different from another.

Timpani: Large drums shaped like kettles consisting of membrane heads stretched over a basin-shaped copper shells. The pitch of the head can be tuned by adjusting screws around the edge or by a foot pedal.

Tom-Tom: A double- or single-headed drum, usually part of a set, each with a different tone.

Tonal memory: The ability to remember a sequence of musical sounds.

Tone: A musical sound.

Treble clef: The sign at the beginning of the staff that indicates the pitches of the staff, from the lowest line, E above middle C on the piano, to the highest line, F, 10 notes above middle C.

Triangle: A steel rod bent into a triangular shape, suspended by a string, and played with a metal beater.

Tribal drumming: A type of drumming rooted in traditional cultures and intended to serve ends other than expressing conventional music.

Trombone: The tenor voice of the brasses and the only ones whose pitch is changed by moving a slide in and out to elongate and shorten the tube. The tone is produced by a cup-shaped mouthpiece. Trombones have cylindrical bores, except at the bell, where they flare.

Trumpet: A brass instrument with the same pitch as the cornet, but whereas the cornet tubing is conical, the trumpet's is mostly cylindrical, giving it a somewhat more brilliant, less mellow tone.

Tuba: The largest and lowest-pitched brass instrument. The tone is produced by the players lips vibrating into a cup-shaped mouthpiece. Tubas have a conical bore and are equipped with three or four valves.

V

Vibes: (see "vibraphone")

Vibraphone: A horizontally arrayed set of tuned metal bars arranged like a piano keyboard and fitted with a set of hollow tubes below to amplify the sound. Discs in the tubes revolve to cause the sound to vibrate.

Viola: The alto voice and second smallest of the bowed strings, consisting of 4 strings stretched over a hollow wood resonating box.

Violin: The soprano voice and smallest of the bowed string instruments, consisting of 4 strings stretched over a hollow wood resonating box.

W

Wah-wah mute: A mute for trumpets and cornets, consisting of a cup-shaped part and a smaller trumpet-shaped tube with a flared, open end. When the player moves a hand over the open end, back and forth, the sound imitates the "wah-wah" of a baby.

Whip: Two thin, narrow pieces of wood that slap together to produce the sound of a leather whip.

Wood block: A rectangular block of hardwood in which slits are cut to form a resonating chamber, and played with drumsticks.

Woodwind: An instrument derived from a hollow pipe with holes along its length, which, when opened or closed, change the length of the vibrating air column inside and raise or lower the pitch.

World music: An imprecise term used for a branch of jazz from the 1960s on that sought roots in the assumed commonality of all folk music and made popular by groups such as the Paul Winter Consort.

X

Xylophone: A horizontally-arranged keyboard, 3 1/2 octaves in range, consisting of tuned hardwood bars with a set of hollow tubes mounted below to amplify the sound.

Chapter 17

Resources

The following resources were selected as potentially useful to adult amateur musicians of various ability levels. The listings are current as of the date of publication. Because Internet sites change rapidly, the addresses below may have changed or even disappeared. You may, however, obtain links that can lead to other related sites.

Associations, Amateur Musicians

Maryland

Montgomery County Chamber Music Society. Welcomes advanced pianists, wind players, string players and vocalists who want to sing/play in an ensemble. Dick Wylie, contact, 1206 Floral St. NW, Washington, DC 20012. 202-726-0392, 202-782-3734. www.rmwylie@aol.com.

Washington, DC
Adult Music Student Forum (AMSF). P.O. Box 6204, Washington, DC 20015-0204. 202-686-3513. www.amsfperform.org.

Associations, Bands and Orchestras

The Association of Concert Bands. c/o Nada Vencl, 6613 Cheryl Ann, Independence, OH 44131. www.afn.org.

National Band Association. c/o Valerie Brown, Office Manager, P.O. Box 121292, Nashville, TN 37212. Phone/fax: 615-385-2650. www.nationalbandassoc.org.

Associations, Instruments

Banjos
American Banjo Fraternity (ABF), 636 Pelis Road, Newark, NJ 14513. www.marmee@red-suspenders.com.

Basses (String)
International Association of Bassists. www.jmu.edu/orgs/bassists/isb.html.

Cellos
Internet Cello Society, www.cello.org

Clarinets
International Clarinet Association (I.C.A.) P.O. Box 7683, Shawnee Mission, KS 66207-0683. 913-268-3064. www.clarinet.org

Concertinas
International Concertina Association, Gillingham, UKP8, England.

Cornets/Trumpets
International Trumpet Guild. www.trumpetguild.org.

Flutes
National Flute Association. Phyllis T. Pemberton, Exec. Dir., 26951 Ruether Ave., Suite H, Santa Clara, CA 91351. 661-250-8920. www.nfacentral@compuserve.com.

French Horns
International Horn Society, 8180 Thunder Street, Juneau AK 99801. 907-789-5477 (tel), 907-790-4066 (fax). www.hvogel@ptialaska.net. IHS Online: www.wmich.edu/horn.

Fretted Instruments
The Fretted Instrument Guild of America (FIGA). 5342 Deer Creek Drive, Orlando, FL 32821.

Lutes
Lute Society of America. Box 1328, Lexington, VA 24450. 540-463-5812. lutesociety@rockbridge.net.

Oboes/Bassoons
International Double Reed Society. http://idrs.colorado.edu.

Pianos
American Pianists Association. Clowes Memorial Hall, Butler University, 4600 Sunset Ave., Indianapolis, IN 46208. 317-940-9945. apainfo@SRonline.com.

Trombones
International Trombone Society, c/o Kansas State University Dept. of Music, 109 McCain, Manhattan, KS 66506. www.//web.missouri.edu/~cceric/index.html.

Tubas, Baritones, and Euphoniums

Tubists Universal Brotherhood Association (T.U.B.A.), c/o Music School of the University of Texas, Austin, TX 78712-1208 (tel), 512-475-6788 (fax). www.chisham.com.

Associations, Internet Links

Cycle of Fifths, a web-ring listing of community music groups around the world, including choirs, theater groups, bands and orchestras. www.geocities.com/Vienna/7076/main.html.

The Community Music Mailing List, a link to large ensembles. www.io.com/~rboerger/community.html.

Instructional Media

Books (with or without cassette tapes or CDs)

Bill Brown's Introduction to the Guitar (2 books, 3 tapes). *Bill Brown's Introduction to the Guitar for the Visually Impaired.* 800-484-1839. BillBrown@guitarbyear.com.

You Can Teach Yourself Drums, You Can Teach Yourself Accordion and others. Music Books Plus. www.musicbooksplus.com.

Technique Through Music (Piano course). Saterna Music Publishing Co., P.O. Box 3172, Mission, BC V2V 4J4 Canada. 604-826-1753. www.saternamusic.com.

Cassette Tapes

Guitar by Ear, Piano By Ear. BillBrown@guitarbyear.com.

Online Media

Brent Hugh's Music Instruction Software. www.cctr.umkc.edu:88/userx/bhugh/musicold.html.

The Woodwind Fingering Guide, a source of basic, alternate, trill, and tremolo fingerings for all woodwind instruments. www.sneezy.org/wfg/fing_noframes.html.

Videos

Music lessons on video for learning bluegrass, country, jazz, rock, and gospel music on autoharp, country fiddle, guitar, banjo, bass, dulcimer, mandolin, drums. Texas Music and Video, P.O. Box 16248, Lubbock, TX 79490-6248. (800) 261-3368. www.musicvideo.com.

Beginning Sax, Play Sax from Day One, Beginning Trumpet with Michael Harris, Anyone Can Play Flute, and other videos, Horn Place, P.O. Box 1016, Lebanon, NH 03766. 603-448-8836. www.hornplace.com.

Instructional Organizations

Adult Music Student Forum, Inc. (AMSF). P.O. Box 6204, Washington, DC 20015-0204. 202-686-3515.

Community Music Center San Francisco, 544 Carp Street, San Francisco, CA 94110. 415-647-6015, 415-647-3890 (fax). www.sfmusic.org.

John Payne Music Center, 9A Station St., Brookline, MA 02146. 617-277-3438. www.artsforalo.com/jp.html.

Old Town School of Folk Music, 4544 North Lincoln Ave., Chicago, IL 60625. 773-728-6000 (phone), 773-728-6999 (fax). www.ci.chi.il.us/WorksMart/culturalaffairs/CulturalDevelopment/Commu.../OldTown.ht

Upper Valley Music Center, 1219 Bragg Hill Road, Norwich, VT 05055. 802-649-8266.

Interactive Computer Products

Discovering Keyboards, Play Guitar with Ross Bolton, Basix Bass Method and others, Music Books Plus. www.musicbooksplus.com.

Music Lab Melody (reading, recognizing sounds), *Guido* (recoginizing intervals, chords, melodies), *Piano* (3-level piano course). Musicware, Inc., Redmond, WA. www.musicwareinc.com.

SmartMusic (formerly *Vivace*), play-along accompaniment with CD ROM disks. Coda Music Technology, 6210 Bury Drive, Eden Prairie, MN 55346-1718. 800-843-2066, 612-937-9760 (fax). www.SmartMusicSales@codamusic.com..

Music Camps, Retreats, and Workshops

The following camps and workshops are for adults of all ability levels, unless otherwise noted.

Band

Las Vegas Adult Band Camp. P&P Educational Services, Inc., 1405 Pine Row Ct., St. Louis, MO 63146. www.adultband.pped.com.

Chamber Music

Improvising Chamber Music. Free-wheeling, playful ensemble improvising on any instrument. Music for People, P.O. Box 397, Goshen, CT 06756. 860-491-4511.

Kinhaven Adult Chamber Music Workshop. Non-competitive, supportive music making in Weston, VT. Mary Watt, 430 West 116th St., New York, NY 10027. 212-749-4976.

Vermont Music and Arts Center. Coached chamber music, recreational playing, concerts. Joan E. Miller, P.O. Box 240, Berkeley Heights, NJ 07922. 908-464-6933. www.jemsoftware@wordnet.att.net.

Waterville Valley Music Center. Intense chamber music experience for strings and woodwinds in New Hampshire's White Mountains. David Siegel. 212-724-0348. www.DSViolin@aol.com.

Country Blues

Port Townsend Country Blues Workshop. Guitar, harmonica, gospel singing, piano, bass, mandolin, accordion. P.O. Box 1158, Port Townsend, WA 98368. 360-385-3102. www.mktcentrum@olympus.net.

Dulcimers

Northeast Dulcimer Workshop. Study in small groups; private and semi-private lessons, at Blue Mountain Lake, NY. Barbara Truex, 434 Preble St., So. Portland, ME 04106-3033. 207-799-6899. www.whitetruex@aol.com.

Early Music

Canto Antiguo Early Music Workshop, coached rehearsals, master classes, Renaissance, baroque music and dance in Ojai, CA. 2518 7th St., Apt. A, Santa Monica, CA 90405. 310-399-0238.

Ethnic/Folk

Mideast Workshop. Ensembles, bands, master class, special topics, dancing, concerts and informal playing at La Roche College, Pittsburgh, PA. 10008 Afton Rd., Columbus, OH 43221-1680. 614-457-1403. www.marilyncarlson@msn.com.

Swannanoa Gathering. Celtic Week, Performance Lab Week, Dance Week, Dulcimer Week, Old-Time Music & Dance Week, Contemporary Folk Week, Guitar Week, at Swannanoa, NC. Jim Magill, Warren Wilson College, P.O. Box 9000, Ashville, NC 28815-9000. 704.298.3325 ext. 426. www.gathering@warren-wilson.

Fiddles

Festival of American Fiddle Tunes. Ethnic and regional styles. P.O. Box 1158, Port Townsend, WA 98368. 360-385-3102.

Valley of Moon Scottish Fiddling School. Fiddle, harp, mandolin, guitar, Gaelic singing, Cape Breton step dance, piano, rhythm &bodhran, at Santa Cruz, CA. 1938 Rose Villa St., Pasadena, CA 91107. 818-792-6323. www.tappan@netcom.com.

Guitars

National Guitar Summer Workshop. All styles, guitar, banjo, keyboard, voice, percussion, MIDI, home recording. Box 222, Lakeside, CT 06758. www.guitarworkshop.com.

Instruments, Various

International Music Camp. Programs for string orchestra, choir, brass band, concert band. 1725 11th St., Minot, ND 58701. 701-838-8472.

CAMMAC Cedar Glen Summer Music Centre. Music theater, jazz ensemble, jazz history, improvisation, African drumming, Baroque, Classical and Contemporary technique and ensemble classes. Sue Carduelis, Music Director, Bruce Redstone, Program & Faculty Advisor. PO Box 400, Stouffville, Ontario L4A 7Z6, Canada. 416-964-3642. cedar_glen@cammac.ca , www.cammac.ca.

Midsummer Musical Retreat. Rich musical experiences for the adult musician: orchestra, wind ensemble, chorus. Folk dancing, skit night, wine tasting, flute choir. 12345 Lake City Way NE, Ste. 255, Seattle, WA 98125. 800-471-2419. www.musicalretreat.org/.

Summer Keys. Come as you are to enjoy the study, work, and beauty of the Maine coast, just across the border from Canada. Piano, jazz piano, clarinet, violin, cello, voice, flute, guitar. Bruce Potterton, 80 Essex Street, Jersey City, NJ 07302. 201-451-2338. www.nemaine.com/summerkeys/.

Jazz

Bud Shank Jazz Workshop. Combo class, theory/improv, master classes, lecture-demonstrations, big band rehearsals. P.O. Box 1158, Port Townsend, WA 98368. 360-385-3102. www.mktcentrum@olympus.net.

Stanford Jazz Workshop (intermediate to advanced). P.O. Box 17291, Stanford, CA 94309. www.sjazzw@netcom.com.

Vermont Jazz Center Summer Workshop. Seminars in jazz genres, theory, style; jam sessions, concerts. 72 Cotton Mill Hill, Brattleboro, VT 05301. 802-254-9088.

Piano

Sonata. 10-day program for adults who want to study piano in a concentrated, creative atmosphere in Southwest Vermont. 5 Catamount Lane, Old Bennington, VT 05201. 802-442-9197. www.polly@sonatina.com.

Recorders

Long Island Recorder Festival Summer Workshop. Baroque, renaissance, country, madrigal, at Central Islip, Long Island, NY. 116 Scudder Place, Northport, NY 11768-3025. 516-261-8242.

Strings

National String Workshop. Multi-level performance skills, pedagogy, improvisation, mind/body approaches, string orchestra, conducting, string and bow repair. Univ. of Wisconsin-Madison, 720 Lowell Hall, 610 Langdon St., Madison, WI 53703. 608-265-5629. www.chelcy.bowles@mailadmin.wisc.edu.

Music Sources Online

Educational Music Service, www.emsmusic.com.

www.burtnco.com.

Frank Music, www.frankmusiccompany.com.

www.intlmusicsuppliers.com.

J.W. Pepper, www.jwpepper.com.

www.sheetmusic/plus.com.

T.F. Front, www.books.TFront.com/music/home.html.

Publications, Print

Keynotes, Newsletter of the Adult Music Student Forum, Inc. P.O. Box 6204, Washington, DC 20015-0204. 202-686-3513. www.amsfperform.org.

Music For the Love of It, Newsletter for amateur musicians published 6 times a year. Ted Rust, editor/publisher. 67 Parkside Drive, Berkeley, CA 94705. 510-654-9134. Fax: 510-654-4656. www.music.holowww.com.

Piper and Drummer, Magazine for bagpipes and drums. 917 Mipissing Road, Milton, Ontario L9T 5E5 Canada. www.ppbso@interlog.com.

Publications, Online

Muzine, the Family-Oriented Web Magazine Devoted to the Non-Professional Musician. www.nmsu.edu/~muzine.htm.

Music Theory Online: The Online Journal of the Society for Music Theory. www.boethius.music.ucsb.edu.

Bagpiper.Com. Online magazine for bagpipers, with links to articles, events, classifieds, and bagpipe lore. www.bagpiper.com.

Index

Quick Order Form

Fax orders: (419) 281-6883. Send this form.
Telephone orders: (800) 247-6553. Have your credit card ready.
E-Mail orders: info@bookmaster.com
Postal orders: BookMasters, Inc., 2541 Ashland Road, P.O. Box 2139, Mansfield, OH 44905.

Please send the following books. I understand that I may return any of them for a full refund--
for any reason, no questions asked.

_____

_____

_____

Name: _____

Address: _____

City: _____ State: _____ Zip code: _____

Telephone: _____

e-mail address: _____

Shipping:

US: $3.50 for the first book and $2.00 for each additional book.

International: $9.00 for first book and $5.00 for each additional book.

Payment: ❏ Check, ❏ Credit card:

❏ Visa, ❏ MasterCard, ❏ Optima, ❏ AMEX, ❏ Discover

Card number: _____

Name on card: _____

Expiration date: _____ / _____